Contemporary Diagnosis and Management of **Allergic Diseases and Asthma**®

James E. Gern, MD
Professor of Pediatrics
University of Wisconsin Medical School
Madison, WI

William W. Busse, MD
Professor of Medicine, and
Director, Allergy and Clinical Immunology Department
University of Wisconsin Medical School

Fifth Edition

D1264029

Published by Handbooks in Health Care Co.,
Newtown, Pennsylvania, USA

Acknowledgments

The authors thank Yvonne Gern for word processing and preparation of tables and figures.

International Standard Book Number: 978-1-931981-82-8

Library of Congress Catalog Card Number: 2007943865

Fifth Edition

Contemporary Diagnosis and Management of Allergic Diseases and Asthma®. Copyright © 2008, 2005, 2003, 2000, 1999, 1998 by Handbooks in Health Care Co., a division of Associates in Medical Marketing Co., Inc. All rights reserved. Printed in the United States of America. No part of this book may be used or reproduced in any manner whatsoever, including but not limited to electronic or mechanical means such as photocopying, recording, or using any information storage or retrieval system, without written permission, except in the case of brief quotations embodied in critical articles and reviews. For information, write Handbooks in Health Care Co., 3 Terry Drive, Suite 201, Newtown, Pennsylvania 18940, (215) 860-9600.

Web site: www.HHCbooks.com

Table of Contents

This book has been prepared and is presented as a service to the medical community. The information provided reflects the knowledge, experience, and personal opinions of William W. Busse, MD, Professor of Medicine, and James E. Gern, MD, Professor of Pediatrics, University of Wisconsin-Madison Medical School, Madison, Wisconsin.

This book is not intended to replace or to be used as a substitute for the complete prescribing information prepared by each manufacturer for each drug. Because of possible variations in drug indications, in dosage information, in newly described toxicities, in drug/drug interactions, and in other items of importance, reference to such complete prescribing information is definitely recommended before any of the drugs discussed are used or prescribed.

Chapter **1**

The Epidemiology of Allergic Diseases

sthma, allergic rhinitis, food allergy, and atopic dermatitis tend to occur in the same families and even in the same individuals. These clinical observations have prompted detailed analysis of the epidemiology of these related disorders and have led to new insights into common and unique pathologic mechanisms, the natural history of these disorders, and the development of new preventive and therapeutic strategies. This chapter reviews the epidemiology of common allergic disorders, including prevalence, risk factors, and natural history, and examines possible causes for recent increases in allergy-related morbidity and mortality.

Role of Genetics and the Environment in the Pathogenesis of Allergy

Atopy, or the propensity to produce allergen-specific or increased total immunoglobulin E (IgE), is a common component of atopic diseases such as asthma, chronic rhinitis, food allergy, and atopic dermatitis (Figure 1-1). Although most patients with asthma or allergic rhinitis produce allergen-specific IgE, some affected patients do not have allergies, and not all patients with clinical manifestations of atopic dermatitis have allergies or increased total serum IgE.

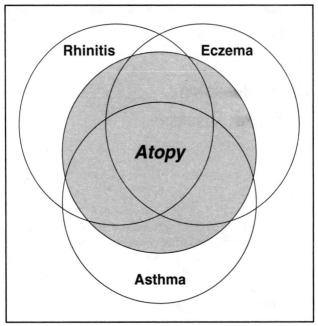

Figure 1-1: Relationship of atopy and allergic diseases.

Another pathogenic factor common to allergic disorders is chronic inflammation involving mast cells, basophils, T cells, and eosinophils. Many of the genes for the cytokines and receptors that regulate allergic inflammation are clustered on a short segment of chromosome 5q, and linkage of total serum IgE levels to these genes has been demonstrated in some families.[1] In contrast, production of IgE specific for some common pollen and pet allergens has been linked to certain class II HLA molecules.[2] These data indicate that the inheritance of allergic disorders is multifactorial. Furthermore, additional factors apparently influence whether a person born into an atopic family will develop allergic rhinitis, asthma, atopic dermatitis, or some combination of these disorders. For example, Dold et al[3] found that families with one parent who had atopic dermatitis were more likely to have a child with atopic dermatitis (odds ratio [OR]=3.4) than were families with one parent with either asthma (OR=1.5) or allergic rhinitis (OR=1.4). Similar trends were observed when inherited asthma or atopic dermatitis was examined, suggesting that additional genetic and environmental factors influence which organ system(s) is affected by allergy.

Although genetics is an important determinant of allergy, environmental exposures undoubtedly contribute to the variability in the expression of allergic diseases in atopic individuals. Environmental factors that may influence the development of allergy include allergen exposure, indoor and/or outdoor air pollution, childhood infections, family size, and rural vs urban lifestyle. The effects of allergen exposure on the development of allergy have been measured prospectively. Infants who are either breast-fed by mothers who restrict their intake of allergenic foods or fed hypoallergenic protein hydrolysate formulas for the first few months of life have a decreased incidence of food allergy and atopic dermatitis, although this effect appears to be temporary.[4] Furthermore, respiratory allergy is more likely to develop in children who are exposed early in life to high levels of indoor allergens such as house dust mites.[5] However, efforts to reduce the risk of allergic diseases by controlling allergen exposure have had mixed results. Adults may also develop respiratory allergy when exposed to a new allergen, and this has been demonstrated in an epidemiologic study of an asthma outbreak in New Guinea.[6] In this case, bringing blankets into the homes led to a sharp increase in exposure to house dust mite proteins, and the development of mite-specific IgE was strongly associated with the onset of asthma. Exposure to new allergens in the workplace can also lead to the development of new-onset allergic rhinitis, dermatitis, or asthma in previously healthy adults.[7]

The relationship between animal exposure and allergy has recently been re-evaluated. It is clear that pet ownership increases symptoms of respiratory allergy and asthma in people who are allergic to their pets. Recently, however, several studies have demonstrated that having a pet in the home during infancy actually reduces the risk of developing allergy.[8] In addition, children raised in rural environments with exposure to farm animals have low rates of allergic diseases and asthma. These results imply that there may be unique mechanisms for developing immune tolerance to allergens in infancy, although these mechanisms have yet to be clearly defined.[9]

The recognition of the high prevalence of respiratory allergy in inner-city neighborhoods such as those in Chicago and New York City has refocused attention on the potential role of air pollution in allergy pathogenesis. Most of the data, however, indicate that while outdoor pollutants such as ozone, NO_2, and diesel particles are important triggers of acute respiratory symptoms,[10] exposure to them is unlikely to cause asthma.[11] More convincing data link the development of asthma to indoor air pollutants such as tobacco smoke. Active or passive exposure to smoke is associated with an increased incidence of many respiratory disorders, including asthma and allergic rhinitis.[12] Exposure to irritants generated by gas stoves or other indoor sources of combustion has also been associated with increased respiratory symptoms and asthma.[13]

The effects of lower respiratory infections in infancy on the subsequent risk for asthma and allergen sensitization have also been prospectively examined. Contracting a wheezy lower respiratory infection (bronchiolitis) at an early age increases the risk of developing additional wheezing illnesses in infancy.[14] In addition, infants with recurrent bronchiolitis who go on to develop allergen-specific IgE are at increased risk for developing typical allergic asthma in childhood.[15] More recent studies indicate that infants who wheeze with rhinoviruses may be at especially high risk of subsequent asthma.[16,17]

In summary, these epidemiologic studies indicate that allergic disorders overlap in clinical expression, genetic linkage, and pathogenic mechanisms. Despite these similarities, genetic and environmental factors likely influence the severity and target organ specificity of allergic disorders.

Incidence, Prevalence, and Natural History of Allergic Disorders

Asthma

According to the US National Health Interview Study (NHIS), the prevalence of asthma rose from 31/1,000 population in 1980 to 54/1,000 during 1993-1994.[18] This 74% increase in asthma prevalence is representative of trends in other developed countries. After 1996, asthma prevalence leveled off, and while outpatient visits for acute asthma have continued to increase, rates of asthma hospitalizations and deaths have decreased.[19] Asthma prevalence and morbidity is highest in blacks and some Hispanic populations, particularly those residing in urban areas. In contrast with national trends, the prevalence of asthma in black, non-Hispanic boys in the United States continued to increase between 2001 and 2004.[20] Finally, after decades of declining death rates from asthma, mortality increased an average of 6.2%/year during the 1980s.[21]

Asthma prevalence and morbidity are not evenly distributed. Worldwide, developed countries have much higher levels of asthma than do Third World countries.[18] In the United States, children, minorities, and inner-city residents are disproportionately affected and have experienced the greatest increase in prevalence and death rates in recent years.[18-21,23]

Asthma often begins during early childhood, and most children have their first episode of asthma before their third birthday.[24] Atopic dermatitis and the development of elevated total or allergen-specific IgE during infancy indicate increased risk for subsequent asthma.[25] Asthma prevalence is strongly related to atopy and especially to positive skin tests for the house dust mite, *Alternaria,* cockroach, or cat.[26,27]

Seventy-five percent to 85% of asthma patients have positive skin reactions to allergies, and there is a strong correlation between the number of positive skin tests in children and the severity of asthma.[28,29] Up to half of asthmatic children will no longer be symptomatic as adults, and the absence of eczema or allergic rhinitis is a good prognostic indicator.[30] Children with severe asthma, however, are likely to continue to have problems as adults.

Allergy is also a contributing factor in most adults with asthma and can involve the same spectrum of allergens associated with asthma in children. Exposure to airborne allergens or chemicals in the working environment should also be considered in evaluating an adult with asthma.[7] Despite the difference in triggers for allergic and nonallergic asthma, the character of the airway inflammation and clinical manifestations are similar. Most adults with asthma date the onset of their respiratory complaints to childhood, or, less often, during the second through the fourth decades. Middle-aged or elderly patients with a new onset of symptoms that suggest asthma should be carefully evaluated for other disorders in the differential diagnosis, such as chronic obstructive pulmonary disease, mechanical obstruction of the airway, gastroesophageal reflux disease (GERD), chronic infections with mycoplasma or chlamydia, or respiratory complaints of cardiac origin. In general, adult-onset asthma is less likely to resolve spontaneously than asthma that begins in childhood.

Allergic rhinitis

Allergic rhinitis is the most common manifestation of atopy, affecting an estimated 20 to 40 million people in the United States.[31] Allergic rhinitis thus has a significant impact on public health and accounts for huge expenditures for prescription and over-the-counter medications. Complications associated with allergic rhinitis include loss of taste and smell, sleep disorders, sinusitis, eustachian tube dysfunction, otitis media, and facial growth abnormalities such as overbite.[32]

Risk factors for the development of allergic rhinitis include asthma, family history of allergy, persistent sensitization to foods in infancy, elevated serum IgE, and exposure to cigarette smoke and environmental allergens.[31,32] Chronic rhinitis from sensitization to perennial allergens such as house dust mite and pet danders can develop in infancy, while rhinitis triggered by seasonal pollen allergens begins to appear in school-age children. The peak prevalence of allergic rhinitis occurs in the teen years or early 20s, and symptoms typically become milder in middle age. Approximately 20% of children with allergic rhinitis eventually become asymptomatic, although other manifestations of atopy, such as asthma, may persist.

Atopic dermatitis

Atopic dermatitis is often the first manifestation of allergy in an atopic child, and approximately 80% of cases begin before the age of 3 years.[33] It is especially common in children and adolescents. Estimates of cumulative prevalence range from 7% to 20% in childhood, while prevalence in adults is estimated to be 2% to 10%.[34-36] As is the case with other common allergic disorders, the prevalence of atopic dermatitis has increased in the past 30 years.[35] The prevalence of atopic dermatitis can be markedly different in similar ethnic populations living in different geographic regions, indicating that environmental factors are important in determining disease expression.[37] The prognosis for atopic dermatitis is generally favorable, and symptoms abate completely in about one third of cases that begin during childhood.

Atopic dermatitis is often associated with other allergic disorders and with overproduction of IgE. In a prospective study of newborns in Tucson, cord blood IgE levels were related to the subsequent incidence of atopic dermatitis.[38] The development of food allergy can also significantly affect the severity of atopic dermatitis. One third to one half of children referred to tertiary-care allergy clinics for severe atopic dermatitis have underlying food allergy.[39,40] Eliminating the offending food from the diet can significantly improve the skin condition, as well as coexistent rhinitis and asthma.[39,41]

Atopic dermatitis in adults is rarely aggravated by food allergy, but occupational exposures frequently contribute to disease severity.[42] Atopic individuals have a much greater incidence of occupational dermatitis, which most commonly affects the hands. Precipitants of occupational dermatitis include irritants and allergens. Careful review of working conditions, household chores, and hobbies often identifies likely antagonists and suggests effective avoidance measures. Nonetheless, occupational dermatitis remains a major cause of work-related disability.

Why Are Atopic Diseases Increasing in Prevalence and Severity?

Asthma, atopic dermatitis, and allergic rhinitis are all increasing in prevalence, even after accounting for time-related differences in diagnostic criteria. These trends, plus the much greater prevalence of allergy in developed vs Third World countries,[22,37] raise the possibility that the causative factors are linked to changes in lifestyles associated with modern industrial society. The underlying reasons to explain the increase in atopic diseases are the subject of intense research, and a number of theories have been proposed.

In the United States, the inner-city environment is associated with particularly high rates of asthma, surpassing 50% in some neighborhoods, and this has prompted large, multicenter studies to identify the causative factors.[43] Allergen exposure can be very high, and the allergy most closely associated with asthma in the inner city is the cockroach. The effect of outdoor air pollution on asthma has also been extensively evaluated. Clearly, polluted air can trigger symptoms in people who already have asthma, but so far there is no clear link between air pollution and increased asthma prevalence.

One of the changes associated with modern lifestyles in Western countries is reduced exposure to infectious disease and, probably, reduced exposure to microorganisms in general. A theory, known as the hygiene hypothesis, states that routine exposure to micro-organisms helps the immune system to develop normally; if this exposure does not occur, the risk for allergic diseases is increased. In support of this hypothesis, the number of older siblings in the family, which presumably determines the exposures to infectious diseases in early childhood, is inversely related to the odds of allergen sensitization.[44] In addition, exposure to pets, farm animals, and consumption of fermented beverages in early childhood are all associated with reduced rates of allergic diseases and asthma.[45] Finally, some data suggest that antibiotic use and lack of breastfeeding change the intestinal microflora in such a way to increase the risk of allergy.[46] Each of these hypotheses is thought provoking, and additional studies are in progress to determine specific mechanisms underlying these epidemiologic associations.

Asthma is increasing not only in frequency, but also in severity, especially in children, minorities, and patients from urban centers.[13] Reasons for these trends appear to be multifactorial and include environmental factors (see above), socioeconomic factors such as access to health care and the ability to purchase asthma medications, underuse of anti-inflammatory medications, and attitudes related to health issues in general. The challenge is to determine which of these factors are important in asthma pathogenesis in individual patient populations so that remedial resources can be mobilized and targeted appropriately.

Summary

Epidemiologic studies have provided important insight into the fundamental issues related to allergic diseases, including determining the contributions of genetics, lifestyle, and environment to pathogenesis and disease expression. Future studies to identify the principal factors driving these trends should enable the creation of better strategies for the prevention and treatment of allergic disorders.

References

1. Finkelman FD, Vercelli D: Advances in asthma, allergy mechanisms, and genetics in 2006. *J Allergy Clin Immunol* 2007;120: 544-550.

2. Howell WM, Holgate ST: HLA genetics and allergic disease. *Thorax* 1995;50:815-818.

3. Dold S, Wjst M, von Mutius E, et al: Genetic risk for asthma, allergic rhinitis, and atopic dermatitis. *Arch Dis Child* 1992; 67:1018-1022.

4. Zeiger RS, Heller S: The development and prediction of atopy in high-risk children: follow-up at age seven years in a prospective randomized study of combined maternal and infant food allergen avoidance. *J Allergy Clin Immunol* 1995;95:1179-1190.

5. Platts-Mills TA, Vaughan JW, Carter MC, et al: The role of intervention in established allergy: avoidance of indoor allergens in the treatment of chronic allergic disease. *J Allergy Clin Immunol* 2000;106:787-804.

6. Dowse GK, Turner KJ, Stewart GA, et al: The association between *Dermatophagoides* mites and the increasing prevalence of asthma in village communities within the Papua New Guinea Highlands. *J Allergy Clin Immunol* 1985;75(1 pt 1):75-83.

7. Chan-Yeung M, Malo JL: Occupational asthma. *N Engl J Med* 1995;333:107-112.

8. Ownby DR, Johnson CC, Peterson EL: Exposure to dogs and cats in the first year of life and risk of allergic sensitization at 6 to 7 years of age. *JAMA* 2002;288:963-972.

9. von Mutius E, Le Souef PN: Early gene-environment interactions: can they inform primary preventive strategies for asthma? *Semin Respir Crit Care Med* 2007;28:255-263.

10. Committee of the Environmental and Occupational Health Assembly of the American Thoracic Society: Health effects of outdoor air pollution. *Am J Respir Crit Care Med* 1996;153:3-50.

11. Koren HS, Utell MJ: Asthma and the environment. *Environ Health Perspect* 1997;105:534-537.

12. von Mutius E: Environmental factors influencing the development and progression of pediatric asthma. *J Allergy Clin Immunol* 2002;109(6 suppl):S525-S532.

13. Ostro BD, Lipsett MJ, Mann JK, et al: Indoor air pollution and asthma. Results from a panel study. *Am J Respir Crit Care Med* 1994;149:1400-1406.

14. Morgan WJ, Martinez FD: Risk factors for developing wheezing and asthma in childhood. *Pediatr Clin North Am* 1992;39:1185-1203.

15. Martinez FD, Wright AL, Taussig LM, et al: Asthma and wheezing in the first six years of life. The Group Health Medical Associates. *N Engl J Med* 1995;332:133-138.

16. Kotaniemi-Syrjanen A, Vainionpaa R, Reijonen TM, et al: Rhinovirus-induced wheezing in infancy—the first sign of childhood asthma? *J Allergy Clin Immunol* 2003;111:66-71.

17. Lemanske RF Jr, Jackson DJ, Gangnon RE, et al: Rhinovirus illnesses during infancy predict subsequent childhood wheezing. *J Allergy Clin Immunol* 2005;116:571-577.

18. Centers for Disease Control and Prevention: Surveillance for asthma—United States, 1960-1995. *MMWR* 1998;47:1-26.

19. Mannino DM, Homa DM, Akinbami LJ, et al: Surveillance for asthma—United States, 1980-1999. *MMWR Surveill Summ* 2002;51:1-13.

20. QuickStats: Percentage of Children Aged <18 Years with Current Asthma, by Race/Ethnicity and Sex—United States, 2001-2004. *MMWR* 2006;55:185.

21. Weiss KB, Wagener DK: Changing patterns of asthma mortality. Identifying target populations at high risk. *JAMA* 1990; 264:1683-1687.

22. Pearce N, Ait-Khaled N, Beasley R, et al, and the ISAAC Phase Three Study Group: Worldwide trends in the prevalence of asthma symptoms: phase III of the International Study of Asthma and Allergies in Childhood (ISAAC). *Thorax* 2007;62:758-766.

23. Lang DM, Polansky M: Patterns of asthma mortality in Philadelphia from 1969 to 1991. *N Engl J Med* 1994;331:1542-1546.

24. Gergen PJ, Mullally DI, Evans R 3rd: National survey of prevalence of asthma among children in the United States, 1976 to 1980. *Pediatrics* 1988;81:1-7.

25. ETAC Study Group: Allergic factors associated with the development of asthma and the influence of cetirizine in a double-blind, randomised, placebo-controlled trial: first results of ETAC.

Early Treatment of the Atopic Child. *Pediatr Allergy Immunol* 1998;9:116-124.

26. Rosenstreich DL, Eggleston P, Kattan M, et al: The role of cockroach allergy and exposure to cockroach allergen in causing morbidity among inner-city children with asthma. *N Engl J Med* 1997;336:1356-1363.

27. Gergen PJ, Turkeltaub PC: The association of individual allergen reactivity with respiratory disease in a national sample: data from the second National Health and Nutrition Examination Survey, 1976-80 (NHANES II). *J Allergy Clin Immunol* 1992;90 (4 pt 1): 579-588.

28. Martin AJ, Landau LI, Phelan PD: Natural history of allergy in asthmatic children followed to adult life. *Med J Aust* 1981;2: 470-474.

29. Zimmerman B, Chambers C, Forsyth S: Allergy in asthma. II. The highly atopic infant and chronic asthma. *J Allergy Clin Immunol* 1988;81:71-77.

30. Aberg N: Asthma and allergic rhinitis in Swedish conscripts. *Clin Exp Allergy* 1989;19:59-63.

31. Skoner DP: Allergic rhinitis: definition, epidemiology, pathophysiology, detection, and diagnosis. *J Allergy Clin Immunol* 2001;108(1 suppl):S2-S8.

32. Howarth PH: Allergic and nonallergic rhinitis. In: Adkinson NF Jr, Yunginger JW, Busse WW, et al, eds: *Allergy: Principles and Practice*. Philadelphia, PA, Mosby, 2003, pp 1391-1406.

33. Ong PY, Leung DY: Atopic dermatitis. *Clin Allergy Immunol* 2002;16:355-379.

34. Croner S; Atopic dermatitis—epidemiology. *Pediatr Allergy Immunol* 1991;2:6-7.

35. Simpson EL, Hanifin JM: Atopic dermatitis. *Med Clin North Am* 2006;90:149-167.

36. Hanifin JM, Reed ML: A population-based survey of eczema prevalence in the United States. *Dermatitis* 2007;18:82-91.

37. Williams H, Robertson C, Stewart A, et al: Worldwide variations in the prevalence of symptoms of atopic eczema in the International Study of Asthma and Allergies in childhood. *J Allergy Clin Immunol* 1999;103:125-138.

38. Halonen M, Stern D, Taussig LM, et al: The predictive relationship between serum IgE levels at birth and subsequent incidences of lower respiratory illnesses and eczema in infants. *Am Rev Respir Dis* 1992;146:866-870.

39. Sampson HA, McCaskill CC: Food hypersensitivity and atopic dermatitis: evaluation of 113 patients. *J Pediatr* 1985; 107:669-675.

40. Jones SM, Sampson HA: The role of allergens in atopic dermatitis. *Clin Rev Allergy* 1993;11:471-490.

41. James JM, Bernhisel-Broadbent J, Sampson HA: Respiratory reactions provoked by double-blind food challenges in children. *Am J Respir Crit Care Med* 1994;149:59-64.

42. Simpson EL, Thompson MM, Hanifin JM: Prevalence and morphology of hand eczema in patients with atopic dermatitis. *Dermatitis* 2006;17:123-127.

43. Busse WW, Mitchell H: Addressing issues of asthma in inner-city children. *J Allergy Clin Immunol* 2007;119:43-49.

44. Strachan DP, Harkins LS, Johnston ID, et al: Childhood antecedents of allergic sensitization in young British adults. *J Allergy Clin Immunol* 1997;99:6-12.

45. Schaub B, Lauener R, von Mutius E: The many faces of the hygiene hypothesis. *J Allergy Clin Immunol* 2006;117:969-977.

46. Bjorksten B, Naaber P, Sepp E, et al: The intestinal microflora in allergic Estonian and Swedish 2-year old children. *Clin Exp Allergy* 1999;29:342-346.

Chapter 2

Differential Diagnosis of Allergic Diseases and Asthma

Allergic disorders can involve the skin, respiratory tract, gastrointestinal (GI) tract, cardiovascular system, and even the central nervous system (CNS) and can thereby cause a wide variety of signs and symptoms. Because allergic diseases are common and varied in their presentation, clinicians need to have a clear understanding of the diagnostic features of allergic disorders and to be able to differentiate allergy from other diseases that present in a similar fashion. For example, although the onset of chronic nasal congestion during the pollen season usually indicates allergic rhinitis, it is important to recognize the patient whose congested nose is an indication of a less common problem, such as a systemic illness (eg, hypothyroidism), a nasal polyp, or cocaine abuse. Not considering the differential diagnosis can lead to delays in appropriate therapy. Conversely, overdiagnosis of allergic disorders can lead to inappropriate or unnecessary prescribed therapy. For example, prescribing an overly restrictive diet for a child who has been mistakenly diagnosed as having food allergy may lead to nutritional deficiencies.

This chapter provides a quick reference to the diagnostic criteria and differential diagnosis for asthma and the most common allergic disorders. Subsequent chapters examine additional information about the diagnostic and therapeutic approaches to allergic disorders.

Allergic Conjunctivitis

Diagnostic features

Allergic conjunctivitis, also known as hay fever conjunctivitis, is immunoglobulin E (IgE)-mediated inflammation of the conjunctiva triggered by outdoor allergens, such as pollen or mold, or indoor allergens, such as pet dander or house dust mites. Symptoms include itching, redness, and tearing of the eyes, often accompanied by swelling of the periocular tissues. One of the cardinal features of allergic rhinoconjunctivitis is the coexistence of allergic rhinitis. The severity of the nasal and ocular symptoms usually changes in parallel. Physical findings include bilateral injection, erythema, and edema of the conjunctiva, accompanied by typical signs of nasal allergy. Skin or in vitro tests for allergen-specific IgE, ie, radioallergosorbent tests (RASTs) or fluoroenzyme immunoassays (FEIAs), can be used to verify the diagnosis of allergy and to guide therapeutic decisions (Table 2-1).[1-3] Allergic conjunctivitis is examined in more detail in Chapter 5.

Allergic Rhinitis

Diagnostic features

Allergic rhinitis usually begins in childhood, and peak prevalence occurs in the second and third decades of life. Symptoms of allergic rhinitis include nasal congestion, rhinorrhea, nasal itching, and sneezing, occurring either seasonally or year round. Associated physical findings include puffy eyes; swollen nasal mucosa that can be pale, bluish, or even red; nasal discharge that is usually clear and thin; serous effusion in the middle ear; and lymphoid aggregates on the soft palate and posterior pharynx. Skin tests or RAST can be used to confirm the diagnosis of respiratory allergy and to guide therapy (Table 2-2).[4,5] Allergic rhinitis is examined in more detail in Chapter 6.

Asthma

Diagnostic features

The diagnosis of asthma is based on the patient's medical history, physical examination, and objective measurements

Table 2-1: Differential Diagnosis of Allergic Conjunctivitis

Disorder	Frequency
Allergic rhinoconjunctivitis	Common
Atopic keratoconjunctivitis	Common
Contact dermatitis	Common
Giant papillary conjunctivitis	Common
Conjunctivitis sicca	Uncommon
Vernal conjunctivitis	Rare

RASTs=radioallergosorbent tests

of pulmonary function.[6] Cough, wheezing, and dyspnea that worsen in the early morning hours or with exercise are typical complaints. Moderate-to-severe asthma usually limits exercise tolerance, affects school or job performance, and wakens the patient at night. Wheezing of the chest is a main characteristic of asthma but is not always present because (1) airway obstruction in asthma is often erratic, so that examination of the chest during scheduled visits can be normal; (2) wheezing is a relatively insensitive sign of small-airway obstruction[7]; and (3) wheezing may be absent during severe exacerbations of asthma when airflow is severely limited. Other physical

Distinguishing Features

Associated with allergic rhinitis
Positive skin tests or RAST
Bilateral conjunctival involvement

Usually associated with atopic dermatitis
elsewhere on the body
Bilateral prominent upper eyelid involvement

Associated with the use of a new eye drop or cosmetic
Distribution of rash corresponds to area where the
offending allergen was applied

Affects contact lens wearers
Papillary response on upper-lid conjunctiva
Symptoms fade if lenses are not worn

Decreased tearing
Associated with autoimmune disorders (Sjogren's
syndrome, mixed connective-tissue disease)

Affects children and young adults in tropical climates
Giant papillae on upper-lid conjunctiva

findings associated with asthma include the use of accessory muscles during tidal breathing (indicating severe airflow obstruction), a prolonged expiratory phase, and a barrel-chested appearance. Pulmonary function tests (PFTs) that suggest asthma include reduction in forced expiratory volume in 1 second (FEV_1), peak expiratory flow (PEF), the ratio of FEV_1 to forced vital capacity (FEV_1/FVC ratio), and the midexpiratory forced expiratory flow rate ($FEF_{25\%-75\%}$).[8,9]

A key feature of asthma is the demonstration of reversible airway obstruction. Reversibility is documented by performing PFTs (PEF or FEV_1) before and then 15 minutes

Table 2-2: Differential Diagnosis of Allergic Rhinitis

Disorder	Frequency
Allergic rhinitis	Common
Viral URI	Common
Bacterial sinusitis	Common
Foreign body	Common (young children)
NARES syndrome	Common
Vasomotor rhinitis	Common
Rhinitis medicamentosa	Common

Medication or drug side effects
  Antihypertensive drugs
  Cocaine abuse
  Oral contraceptive pills
	Common

Systemic conditions Pregnancy	Common
Hypothyroidism	Uncommon
Granulomatous diseases (ie, Wegener's granulomatosis, sarcoidosis, infection)	Rare
Neoplasm	Rare
Mastocytosis	Rare

NARES=nonallergic rhinitis with eosinophilia; RASTs=radio-allergosorbent tests; URI=upper respiratory infection

Distinguishing Features

Chronic seasonal or perennial symptoms
Onset usually occurs in childhood
Positive skin tests or RAST

Self-limited illness lasting 5-10 days
Malaise or fever
Lymphadenopathy

Sinus radiographs abnormal
Halitosis
Purulent postnasal drip
Chronic cough: often follows a viral URI

Unilateral nasal discharge
Halitosis
Children <6 years of age

Eosinophilia of nasal secretions
Negative skin tests or RAST

Triggered by strong odors, tastes, or changes in climate
Negative skin tests or RAST

Use of topical vasoconstrictors for >5 days
Severe mucosal edema and erythema

Congestion temporally associated with beginning
a new medication

History and physical examination

Granulomatous lesions on rhinoscopy

Lesion seen on rhinoscopy

Mast cell infiltration of the skin, bone marrow, liver, spleen

Table 2-3: Differential Diagnosis of Asthma in Children

Disorder	Frequency
Asthma	Common
Bronchiolitis	Common
Chronic sinusitis	Common
Hyperventilation	Common
Laryngotracheomalacia	Common
Foreign body aspiration	Common
Vocal cord dysfunction	Common
Gastroesophageal reflux with recurrent aspiration	Common
Bronchopulmonary dysplasia	Uncommon
Cystic fibrosis	Uncommon
Allergic bronchopulmonary aspergillosis	Rare

Congenital anatomic airway abnormality
    Vascular ring
    Laryngeal web
	Rare

IgE=immunoglobulin E

Distinguishing Features

Variable cough, wheeze, dyspnea
Worse at night and after exercise
Pulmonary function tests—reversible airway obstruction
Often associated with other atopic diseases
Symptoms relieved by β-agonist administration
Age <2 years
Associated with respiratory virus infection
Chronic cough and nasal congestion
Abnormal sinus radiographs but normal pulmonary function
Triggered by anxiety or exercise
Normal pulmonary function tests, no hypoxia
Tingling or numbness of extremities
Rapid resolution of symptoms with calming
Stridor
Early onset of symptoms
No response to bronchodilator
Sudden onset of symptoms
Coughing or choking while eating
Abnormal expiratory chest radiograph (air trapping)
Bronchoscopy is the definitive study
Pulmonary function tests—decreased inspiratory flow
Hoarseness, stridor
Symptoms do not respond to asthma therapy
Nocturnal symptoms common
Vomiting or cough when recumbent
Barium swallow abnormal
Chronic airway disease with exacerbations
History of premature delivery and respiratory support
Abnormal sweat test and abnormal chest radiograph
Poor growth, fat malabsorption
Migratory infiltrates on chest radiograph
Positive skin test for *Aspergillus* (often with serum precipitins)
Elevated total IgE
Early onset of stridor, no response to bronchodilator
Airway compromised on chest radiograph or with barium swallow
Bronchoscopy

Table 2-4: Differential Diagnosis of Asthma in Adults

Disorder	Frequency
Asthma	Common
Chronic obstructive pulmonary disease (COPD)	Common
Cardiac asthma	Common
Gastroesophageal reflux with recurrent aspiration	Common
Hyperventilation	Common
Vocal cord dysfunction	Common
Pulmonary embolism	Common
Hypersensitivity pneumonitis	Uncommon
Drug-induced cough	Uncommon

Distinguishing Features

Variable cough, wheeze, dyspnea
Onset usually in childhood
Worse at night and with exercise
Pulmonary function tests (PFTs)—reversible airway obstruction
Often associated with other atopic diseases
Symptoms relieved by β-agonist administration

Progressive small airway obstruction
Poor response to bronchodilator
History of tobacco smoking

Physical signs of cardiac dysfunction
Chest radiograph—cardiomegaly
Abnormal echocardiogram

Nocturnal symptoms common
Vomiting or heartburn
Barium swallow

Triggered by anxiety or exercise
Normal PFTs, no hypoxia
Tingling or numbness of extremities
Rapid resolution of symptoms with calming

Hoarseness, stridor
PFTs—limited inspiratory flow
Poor response to asthma therapy

Tachypnea, tachycardia
Hypoxia
Chest pain
PFTs—restricted lung volume
Abnormal ventilation/perfusion scan

Occupational or recreational exposure to molds,
organic dusts, or chemical solvents
Antigen-specific, precipitating antibodies in serum
PFTs—restricted lung volumes

Angiotensin-converting enzyme (ACE) inhibitors

(continued on next page)

Table 2-4: Differential Diagnosis of Asthma in Adults (continued)

Disorder	Frequency

Fixed large-airway obstruction
  Vocal cord paralysis
  Tracheal stenosis
  Glottic web
  Foreign body
  Neoplasms
	Uncommon

Allergic bronchopulmonary aspergillosis	Rare
Pulmonary infiltrates with eosinophilia syndromes	Rare
α_1-antitrypsin deficiency	Rare

IgE=immunoglobulin E

after administration of a short-acting inhaled β-adrenergic agonist or by performing PFTs before and after a 2-week to 3-week course of oral or inhaled corticosteroid. An increase in PEF or FEV_1 of >12% from baseline values strongly supports the diagnosis of asthma (Tables 2-3 and 2-4).[10,11] More information on asthma and its management is provided in Chapters 7 and 8.

Atopic Dermatitis
Diagnostic features

Atopic dermatitis is a chronic skin disorder characterized by pruritus, dry skin, and excoriation. It can be localized to a few patches or involve large portions of the body. Atopic dermatitis usually begins early in life, typically in the second half of the first year. The pattern of distribution

Distinguishing Features

Stridor
PFTs—decreased inspiratory and
expiratory flow
No bronchodilator response
Abnormal chest radiograph (neoplasm)
Bronchoscopy

Migratory infiltrates on chest radiograph
Positive skin test for *Aspergillus*
Elevated total IgE
Aspergillus precipitins in serum

Pulmonary infiltrates
Peripheral blood eosinophilia

Emphysema
Low or undetectable serum α_1-antitrypsin
α_1-antitrypsin phenotype abnormal

of atopic dermatitis lesions changes with age. Affected areas in infants include the cheeks, trunk, and extensor surfaces of the extremities. During childhood and adolescence, the distribution shifts to involve the neck and flexural areas of the extremities.

Early lesions of atopic dermatitis are red and dry, with small papules, mild scaling, and areas of excoriation. Skin infections are common, and appear as moist and oozing lesions, or as sudden onset of increased erythema of the affected skin. Chronically affected areas show accentuated skin lines and thickening of the skin (lichenification) and postinflammatory pigmentation abnormalities. Pruritus is universally present, and scratching is a major factor in the pathogenesis of the acute and chronic skin lesions (Table 2-5).[12] Atopic and contact dermatitis are examined in Chapter 10.

Table 2-5: Differential Diagnosis of Atopic Dermatitis

Disorder	Frequency
Atopic dermatitis	Common
Seborrheic dermatitis	Common
Scabies	Common
Contact dermatitis	Common
Nummular eczema	Common
Drug eruption	Common
Immune deficiency	
Wiskott-Aldrich syndrome (infants)	Rare
Severe combined immunodeficiency (infants)	Rare
Hyperimmunoglobuli-nemia E syndrome	Rare

IgE=immunoglobulin E

Food Allergy

Diagnostic features

Food-induced allergic reactions usually begin soon after the ingestion of the offending food, often within minutes and nearly always within 2 hours. The GI tract and the skin

Distinguishing Features

Pruritus
Characteristic distribution:
- Infants—cheeks, trunk, and extensor surfaces
- Children and adults—flexor surfaces

Associated with other atopic diseases
Nonpruritic
Greasy scale on scalp, nasal folds, behind ears
Onset soon after birth
Intertriginous papules
Mites visualized in scraping of lesions
Contagious
Onset corresponds with use of new medicine or skin cream
Distribution of rash corresponds to area of contact
with the offending allergen
Lesions limited to small, round, scaly plaques
Coincides with beginning a new oral or
parenteral medication
Thrombocytopenia
Chronic diarrhea
Recurrent infections
Lymphopenia
Chronic diarrhea and recurrent infections
Staphylococcal abscesses and pneumonitis
Very high total serum IgE (but IgE levels overlap
with those of atopic dermatitis)

are the most commonly affected organ systems. Reactions range in severity from flushing or mild itching of the mouth to wheezing, upper airway obstruction, and cardiovascular collapse (see Anaphylaxis, below). Abdominal pain, nausea,

Table 2-6: Differential Diagnosis of Food Allergy

Disorder	Frequency
Food allergy	Common
Toxic contamination of food • Bacterial toxins • Scombroid poisoning (fish)	Common
Impaired food absorption • Lactase deficiency (milk) • Fructose overload (fruit juice) • Sorbitol (sugarless gum or candy)	Common
Pharmacologic properties of food • Coffee (caffeine) • Aged cheese (tyramine)	Common
Idiosyncratic responses • Alcohol flushing • Chinese restaurant syndrome	Common
Psychosomatic reactions	Uncommon
Allergy to food dyes or preservatives	Uncommon
Inflammatory bowel disease (IBD)	Uncommon
Anorexia nervosa/bulimia	Uncommon
Inborn errors of metabolism • Sucrase-isomaltase deficiency • Phenylketonuria • Many others	Rare

RASTs=radioallergosorbent tests

Distinguishing Features

Typical organ systems involved
Temporally associated with causative food
Reproducible each time offending food is eaten
Associated with other atopic diseases
Positive skin tests or RASTs in most cases

Affects a large percentage of people ingesting the food
Includes toxins from *S aureus*, *Shigella*, *E coli*
Elevated histamine levels from breakdown of
histidine in the meat of deep-sea fish

Bloating, diarrhea, and intestinal gas
Small amounts are usually tolerated but symptoms
develop if absorption capacity is exceeded

Symptoms are produced only when large quantities of
the food are ingested

Reproducible, but mechanisms are unknown

Not reproducible with double-blind, placebo-
controlled food challenges

Verify with double-blind, placebo-controlled food
challenge

Abnormal abdominal radiographs
Elevated erythrocyte sedimentation rate
Intolerance for a broad range of foods

Distorted body image
Intolerance for a broad range of foods

Failure to thrive
Vomiting, diarrhea
Seizures

Table 2-7: Differential Diagnosis of Anaphylaxis

Disorder	Frequency
Anaphylaxis	Common
Vasovagal reactions	Common
Asthma	Common
Arrhythmia, myocardial infarction (MI)	Common
Food aspiration	Common
Serum sickness	Common
Idiopathic urticaria	Common
Pulmonary embolus	Uncommon
Sepsis	Uncommon
Flushing syndrome	
• Mastocytosis	Rare
• Carcinoid tumor	Rare
Scombroid poisoning (fish)	Rare

GI=gastrointestinal

vomiting, and diarrhea are GI symptoms commonly associated with food allergy. Multiple vague complaints, such as lethargy and headache, without signs or symptoms of hypersensitivity, are unlikely to be from food allergy.[13]

Distinguishing Features

Typical organ systems involved (skin, respiratory, cardiovascular, GI tract)
Usually abrupt onset
Hypotension and tachycardia
Elevated serum tryptase (retrospectively)

Triggered by pain or anxiety
Hypotension and bradycardia
Pallor, diaphoresis
Rapid recovery when feet are elevated

No skin manifestations or hypotension

Abnormal electrocardiogram (ECG)
Findings limited to cardiovascular compromise

Abrupt onset of coughing and choking during a meal

Gradual onset of rash, fever, arthritis
Occurs 7-21 days after starting a new medication

Findings limited to the skin

Tachypnea and tachycardia
Absence of wheezing and urticaria

Fever, progressive illness

Mast-cell infiltration of the skin, bone marrow, liver, spleen
Elevated urine 5-hydroxyindoleacetic acid

Flushing, sometimes wheezing, after eating deep-sea fish (due to histamine in the meat)

Testing for food-specific IgE either by prick skin testing or RAST can provide data to support or disprove the possibility of food allergy, but both tests have a low positive predictive value. Double-blind, placebo-controlled food challenge is the best method for confirming the diagnosis of food allergy (Table 2-6).[14,15] More information on food allergy is provided in Chapter 11.

Anaphylaxis

Diagnostic features

Anaphylaxis is usually a clinical diagnosis. In most cases, there is a clear history of a sudden and sometimes catastrophic reaction that closely follows the administration of an inciting agent, but in some cases, no cause can be identified. Signs and symptoms of anaphylaxis include (1) urticaria, angioedema, and flushing; (2) rhinorrhea, bronchospasm, hoarseness, and laryngeal edema; (3) capillary leakage, diminished cardiac output, tachycardia, and hypotension; (4) nausea, vomiting, abdominal pain, and diarrhea; and (5) loss of consciousness. Laboratory evaluation is usually not helpful during the acute reaction; however, finding an increase in serum tryptase, a mast-cell mediator, can retrospectively confirm the diagnosis of anaphylaxis (Table 2-7).[16,17] Anaphylaxis is examined in more detail in Chapter 15.

References

1. Weiss A, Brinser JH, Nazar-Stewart V: Acute conjunctivitis in childhood. *J Pediatr* 1993;122:10-14.

2. Ono SJ, Abelson MB: Allergic conjunctivitis: update on pathophysiology and prospects for future treatment. *J Allergy Clin Immunol* 2005;115:118-122.

3. Bielory L: Allergic and immunologic disorders of the eye. Part II: ocular allergy. *J Allergy Clin Immunol* 2000;106:1019-1032.

4. Skoner DP: Allergic rhinitis: definition, epidemiology, patho-physiology, detection, and diagnosis. *J Allergy Clin Immunol* 2001;108(1 suppl):S2-S8.

5. Jacobs RL, Freedman PM, Boswell RN: Nonallergic rhinitis with eosinophilia (NARES syndrome). Clinical and immunologic presentation. *J Allergy Clin Immunol* 1981;67:253-262.

6. Busse WW, Holgate ST, eds: *Asthma and Rhinitis*. Oxford, England, Blackwell Scientific Publications, 2000.

7. Shim CS, Williams MH Jr: Relationship of wheezing to the severity of obstruction in asthma. *Arch Intern Med* 1983;143: 890-892.

8. National Asthma Education and Prevention Program, National Heart, Lung, and Blood Institute, National Institutes of Health: Expert Panel Report 3: *Guidelines for the Diagnosis and Management of Asthma (Full Report 2007)*. Bethesda, MD, US Department of Health and Human Services, 2007, NIH publication number 08-5846. Available at: http://www.nhlbi.nih.gov/guidelines/asthma/asthgdln.htm. Accessed January 21, 2008.

9. National Asthma Education and Prevention Program: Expert Panel Report EPR-3: Guidelines for the Diagnosis and Management of Asthma—Summary Report 2007. Available at: http://nhlbi.nih.gov/guidelines/archives. Accessed January 21, 2008.

10. American Thoracic Society: Lung function testing: selection of reference values and interpretative strategies. *Am Rev Respir Dis* 1991;144:1202-1218.

11. American Thoracic Society: Standards for the diagnosis and care of patients with chronic obstructive pulmonary disease (COPD) and asthma. *Am Rev Respir Dis* 1987;136:225-244.

12. Boguniewicz M, Leung DY: 10. Atopic dermatitis. *J Allergy Clin Immunol* 2006;117(2 suppl mini-primer):S475-S480.

13. Pearson DJ, Rix KJ, Bentley SJ: Food allergy: how much in the mind? A clinical and psychiatric study of suspected food hypersensitivity. *Lancet* 1983;1:1259-1261.

14. Bock SA, Sampson HA, Atkins FM, et al: Double-blind, placebo-controlled food challenge (DBPCFC) as an office procedure: a manual. *J Allergy Clin Immunol* 1988;82:986-997.

15. Sicherer SH, Sampson HA: 9. Food allergy. *J Allergy Clin Immunol* 2006;117(2 suppl mini-primer):S470-S475.

16. Joint Task Force on Practice Parameters; American Academy of Allergy, Asthma and Immunology; American College of Allergy, Asthma and Immunology; Joint Council of Allergy, Asthma and Immunology: The diagnosis and management of anaphylaxis: an updated practice parameter. *J Allergy Clin Immunol* 2005;115 (3 suppl 2):S483-S523.

17. Winbery SL, Lieberman PL: Anaphylaxis. In: Virant SL, ed: *Systemic Reactions.* Philadelphia, PA, WB Saunders & Co, 1995, pp 447-475.

Chapter 3

Pathogenesis of Allergies and Asthma

Overview of Allergic Mechanisms

Allergy and hypersensitivity are terms that are used interchangeably to describe an adverse clinical reaction to a foreign substance caused by an immunologic mechanism. Gell and Coombs originally proposed several different mechanisms for immunologic hypersensitivity, and Shearer and Huston[1] have modified the classification system to accommodate more recent discoveries (Table 3-1). Common respiratory, food, and stinging insect allergies and some drug reactions are mediated by mast cells. These are known as type I hypersensitivity reactions, or immediate hypersensitivity. Mast cells can be triggered via either immunoglobulin E (IgE)-dependent or IgE-independent (anaphylactoid) pathways. Several drugs, such as codeine and radiocontrast media, can precipitate anaphylactoid reactions by inducing degranulation of mast cells without binding to IgE.[2] Aspirin and other nonsteroidal anti-inflammatory drugs (NSAIDs) can produce similar reactions but do so through a distinct mechanism. NSAIDs inhibit the enzyme prostaglandin synthase (cyclo-oxygenase) and thereby block the synthesis of prostaglandins from arachidonic acid. In aspirin-sensitive individuals, however, the reduction in prostaglandin synthesis is accompanied by increased production of the other major derivatives of

Table 3-1: Classification of Hypersensitivity Reactions*

Type I	Mast-cell mediated a) IgE dependent (anaphylactic) b) IgE independent (anaphylactoid)
Type II	Antibody mediated (non-IgE)
Type III	Immune complex
Type IV	Cell mediated

*Modified from Shearer and Huston,[1] used with permission.
IgE=immunoglobulin E

arachidonic acid, the leukotrienes.[3] Overproduction of leukotrienes, which are potent bronchoconstrictors and vasodilators, may produce severe allergic symptoms.

Type II hypersensitivity reactions occur when antibodies (other than IgE) bind to the surface of cells or to extracellular tissues, leading to activation of complement and phagocytic cells. Penicillin can produce type II reactions by binding to the surface of red blood cells, creating a neoantigen that may be recognized by circulating antibodies. Binding of the antibody to the surface of the red cell leads to activation of complement and cell lysis.[4]

Type III reactions occur when antibodies bind to circulating antigens and form immune complexes, which are also potent activators of complement. This type of reaction was first recognized by Clemens von Pirquet, who observed that patients receiving horse serum as treatment for diphtheria developed skin rash, arthritis, and fever. Similar reactions have recently been observed in patients receiving antithymocyte globulin as treatment for bone marrow failure, and in those receiving extended courses of antibiotics.[5]

Finally, type IV reactions, also known as delayed-type hypersensitivity reactions, are mediated by T lymphocytes or natural killer cells. Examples include skin rashes that occur 1 to 2 days after contact with poison ivy, nickel, or other skin sensitizers in susceptible individuals. Type IV reactions require a sensitization phase, during which the antigen is processed by antigen-presenting cells that then activate CD4+ T cells.[6] Within 48 hours of re-exposure, both antigen-specific and antigen-nonspecific T cells home to the area of exposure. Cytokines secreted by activated T cells recruit additional mononuclear cells into the area and potentiate the inflammatory functions of cells in the affected tissue.

These different types of reactions are not mutually exclusive, and an allergen can produce more than one type of reaction even in a single individual. For example, reactions to latex gloves may progress over time from contact dermatitis to contact urticaria to anaphylaxis.[7] Of course, many types of adverse reactions to foreign substances do not involve immunologic mechanisms. Examples include irritant reactions (nasal irritation after exposure to tobacco smoke), pharmacologic effects of a substance (local swelling after a bee sting), metabolic deficiencies (diarrhea secondary to lactase deficiency), and idiosyncratic reactions for which no mechanism has been identified. In most cases, these reactions may be distinguished from allergy by careful evaluation of the history and physical findings.

Allergens

Allergens are substances that lead to sensitization (ie, production of allergen-specific IgE) followed by induction of clinical symptoms of allergy upon reexposure. Most allergens are medium-sized proteins that bind to specific IgE molecules on the surface of mast cells and basophils, triggering the release of a cascade of inflammatory mediators. Low-molecular-weight substances (haptens) such as penicillin metabolites are too small to cross-link IgE on their own, but they may serve as allergens after binding to carrier proteins such as albumin.

Table 3-2: Common Allergens

Inhaled	Ingested	Injected

• Pollens
  - Trees
  - Grasses
  - Weeds
• Molds
  - *Alternaria*
  - *Aspergillus*
• Arthropods
  - House dust mite
  - Cockroach
• Animal proteins
  - Cat
  - Rodents
  - Dog
• Latex
	• Foods
	  - Egg
	  - Milk
	  - Soy
	  - Peanut
	  - Tree nuts
	  - Fish
	• Medications
	  - Penicillin
	  - Cephalo-sporins
	  - Sulfonamide
	  - Erythromycin
	  - Codeine*
		• Insect venom
		  - Yellow jacket
		  - Bee
		  - Wasp
		  - Fire ant
		• Medications
		  - Penicillin
		  - Cephalo-sporins
		  - Morphine*
		• Intravenous contrast dye*

*Substances that provoke allergic reactions through IgE-independent mechanisms

Allergens come from a wide variety of sources, and exposure may occur by inhalation, ingestion, or injection (Table 3-2). Respiratory allergens may be classified as either perennial (year round) or seasonal, depending on their patterns of exposure. Common perennial allergens include proteins from house dust mites, pets, cockroaches, rodents, and indoor molds. Seasonal allergens include pollens from trees, grasses, and weeds, in addition to outdoor molds such as *Alternaria*. Extracts prepared from these allergens have long been used in the diagnosis and treatment of allergy and naturally contain many proteins and other soluble substances. The past three decades have witnessed a significant effort to identify the specific proteins responsible for producing allergic symptoms and to develop standardized extracts containing defined amounts of allergenic protein.[8]

The major allergenic proteins for house dust mite, cat, ragweed, and many other major allergens have been identified, and in some instances, the genes have been cloned and sequenced. These allergenic extracts are now being standardized according to allergen content and skin test reactivity, and this has improved the potency, reliability, efficacy, and safety of these preparations.

Allergen Sensitization

Allergen sensitization refers to a process in which a foreign protein interacts with the immune system, leading to the production of allergen-specific IgE. Once an individual becomes sensitized, additional contacts with the allergen may produce signs and symptoms of allergy. Several factors determine the likelihood of sensitization to a particular antigen. Sensitization most readily occurs with repetitive exposure to an allergen via the mucous membranes, skin, or gastrointestinal (GI) tract. High doses of inhaled or cutaneous allergen are also more likely to produce sensitization.[9] Host factors that influence sensitization rates include age (peak incidence in the second decade of life) and genetic factors. Although the genetics of allergy are far from clear, detailed analyses of allergic families have revealed that certain class II major compatibility loci are linked to the production of allergen-specific IgE.[10] In contrast, total serum IgE levels show linkage to several markers on chromosome 5, including the gene for interleukin-4 (IL-4), a cytokine that is required for IgE production.[11]

Regulation of IgE Synthesis

Production of allergen-specific IgE is prerequisite to the development of type I allergic reactions. Thus, defining the

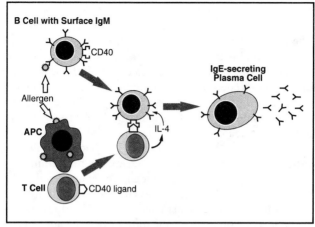

Figure 3-1: Regulation of IgE synthesis. A protein allergen activates a resting B cell by binding to surface IgM and activates T cells after first being processed by an antigen-presenting cell (APC). For IgE synthesis to occur, the T cell must furnish two signals by binding to CD40 on the B cell and secreting interleukin-4. These stimuli allow for isotype switching from IgM to IgE, followed by differentiation of the B cell into an IgE-secreting plasma cell. IgE=immunoglobulin E; IgM=immunoglobulin M

regulation of this process is important in efforts to find effective treatments and perhaps even a cure for allergy. Production of IgE requires a cooperative effort of CD4$^+$ T cells (T helper cells) and B cells (Figure 3-1). After maturing in the bone marrow, B cells have IgM or IgD immunoglobulin on their cell membranes (surface immunoglobulins). The immunoglobulin produced by each B cell has a unique structure in the antigen-binding region (variable portion of the Fab region). As a result, each B cell can bind a unique antigen, such as house dust mite protein. For a B cell to become activated to produce the secreted form of immunoglobulin, there must be at least two signals.[12] One signal occurs when the surface immunoglobulin on the

43

B cell binds to an antigen. The second signal is provided by T helper cells that are activated by the same antigen. The activated T cells make contact with the B cell, and a second signal is transmitted via the CD40 surface protein on the B cell. These two signals cause the B cell to further differentiate into immunoglobulin-secreting plasma cells. The signals also cause an isotype shift in the type of immunoglobulin produced, so that IgG, IgA, or IgE is produced instead of IgM or IgD. A major breakthrough in allergy research was the discovery that T cells and other cells secrete cytokines that determine which immunoglobulin isotype will be produced. For example, IL-4 or interleukin-13 (IL-13) is necessary for the switch from IgM to IgE secretion, while interferon-γ (IFN-γ) favors the production of IgG.[12] Identification of the mechanism for the production of allergen-specific IgE has led to the development of new experimental approaches to controlling allergies and asthma.

Pathogenesis of Type I Hypersensitivity Reactions

Symptoms of respiratory allergy are directly related to an allergen-driven chronic inflammation of the respiratory mucosa. Whether it is present in the eye, nose, or small airways of the lung, allergic inflammation acts on local structures such as smooth muscle, epithelial cells, and nerves to produce an increased sensitivity of the affected tissue to specific allergens (eg, pollen, house dust mite) and irritants (eg, tobacco smoke, cold air). This heightened sensitivity to allergic as well as nonspecific stimuli is called hyperresponsiveness.[13] Bronchial hyperresponsiveness can be measured by performing an inhalational challenge using a nonspecific stimulus such as methacholine, histamine, or cold air and then measuring the degree of bronchoconstriction using spirometry.[13] This concept has been valuable in understanding the relationship between inflammation and clinical symptoms and as a diagnostic tool in patients with symptoms that suggest asthma.

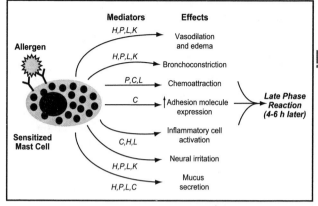

Figure 3-2: Effects of allergen-induced release of mast-cell mediators. C=cytokines; H=histamine; K=kinins; L=leukotrienes; P=prostaglandin D$_2$

Although many cells and mediators participate in allergy pathogenesis, it is clear that a few are key in this process. Allergens that reach the target tissue bind to allergen-specific IgE on the surface of mast cells, basophils, and other cells bearing IgE receptors. When IgE molecules are cross-linked by an allergen, the mast cell releases preformed mediators present in intracellular granules and begins to synthesize and secrete additional mediators and cytokines (Figure 3-2). Alternately, mast cells may be triggered directly by low-molecular-weight substances such as codeine or intravenous contrast material. Mediators contained in granules, such as histamine, produce vasodilation and increase capillary leakage within minutes, and newly synthesized leukotrienes and prostaglandins exacerbate local inflammation and attract new inflammatory cells such as eosinophils, basophils, and activated T cells into the area.[14]

Cytokines produced by mast cells, T cells, and other inflammatory cells have many proinflammatory effects, including enhancement of endothelial cell adhesion mol-

Table 3-3: Cytokines Implicated in Allergic Inflammation

Cytokine	Cell Sources	Pertinent Effects
Eotaxin	Mononuclear cells, epithelial cells	• Eosinophil chemoattractant
IL-3	T cells	• Mast cell and basophil growth factor
IL-4	T cells, basophils	• IgE synthesis • Recruits eosinophils to site via effects on adhesion molecule VCAM-1
IL-5	T cells, mast cells	• Eosinophil growth factor • Potent eosinophil activator

ecule expression leading to additional cell recruitment and augmentation of inflammatory cell function (Table 3-3). These inflammatory cells, particularly eosinophils, secrete additional mediators and cytokines that damage epithelial cells, stimulate mucous secretion and neurogenic inflammation, and promote vascular leakage and tissue edema (Table 3-4).[15]

In the respiratory tract, each of these factors contributes to nasal and lower airway obstruction, leading directly to clinical symptoms. With continued allergen exposure, inflammation may progress to structural changes in the

Cytokine	Cell Sources	Pertinent Effects
GM-CSF	T cells, epithelial and endothelial cells, eosinophils	• Granulocyte growth factor • Eosinophil activator
RANTES	Platelets, epithelial cells, macrophages	• Eosinophil chemoattractant
TNF-α	Macrophages, mast cells	• ↑Adhesion molecule expression • ↑Capillary permeability • ↑Mucous secretion

GM-CSF=granulocyte monocyte colony stimulating factor; IgE=immunoglobulin E; IL=interleukin; RANTES=regulated upon activation, normal T cell expressed and secreted; TNF-α=tumor necrosis factor-α.

airway, such as increased collagen deposition, hypertrophy of airway smooth muscle, and vascular hyperplasia. These changes, known as airway remodeling, are likely to contribute to long-term, perhaps irreversible, deterioration in lung function.[16]

Summary

Because many factors contribute to the pathogenesis of allergy and asthma, interventions at multiple levels may be required to control these disorders. Defining allergic mechanisms has permitted the development of therapies that affect

Table 3-4: Cells Involved in Chronic Allergic Inflammation

Cell	Mediators	Comments
Basophil, mast cell	Histamine, LTB_4, C_4, cytokines (IL-4, TNF-α)	Has high-affinity IgE receptors on surface and is triggered by allergen
Dendritic cell	Cytokines (IL-1, TNF-α)	Avid antigen-presenting cell and T-cell activator
Eosinophil	Cationic granular proteins, superoxide, LTC_4, cytokines (GM-CSF)	Granule proteins are toxic to epithelial cells, irritating to neurons
Macrophage	Superoxide, nitric oxide (NO), PGE_2, LTB_4, cytokines (IL-1, TNF-α, GM-CSF)	Macrophages have considerable inflammatory capabilities and can activate other cells via antigen presentation or cytokine secretion
T cell	Cytokines (IL-3, IL-4, IL-5, GM-CSF)	Cytokines secreted by allergen-specific T cells are potent activators of eosinophils and IgE production

GM-CSF=granulocyte monocyte colony stimulating factor; IgE=immunoglobulin E; IL=interleukin; LTB_4=leukotriene B_4; LTC_4=leukotriene C_4; PGE_2=prostaglandin E_2; TNF-α=tumor necrosis factor-α.

one or more specific mediators or effector cells described in this review. A clear understanding of the pathogenesis of allergy will enable clinicians to most effectively use current and future generations of antiallergic therapies.

References

1. Shearer WT, Huston DP: The immune system. In: Middleton E Jr, Reed CE, Ellis EF, et al, eds: *Allergy: Principles and Practice*. St. Louis, MO, Mosby-Year Book, 1993, pp 3-21.

2. VanArsdel PP Jr: Pseudoallergic drug reactions. *Immunol Allergy Clin North Am* 1991;11:635-644.

3. Israel E, Fischer AR, Rosenberg MA, et al: The pivotal role of 5-lipoxygenase products in the reaction of aspirin-sensitive asthmatics to aspirin. *Am Rev Respir Dis* 1993;148(6 pt 1):1447-1451.

4. Dove AF, Thomas DJ, Aronstam A, et al: Haemolytic anaemia due to penicillin. *Br Med J* 1975;3:684.

5. Lawley TJ, Bielory L, Gascon P, et al: A prospective clinical and immunologic analysis of patients with serum sickness. *N Engl J Med* 1984;311:1407-1413.

6. Wood GS, Volterra AS, Abel EA, et al: Allergic contact dermatitis: novel immunohistologic features. *J Invest Dermatol* 1986;87:688-693.

7. Ownby DR: Manifestations of latex allergy. *Immunol Allergy Clin North Am* 1995;15:31-43.

8. Becker WM, Vogel L, Vieths S: Standardization of allergen extracts for immunotherapy: where do we stand? *Curr Opin Allergy Clin Immunol* 2006;6:470-475.

9. Bachmann MF, Rohrer UH, Steinhoff U, et al: T helper cell unresponsiveness: rapid induction in antigen-transgenic and reversion in non-transgenic mice. *Eur J Immunol* 1994;24:2966-2973.

10. Meyers DA, Freidhoff LR, Marsh DG: Predicting skin test sensitivity and total serum IgE levels in family members. *J Allergy Clin Immunol* 1986;77:608-615.

11. Barnes KC: Evidence for common genetic elements in allergic disease. *J Allergy Clin Immunol* 2000;106(5 suppl):S192-S200.

12. Geha RS, Jabara HH, Brodeur SR: The regulation of immunoglobulin E class-switch recombination. *Nat Rev Immunol* 2003;3: 721-732.

13. Cockcroft DW, Davis BE: Mechanisms of airway hyperre-sponsiveness. *J Allergy Clin Immunol* 2006;118:551-559.

14. Busse WW, Lemanske RF Jr: Asthma. *N Engl J Med* 2001; 344:350-362.

15. Jacobsen EA, Ochkur SI, Lee NA, et al: Eosinophils and asthma. *Curr Allergy Asthma Rep* 2007;7:18-26.

16. Slade DJ, Kraft M: Airway remodeling from bench to bedside: current perspectives. *Clin Chest Med* 2006;27:71-85.

Chapter 4

Testing for Allergy

B ecause seasonal allergies are often clinically obvious, they usually can be treated appropriately without skin testing or in vitro assays. In more ambiguous
cases or in those involving perennial symptoms, testing for
allergy provides information that helps to establish the correct diagnosis, to formulate measures that control exposure
to environmental allergens, and to prescribe medication or
immunotherapy. The detection of allergen-specific immunoglobulin E (IgE) is the most useful test in evaluating the
possibility of immediate hypersensitivity,[1,2] although other
tests can provide supportive information or be used to rule
out other disorders in the differential diagnosis. This chapter
reviews the indications, methods, and interpretation of skin
and laboratory testing for allergy.

Laboratory Tests

Eosinophil count

Allergic individuals often have increased circulating eosinophils, and blood eosinophil counts correlate with disease
severity in atopic dermatitis[3] and asthma.[4] However, because of
large variations among individuals, the eosinophil count cannot
be relied upon as a sensitive marker for either the presence or
the severity of allergic disease in a particular individual.

Table 4-1: Indications to Test for Allergen-Specific IgE

Inhalant sensitivity
- Allergic rhinitis
- Asthma

Food sensitivity
- Severe atopic dermatitis (children)
- Food-induced respiratory symptoms
- Food-induced gastrointestinal (GI) symptoms
- Food-induced urticaria or anaphylaxis

Drug reactions
- Penicillin sensitivity
- Local anesthetic reactions

Stinging insect anaphylaxis
Latex hypersensitivity

IgE=immunoglobulin E

Examining nasal secretions for eosinophils is sometimes useful in diagnosing allergic rhinitis in patients with chronic nasal symptoms.[5] During active allergic rhinitis, the nasal secretions may contain >25% eosinophils. However, nonallergic individuals with nonallergic rhinitis with eosinophilia syndrome (NARES) also have eosinophilia of the nasal secretions without respiratory allergies.[6] Many individuals with NARES have a good clinical response to topical corticosteroids.

Total serum IgE
There is no doubt that the mean total serum IgE level of allergic patients is elevated; however, there is considerable

Table 4-2: Selection of Skin Tests vs RAST

Skin Tests	*RAST*
• Greater sensitivity	• Not affected by antihistamines
• Measure biological response	• Not affected by skin disease
• Less expensive	• No risk of anaphylaxis
• Rapid results	• Widely available

RASTs=radioallergosorbent tests

overlap with total serum IgE levels of nonallergic individuals.[7] As a result, the total serum IgE level is not useful in evaluating individuals with suspected allergy.[2,7] The preferred diagnostic test for allergy is the detection of allergen-specific IgE antibodies using an appropriate panel of allergen skin tests or radioallergosorbent test (RAST).

Detection of allergen-specific IgE

Allergen-specific IgE can be measured using immediate hypersensitivity skin tests or in vitro methods, such as the RAST or analogues thereof. Indications for skin testing or RAST include the clinical suspicion of respiratory allergy (ie, rhinoconjunctivitis or asthma) or allergy to foods, stinging insects, or latex (Table 4-1).

The decision to use skin tests or RAST to detect allergen-specific IgE is based largely on availability and expertise, but each technique has advantages and disadvantages that affect its clinical utility (Table 4-2). Because the reliability of allergy test results strongly depends on technical factors, health-care providers should refer to qualified allergists or laboratories who use strict quality control measures. Skin testing is somewhat more sensitive and specific, yields information quickly, is relatively inexpensive, and is the

Table 4-3: Contraindications to Allergen Skin Testing

Absolute

- Patient is on β-blocker therapy
- Pregnancy
- Generalized skin disease

Relative

- History of severe anaphylaxis
- Dermatographism
- Use of H_1 antihistamines, which inhibit the skin-test response for variable periods:
  - Hydroxyzine, cetirizine, loratadine—3-10 days
  - Fexofenadine—2 days
  - Other antihistamines—1-3 days
  - Tricyclic antidepressants (TCAs)—5 days

preferred method for detecting IgE-mediated reactions to medications such as penicillin.[8]

Contraindications to skin testing (Table 4-3) include the use of β-blockers such as propranolol (Inderal®, Inderal® LA) or metoprolol (Lopressor®, Toprol-XL®). If anaphylaxis occurs in a patient taking β-blockers, resuscitative efforts with epinephrine (EpiPen®, EpiPen® Jr.) may be unsuccessful, so there is an increased risk for a fatal reaction.[9] Pregnancy is also a contraindication to skin testing. Although the risk of anaphylaxis induced by skin testing is low, such a reaction during pregnancy could harm the fetus.[10] Skin tests are not useful in patients with extensive skin disease or in those receiving certain medications such as antihistamines because these factors may obscure wheal and flare responses (Table 4-3).

RAST and RAST analogues are useful when skin tests are contraindicated or cannot be interpreted because of concurrent skin disorders such as severe atopic dermatitis or dermatographism, or when it is not desirable to stop antihistamine therapy (Table 4-2). Disadvantages of RAST include the relatively high cost, decreased sensitivity and specificity compared to skin tests, and a turnaround time of several days or more.

Methods

Skin testing can be performed using either the prick or the intradermal technique.[11,12] Prick skin tests are simple, rapid, relatively painless, and commonly used as screening tests. Prick skin tests are generally considered to be more specific than intradermal skin tests because there are fewer false-positive reactions. Also, adverse reactions are more common with intradermal testing because of the larger dose of antigen administered; therefore, prick skin testing should be done first to minimize the risk of systemic allergic reactions. Prick skin tests are also preferred in testing for food allergy because of the lower incidence of false-positive tests compared to intradermal testing. The extracts used in prick skin testing are usually 1:10 to 1:20 weight/volume extracts in 50% glycerine, and every effort should be made to use standardized extracts from reputable sources. Control solutions include histamine (1 mg/mL for prick testing) and the diluent used to prepare the extract. After application of a drop of extract, the skin is pricked with a bifurcated needle, blood lancet, or commercially available multitest device.[13] Intradermal testing involves the intradermal injection of 0.03 to 0.05 mL of diluted (1:100 to 1:1,000) extract. The test results (size of wheal and flare) of either mode of testing are read 10 to 15 minutes later.

Skin test results depend on a number of factors besides the presence of IgE, such as mast cell degranulation and the responsiveness of the skin to inflammatory mediators such as histamine. Therefore, skin testing provides a more

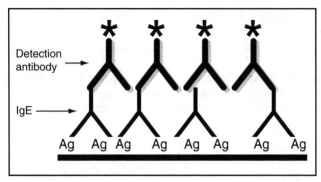

Figure 4-1: Radioallergosorbent test (RAST). Antigen (Ag) is bound to a solid support such as nitrocellulose, paper disks, or beads. Test serum is then incubated with the solid-phase antigen, and antigen-specific antibody (if present) binds to antigen. To detect allergen-specific IgE, a labeled (*) detection antibody specific for IgE is added, and quantitative measurements are performed in either a scintillation counter (radioactivity) or an ELISA plate reader (enzyme detection system). ELISA=enzyme-linked immunosorbent assay, IgE=immunoglobulin E

informative evaluation of the effect of the allergic reaction than simply measuring specific IgE antibodies in serum. However, antihistamines may suppress skin-test responses for variable periods (Table 4-3).[14,15] Tricyclic antidepressants (TCAs) can also blunt the skin test response for up to 5 days.

The RAST and RAST analogues are in vitro tests designed to detect allergen-specific IgE antibodies in serum.[16] The test involves the coupling or absorption of an allergenic protein onto a solid-phase support such as microcrystalline cellulose, paper disks, sepharose beads, or nitrocellulose (Figure 4-1). Human serum is incubated with the solid-phase antigen, and the allergen-specific IgE antibodies are detected by the addition of antihuman IgE antibodies labeled with radioactive iodine or an enzyme.

Selection of Specific Allergens for Testing

The number of skin tests or RASTs performed should not be excessive because the information gained from a few tests chosen based on the pattern of symptoms and history of exposure is more relevant than information derived from a large number of tests selected as a panel (Table 4-4). When selecting allergens for testing, either by in vivo or in vitro methods, clinicians should consider several factors.[16] First, what is the likelihood that identification of these allergens will improve the quality of the patient's care, either by avoidance measures or by intervention with medications or immunotherapy? Second, the specific allergens used in the testing should be chosen according to the nature of the allergens found in the patient's locale. Pollens from trees, grasses, and weeds vary in different parts of the United States. Thus, a knowledge of the botany of the area where the patient lives will be of use in determining which materials to choose for testing and whether treatment with immunotherapy is appropriate. Third, the age of the patient should influence allergen selection. For example, children may develop allergies to foods in the first few months of age but are rarely allergic to indoor allergens before the age of 1 to 2 years, or to pollens before 4 to 5 years of age.[17] Finally, the availability of standardized materials for skin testing or RAST should be considered. The use of poorly characterized reagents or inappropriate allergens such as butterfly, tobacco smoke, or facial tissue extracts should be avoided.

Indoor Allergens

Because house dust mite sensitivity is a major cause of allergic respiratory disease, testing for house dust mites is essential in areas of the country with sufficient humidity to support their growth. The two chief species of house dust mite in the United States are *Dermatophagoides pteronyssinus* and *D farinae*, and standardized extracts are available for testing.

Pet proteins are another major source of indoor allergens and have been linked to allergic rhinitis and asthma.[18] The

57

Table 4-4: Selection of Tests for Allergen-Specific IgE

Indoor

- House dust mite
- Molds
  - *Aspergillus*
  - *Penicillium*
  - *Cladosporium*
- Pets and pests
  - Cat
  - Dog
  - Mouse
  - Cockroach

IgE=immunoglobulin E

main allergen responsible for cat allergy is the protein *Fel d* 1, which is found in cat dander and cat saliva. The chief allergens responsible for dog allergy are less well characterized than cat antigens and may be specific for a particular breed.[18] Rodents such as mice, hamsters, and gerbils are also highly allergenic. The major rodent allergens are excreted in the urine.[19]

Molds such as *Aspergillus* and *Penicillium* are also indoor allergens.[20] These grow best on moist areas such as basements, bathroom tiles, and windowsills. Finally, cockroach allergens are an important precipitant of asthma and rhinitis, especially in inner-city areas.[21,22]

Outdoor Allergens

Outdoor allergens vary widely with season and location but may be broadly divided into grasses, trees, and weeds. Grass pollens are among the most common triggers of allergic symptoms, affecting 10% to 30% of allergic patients worldwide. Although many species of grass have been implicated in allergic disease, the allergenic proteins of most species have extensive immunologic cross-reactivity. As a result, mixtures of grass pollen extracts identify grass pollen-sensitive individuals, and there is seldom a need to

Outdoor

Season	Predominant Allergens
Spring	• Trees
Summer	• Grasses, molds (late)
Fall	• Molds (*Alternaria*), weeds

test for each grass pollen individually because of this high degree of cross-reactivity. Exceptions include Johnson and Bermuda grasses, which are found primarily in the South and possess unique allergenic components.

Most tree pollens associated with allergy in North America are from deciduous trees, including birch, beech, oak, maple, elm, willow, poplar, aspen, olive, and ash trees. One coniferous tree, the mountain cedar, which is found in abundance in Texas and portions of the southwestern United States, also contributes substantially to seasonal allergic rhinitis and asthma. Tree pollen seasons typically occur in the early spring and usually are brief (ie, 4 to 6 weeks).

The main weed pollen in the United States is ragweed. There are two major forms of this plant, short ragweed (*Ambrosia artemisifolia*) and giant ragweed (*Ambrosia trifida*), although other species are found in different locales throughout the United States. Other weeds that cause difficulty include *Amaranthus* and chenopods. The cross-reactivity of these weed pollens appears to be extensive, although some possess unique allergens.

A great number of fungi are allergenic, but the complexity of these allergens has hindered the development of standardized extracts.[20] Many of the extracts are of poor quality, and, with a few exceptions, justification for their use as either testing or treatment reagents is questionable. The most important species appear to be *Cladosporium*, *Alternaria*, *Aspergillus*, and *Penicillium*. *Alternaria* is primarily found outdoors and is a particularly potent allergen that has been linked to allergic rhinitis and asthma.[23]

Foods

Although food allergy can occur at any age, it is most common in young children who have respiratory, gastrointestinal, or dermatologic symptoms that appear soon after food ingestion.[24] The kinds of foods that cause allergic reactions vary with age: children are most often allergic to milk, eggs, soy, peanuts, or wheat, while adults are more likely to be allergic to seafood or nuts. In some instances, testing directly with fresh foods, such as a fruit or vegetable, by applying it to the skin and conducting a prick skin test may be useful.[25] Because of the high frequency of false-positive results with food skin tests, it is important to carefully correlate skin test results with data obtained from the history and food challenge test results before recommending dietary changes.[24]

Latex

Latex allergy is being recognized with increasing frequency, especially in high-risk groups such as health-care workers, spina bifida patients, and other patients who have had increased latex exposure from repeated surgical procedures.[26] A well-defined latex skin test reagent has been tested in a multicenter study and appears to have good sensitivity and specificity.[27] Its approval by the US Food and Drug Administration (FDA) is pending. A RAST to detect latex-specific IgE is available, but false-negative tests are relatively common.

Risks of Skin Tests

Although skin testing is generally safe, anaphylactic reactions, including cases of fatal reactions, do occur rarely.[28] To minimize the chance of severe adverse reactions, it is important to ensure the availability of a physician with the equipment and expertise to treat anaphylaxis and to evaluate patients for risk factors. Contraindications to skin testing include pregnancy, severe allergic symptoms, or the use of medications that block β-adrenergic receptors.[9]

Interpretation

Skin tests are interpreted by comparing the size of the wheal and flare responses to positive (histamine) or negative (diluent) controls.[29] The tests may be scored using either qualitative (0 to 4+) or quantitative (diameter of wheal and flare in millimeters) measurements.[11] A prick test producing a wheal at least 3 mm larger than the negative control, or an intradermal test producing a wheal larger than 5 to 10 mm, usually indicates a clinically significant response. Results of RAST can be expressed qualitatively or in comparison to test results performed with a pool of serum from nonallergic individuals. Regardless of the scoring system, it is imperative that treatment recommendations not be based solely on results of skin tests or RAST.[30] Data pertaining to allergen-specific IgE must be correlated with a complete evaluation of allergen exposure, allergic symptoms, the physical examination, and the response to any previous medical therapy.

Unproved Methods of Allergy Testing

There are a variety of other tests that are inappropriately marketed as allergy tests (Table 4-5).[31-34] Some of these tests, such as measurement of T cell subsets by flow cytometry, are valid diagnostic tests but are of no value in the diagnosis of IgE-mediated allergic disorders. Other methods have never been rigorously tested or are of no value at all. Some tests are useful in allergy research or in a limited number of clinical scenarios, but their value as diagnostic procedures is limited by added costs or by a higher degree of precision than is warranted for general clinical use. To avoid results that may be misleading or of questionable significance, health-care providers should limit their diagnostic testing to methods of proven value in the clinical setting.[33,34]

Table 4-5: Controversial or Unproved Methods of Allergy Testing[29]

Procedures incapable of any measurement

- Cytotoxic tests
- Provocation/neutralization
- Electrodermal diagnosis
- Applied kinesiology
- Reaginic pulse test
- Body chemical analysis

Valid tests that are inappropriate in the diagnosis of IgE-mediated allergy

- Allergen-specific IgG RAST or ELISA test
- Immune complexes containing food proteins
- Certain measures of immunity
  - Quantitative IgG, IgA, IgM, IgD
  - Complement components
  - Lymphocyte subset analysis

Valid diagnostic allergy tests that are inappropriate for general use*

- Basophil histamine release
- In vitro lymphocyte proliferation

*These tests are often used in research protocols and may be indicated in certain clinical situations.

ELISA=enzyme-linked immunosorbent assay; Ig=immunoglobulin; RAST=radioallergosorbent test

Summary

Techniques such as skin testing or RAST, when used in conjunction with a careful evaluation of the history and physical examination, are an important part of the diagnostic evaluation of allergy. This information can dramatically improve treatment by allergen avoidance, medical management, and immunotherapy. The use of well-standardized testing procedures and careful quality control ensure that reliable data are provided, leading to sound clinical decisions.

References

1.   Gergen PJ, Turkeltaub PC: The association of allergen skin test reactivity and respiratory disease among whites in the US population. Data from the Second National Health and Nutrition Examination Survey, 1976 to 1980. *Arch Intern Med* 1991;151:487-492.

2.   Brand PL, Kerstjens HA, Jansen HM, et al: Interpretation of skin tests to house dust mite and relationship to other allergy parameters in patients with asthma and chronic obstructive pulmonary disease. The Dutch CNSLD Study Group. *J Allergy Clin Immunol* 1993;91:560-570.

3.   Magnarin M, Knowles A, Ventura A, et al: A role for eosinophils in the pathogenesis of skin lesions in patients with food-sensitive atopic dermatitis. *J Allergy Clin Immunol* 1995;96:200-208.

4.   Jacobsen EA, Ochkur SI, Lee NA, et al: Eosinophils and asthma. *Curr Allergy Asthma Rep* 2007;7:18-26.

5.   Feather IH, Wilson SJ: Eosinophils in rhinitis. In: Busse WW, Holgate ST, eds: *Asthma and Rhinitis*. Cambridge, MA, Blackwell Scientific Publications, 1995, pp 347-363.

6.   Jacobs RL, Freedman PM, Boswell RN: Nonallergic rhinitis with eosinophilia (NARES syndrome). Clinical and immunologic presentation. *J Allergy Clin Immunol* 1981;67:253-262.

7.   Klink M, Cline MG, Halonen M, et al: Problems in defining normal limits for serum IgE. *J Allergy Clin Immunol* 1990;85:440-444.

8.   Sogn DD, Evans R 3d, Shepherd GM, et al: Results of the National Institute of Allergy and Infectious Diseases Collaborative Clinical Trial to test the predictive value of skin testing with major

and minor penicillin derivatives in hospitalized adults. *Arch Intern Med* 1992;152:1025-1032.

9. Toogood JH: Risk of anaphylaxis in patients receiving beta-blocker drugs. *J Allergy Clin Immunol* 1988;81:1-5.

10. Erasmus C, Blackwood W, Wilson J: Infantile multicystic encephalomalacia after maternal bee sting anaphylaxis during pregnancy. *Arch Dis Child* 1982;57:785-787.

11. Yunginger JW, Ahlstedt S, Eggleston PA, et al: Quantitative IgE antibody assays in allergic diseases. *J Allergy Clin Immunol* 2000;105(6 pt 1):1077-1084.

12. Ten RM, Klein JS, Frigas E: Allergy skin testing. *Mayo Clin Proc* 1995;70:783-784.

13. Nelson HS, Rosloniec DM, McCall LI, et al: Comparative performance of five commercial prick skin test devices. *J Allergy Clin Immunol* 1993;92:750-756.

14. Simons FE: Comparative pharmacology of H1 antihistamines: clinical relevance. *Am J Med* 2002;113 (suppl 9A):38S-46S.

15. Simons FE, Silver NA, Gu X, et al: Clinical pharmacology of H1-antihistamines in the skin. *J Allergy Clin Immunol* 2002;110:777-783.

16. Hamilton R: Assessment of human allergic disease. In: Rich RR, Fleisher TA, Shearer WT, et al, eds: *Clinical Immunology*, 2nd ed. St. Louis, MO, Mosby Ltd., 2001, pp 124.1-124.14.

17. Ownby DR, Adinoff AD: The appropriate use of skin testing and allergen immunotherapy in young children. *J Allergy Clin Immunol* 1994;94:662-665.

18. Lindgren S, Belin L, Dreborg S, et al: Breed-specific dog-dandruff allergens. *J Allergy Clin Immunol* 1988;82:196-204.

19. Krop EJ, Matsui EC, Sharrow SD, et al: Recombinant major urinary proteins of the mouse in specific IgE and IgG testing. *Int Arch Allergy Immunol* 2007;144:296-304.

20. Bush RK: Fungal extracts in clinical practice. *Allergy Proc* 1993;14:385-390.

21. Garcia DP, Corbett ML, Sublett JL, et al: Cockroach allergy in Kentucky: a comparison of inner city, suburban, and rural small town populations. *Ann Allergy* 1994;72:203-208.

22. Rosenstreich DL, Eggleston P, Kattan M, et al: The role of cockroach allergy and exposure to cockroach allergen in causing morbidity among inner-city children with asthma. *N Engl J Med* 1997;336:1356-1363.

23. Perzanowski MS, Sporik R, Squillace SP, et al: Association of sensitization to *Alternaria* allergens with asthma among school-age children. *J Allergy Clin Immunol* 1998;101:626-632.

24. Sicherer SH, Sampson HA: 9. Food allergy. *J Allergy Clin Immunol* 2006;117(2 suppl mini-primer):S470-S475.

25. Rosen JP, Selcow JE, Mendelson LM, et al: Skin testing with natural foods in patients suspected of having food allergies: is it a necessity? *J Allergy Clin Immunol* 1994;93:1068-1070.

26. Slater JE: Latex allergy. *J Allergy Clin Immunol* 1994;94(2 pt 1): 139-149.

27. Hamilton RG, Adkinson NF Jr: Diagnosis of natural rubber latex allergy: multicenter latex skin testing efficacy study. Multicenter Latex Skin Testing Study Task Force. *J Allergy Clin Immunol* 1998;102:482-490.

28. Reid MJ, Lockey RF, Turkeltaub PC, et al: Survey of fatalities from skin testing and immunotherapy 1985-1989. *J Allergy Clin Immunol* 1993;92(1 pt 1):6-15.

29. Bernstein IL, Storms WW: Practice parameters for allergy diagnostic testing. *Ann Allergy Asthma Immunol* 1995;75(6 pt 2): 553-625.

30. Nelson HS, Areson J, Reisman R: A prospective assessment of the remote practice of allergy: comparison of the diagnosis of allergic disease and the recommendations for allergen immunotherapy by board-certified allergists and a laboratory performing in vitro assays. *J Allergy Clin Immunol* 1993;92:380-386.

31. Condemi JJ: Unproved diagnostic and therapeutic techniques. In: Metcalfe DD, Sampson HA, Simon RA, eds: *Food Allergy: Adverse Reactions to Foods and Food Additives*. Boston, MA, Blackwell Scientific Publications, 1997, pp 541-550.

32. VanArsdel PP Jr, Larson EB: Diagnostic tests for patients with suspected allergic disease. Utility and limitations. *Ann Intern Med* 1989;110:304-312.

33. Executive Committee of the American Academy of Allergy and Immunology: Clinical ecology. *J Allergy Clin Immunol* 1986;78:269-271.

34. American Academy of Allergy and Immunology: Unproven procedures for diagnosis and treatment of allergic and immunologic diseases. *J Allergy Clin Immunol* 1986;78:275-277.

Chapter 5

Allergic Conjunctivitis

Allergic eye symptoms are especially alarming to patients because, in addition to the annoying symptoms of itching and burning, the swelling and redness of the eyes are noticeable to family, friends, and co-workers. Consequently, when these symptoms occur, the health-care provider is expected to arrive at the correct diagnosis quickly and to prescribe fast-acting and effective remedies. This chapter reviews the diagnostic features of and treatments for the major forms of ocular allergy.

The three most common forms of ocular allergy are allergic rhinoconjunctivitis, atopic keratoconjunctivitis, and ocular contact dermatitis. Although these disorders are each associated with inflammation of the eyes and surrounding tissues, they can be distinguished by their clinical presentation (Table 5-1).

Allergic Rhinoconjunctivitis

Allergic rhinoconjunctivitis, also known as hay fever conjunctivitis, results from immunoglobulin E (IgE)-mediated inflammation of the conjunctiva triggered by outdoor allergens such as pollen or mold, or by indoor allergens such as pet dander or house dust mites.[1] Symptoms include itching, redness, and tearing of the eyes, often accompanied by

Table 5-1: Clinical Features of Allergic Eye Disease

	Allergic Rhinoconjunctivitis
Patient History	
Seasonal occurrence	Associated with pollen season and rhinitis symptoms
Atopic dermatitis	Sometimes
Pruritus	Yes
Discharge	Clear
Physical Examination	
Pattern	Bilateral
Conjunctiva	Red and edematous, papillary response
Cornea	Usually not involved
Eyelid	Mild edema and redness with periocular edema
Cataracts	Unusual
Helpful Adjuncts	
Skin tests or RAST	Yes
Patch tests	No
Conjunctival scrapings	Eosinophils

RAST=radioallergosorbent test

Atopic Keratoconjunctivitis	Contact Keratoconjunctivitis
Often worse in extremes of hot and cold weather	No
Yes	No
Yes	Yes
Stringy	Sometimes
Bilateral	Unilateral or bilateral, depending on mode of exposure
Red and edematous, Trantas' dots	Red, edematous (especially if caused by eyedrops)
May be involved	May be involved
Thickened with fissures, excoriations, scaling; especially upper lids	Erythema and edema prominent, papules or vesicles may be present
Develop after pro- longed inflammation	Unusual
No	No
No	Yes
Eosinophils	Neutrophils, mononuclear cells, or eosinophils

swelling about the eye. One of the cardinal features of allergic rhinoconjunctivitis is the coexistence of allergic rhinitis, and the severity of the nasal and ocular symptoms usually changes in parallel. Pollen allergy is the most common trigger of allergic rhinoconjunctivitis, and symptoms usually occur at predictable times of the year, with peak symptoms usually limited to a few weeks. Many patients, however, are allergic to multiple pollens and thus experience the effects of several pollen seasons in series over the spring, summer, and fall. Patients allergic to indoor allergens usually have milder symptoms, but these may occur year-round, depending upon the exposure. Patients allergic to animals can experience dramatic eye swelling and inflammation after contact with pets.

Physical findings include injection, erythema, and edema of the conjunctiva. The edema may sometimes be severe, producing chemosis, which is gross swelling of the bulbar conjunctiva. The palpebral conjunctiva may show a papillary response, consisting of erythema and fine polygonal papules from epithelial hypertrophy with inflammatory cell infiltration. The eyelids and the loose tissues below the eye may appear swollen, and the infraorbital region may have a bluish discoloration, producing 'allergic shiners.' The nasal mucosa is usually edematous, with increased mucoid secretions. The color of the mucosa varies—red, pale, or, with severe edema of the mucosa, bluish from venous congestion.

Most of the time, the patient history and physical examination provide sufficient information to make the diagnosis and initiate therapy, but allergy testing can be useful under several circumstances.[2] First, skin testing or radioallergosorbent test (RAST) can help identify triggers for allergic symptoms so that efforts can be made to limit exposure to allergens in the home or work environment. Second, patients who have seasonal allergies and have not had a good response to medical therapy should be tested to confirm the diagnosis. The allergy test results can also be used to direct immunotherapy, if this is a consideration.

Treatment of allergic conjunctivitis is based on the same principles as treating allergic rhinitis (see Chapter 6). If allergies are identified, efforts should be made to minimize allergen exposure, especially in the case of indoor allergens. Unfortunately, short of closing up the home or workspace and living in an air-conditioned environment, pollen is difficult to avoid, so medical therapy is necessary to control symptoms (Table 5-2).

Antihistamines, with or without decongestants, can provide quick relief of mild-to-moderate itching and redness of the eye. Although oral antihistamines (Table 5-2) provide adequate relief for many patients, topical antihistamines (eg, levocabastine) provide more rapid relief (within minutes) and are generally more effective.[3] Azelastine (Optivar®), ketotifen (Zaditor®), and olopatadine (Patanol®) are topical H_1-receptor blockers that also inhibit allergen-induced mast-cell histamine release.[4] In addition to their effects on mast cells, ketotifen and azelastine inhibit eosinophil migration and mediator release.[5,6]

The topical nonsteroidal anti-inflammatory agent ketorolac (Acular®), can be used to treat acute allergic symptoms, although it has few advantages over other medications.[7] Patients with more severe rhinoconjunctivitis or who experience suboptimal relief with antihistamines alone may benefit from the use of a preventive medicine, such as lodoxamide (Alomide®) or nedocromil (Alocril®).[8,9] These mast cell stabilizing drugs are most effective when started before the onset of the pollen season and then continued daily for the duration of the season.[10]

In addition to medications, cool compresses can provide significant relief from pruritus and acute swelling. Nonmedicated artificial tears also provide symptomatic relief and can help to wash away the allergens and inflammatory mediators.

Additional measures are required for patients who experience unrelenting symptoms despite the measures discussed above. Corticosteroids are potent anti-inflamma-

Table 5-2: Medications for Allergic Eye Disease

Category	Medication
Topical Medications	
Artificial tears and lubricants	cellulose esters petrolatum polyvinyl alcohol
Vasoconstrictors	naphazoline hydrochloride 0.01%-0.05% tetrahydrozoline 0.05% (Visine®)
Antihistamines	levocabastine 0.05% emedastine 0.05% (Emadine®)
Combination antihistamine/ vasoconstrictor	naphazoline 0.025%/ pheniramine 0.3% (Naphcon® A, Opcon® A)
Mast-cell stabilizers	cromolyn 4% lodoxamide 0.1% (Alomide®) nedocromil 2% (Alocril®) pemirolast 0.1% (Alamast®)
Antihistamine/ mast-cell stabilizers	azelastine 0.05% (Optivar®) ketotifen 0.025% (Zaditor®) olopatadine 0.1% (Patanol®) olopatadine 0.2% (Pataday™)
Nonsteroidal anti-inflammatories	ketorolac 0.5% (Acular®)
Glucocorticoids	loteprednol 0.2% (Alrex®, Lotemax®)

Dose	Comments
1 drop p.r.n. Small bead to lower eyelid p.r.n.	Blurred vision (especially ointments). Sensitivity to vehicle or preservatives may develop.
1 drop q.i.d. p.r.n.	Temporarily suppress redness, but rebound effect may occur after prolonged use.
1 drop q.i.d. p.r.n. 1 drop q.i.d. p.r.n.	Rapid onset, but short duration. Approved for use in children ≥3 years.
1 drop q.i.d. p.r.n.	See above comments.
1 drop q.i.d. 1 drop q.i.d. 1 drop b.i.d. 1 drop q.i.d.	Best if started 1-2 weeks before and continued through the hay fever season. Approved for use in children ≥3 years.
1 drop b.i.d. 1 drop q 8-12 h 1 drop b.i.d. q 6-8 h 1 drop q.d.	Approved for use in children ≥3 years. Approved for use in children ≥3 years. Approved for use in children ≥3 years. Approved for use in children ≥3 years.
1 drop q.i.d. p.r.n.	Use with caution in patients with bleeding disorders.
Begin with 1 drop q.i.d., taper to mini- mum effective dose	Prolonged use associated with glaucoma and cataracts; contra- indicated in ocular herpes infection.

(continued on next page)

5

Table 5-2: Medications for Allergic Eye Disease *(continued)*

Category	Medication
Oral Medications	
Antihistamines	
First-generation	diphenhydramine (Benadryl®)
	chlorpheniramine (Chlor-Trimeton®)
	hydroxyzine
Second-generation	fexofenadine (Allegra®)
	cetirizine (Zyrtec®)
	levocetirizine (Xyzal®)
	desloratadine (Clarinex®)
	loratadine (Claritin®)
Corticosteroids	prednisone
	prednisolone

tory medications that are effective at relieving allergic inflammation when used topically or systemically. Although topical corticosteroids are safe when used in the nose, their chronic use in the eye can produce significant side effects, such as increased intraocular pressure or cataracts.[11] The use of corticosteroids in an eye with herpetic infection also can lead to extensive corneal ulceration and, ultimately,

Dose	Comments
Short-acting or extended-release	Inexpensive, but side effects may limit clinical usefulness
60 mg PO b.i.d. 180 mg PO q.d. 30 mg PO b.i.d.	Active metabolite of terfenadine Children 2-11 years
5-10 mg PO q.d. 2.5 mg PO q.d.	Incidence of sedation 11%-14% Children 2-5 years
5 mg PO q.d. 2.5 mg PO q.d.	≥12 years Children 6-11 years
5 mg PO q.d.	
10 mg PO q.d. 5 mg PO q.d.	Children >6 years and adults Children 2-5 years
20 mg PO b.i.d. (adults) 1 mg/kg/d (children) in split doses for 3-7 days	Very effective for quick relief of severe symptoms, but unsuitable for long-term use because of side effects

opacification. For these reasons, corticosteroid use in the eye should be minimized and, if necessary, done in collaboration with an ophthalmologist. Recently, 'soft' corticosteroids, such as loteprednol (Alrex®, Lotemax®) have been shown to be effective in treating allergic conjunctivitis. Loteprednol may be less likely to cause side effects because it is rapidly metabolized in the anterior chamber.

Even so, the lowest effective dose should be prescribed, and long-term use should be avoided.

Immunotherapy has proven to be an effective treatment for allergic rhinoconjunctivitis in carefully conducted clinical trials (see Chapter 16).[12] In general, patients experience a one-third to one-half reduction in symptoms, which may make medical management easier or even unnecessary. Immunotherapy works better in patients with a few well-defined allergies, as opposed to those individuals who are 'allergic to everything.' Contraindications to immunotherapy include the use of a β-adrenergic blocking agent or the presence of severe or unstable asthma. Most patients derive lasting benefits after 3 to 5 years of allergy injections, after which immunotherapy can usually be discontinued.[12]

Atopic Keratoconjunctivitis

Atopic dermatitis commonly involves the eyelids or cornea in older children and adults. This condition is known as atopic keratoconjunctivitis. Since allergic rhinoconjunctivitis and atopic keratoconjunctivitis are both found in atopic individuals, these conditions may coexist. The pathogenesis of atopic keratoconjunctivitis is thought to be similar to that of atopic dermatitis (see Chapter 10), but it has not been clearly defined. Biopsies of affected conjunctival tissue show increased numbers of mast cells, activated T lymphocytes, and goblet cells and stain positive for eosinophil granular proteins.[13] Although total and allergen-specific IgE levels are usually elevated in the serum and in tears,[14] allergies that are clearly related to the skin manifestations are the exception and not the rule.

Most patients with atopic keratoconjunctivitis have atopic dermatitis elsewhere on the body, although the ocular manifestations are sometimes the most prominent complaint. Symptoms include pruritus, crusting in the morning, and redness. Corneal involvement may be heralded by photophobia. Physical findings include changes typical of atopic dermatitis, with thickened and red eyelids, accentuated skin lines, and small papular lesions that may be weepy or dry.[15] Skin changes are usually most prominent on the upper eyelids. Scaling and lichenification appear with chronic lesions. The lid margins can appear thickened and scaly, with discharge that is most prominent in the early morning. The conjunctiva can be injected and edematous, with increased secretions, and scarring can develop after chronic inflammation. Trantas' dots, which are localized collections of eosinophils, may be present at the limbus. Corneal involvement, which can be detected by fluorescein staining, consists of punctate erosions. Patients with severe disease can also develop corneal scarring and keratoconus, a cone-shaped cornea associated with corneal thinning.[16] Finally, patients with atopic keratoconjunctivitis can develop anterior or posterior subcapsular cataracts.[16]

Treatment of atopic keratoconjunctivitis should address both the corneal/conjunctival inflammation and the eyelid dermatitis. The possibility of specific allergies should be explored, and if present, allergen avoidance measures should be recommended. Itching, burning, and tearing of the eyes can be treated with dual-action antihistamines such as olopatadine (Pataday™, Patanol®) or azelastine (Astelin®, Optivar®). It is best to avoid long-term use of topical corticosteroids because of the high incidence of local complications.[11] Patients with corneal inflammation, which can be sight-threatening, should be referred to an ophthalmologist for management. Short courses (7 to 10 days) of topical corticosteroid eye drops such as loteprednol (Alrex®) can be used to treat acute exacerbations, but long-term use of these medications should be avoided due to the risk of complications, such as glaucoma and cataracts. For patients with refractory symptoms, topical cyclosporine 0.05% eye drops have been used for their steroid-sparing effect.[17]

Eyelid dermatitis is treated the same as atopic dermatitis elsewhere on the face, with mild topical corticosteroid creams such as 1% hydrocortisone. The patient should be instructed to avoid getting the ointments into the eye itself. Blepharitis is treated with daily cleansing of the eyelids by gently scrub-

Table 5-3: Common Causes of Contact Allergy of the Eye

Eyedrops or ointments

- Antibiotics
  - neomycin
  - erythromycin (ERYC®)
  - sulfacetamide (Klaron®)
  - gentamicin (Genoptic®)
  - penicillin

- Other medications
  - benzocaine
  - pilocarpine (Pilopine HS®, Salagen®)
  - atropine (Atropen®)
  - antazoline
  - phenylephrine
  - thimerosal
  - dorzolamide (Trusopt®)
  - apraclonidine (Iopidine®)

Other causes

- Occupational exposures
- Cosmetics
  - eyeliner
  - mascara
  - facial cream
- Fragrances
- Nail polish
- Hand creams
- Hairsprays

bing with baby shampoo or a mild soap to remove scales and crusting. *Staphylococcus* infection of the eyelids can contribute to the pathophysiology, and can be treated with antibiotics such as topical erythromycin ointment.

Ocular Contact Dermatitis

The skin of the eyelid and the surrounding area is thin and highly vascular and thus highly susceptible to ocular contact dermatitis. Sources of the allergen include eyedrops, cosmetics, and materials that first contact the hands and are then inoculated into the eyes by rubbing (Table 5-3). Because of the heightened sensitivity of the periocular tissues, the dermatopathology may be limited to the eyelids, even if the first contact with the allergen was via the hands. Ocular contact dermatitis is mediated by a type IV hypersensitivity reaction, and both activation of innate immune responses of resident skin cells and allergen-sensitized T lymphocytes are instrumental in producing tissue inflammation.[16,18]

A common scenario for ocular contact dermatitis is a patient who is treated for an ocular condition with eyedrops, experiences transient improvement, and then develops intense itching, tearing, and redness of the eyes. Alternately, patients may experience similar symptoms without any clear trigger. On examination, the eyelids are usually very red and edematous, and microvesicles or shallow ulcers may be present. When eyedrops are involved, lower eyelid inflammation may be prominent, and the distribution of the dermatitis may correspond to the path of drops running down onto the face. The conjunctiva are usually intensely red, with a variable amount of edema. Severe cases may be accompanied by erosions of the corneal epithelium, which can be detected by fluorescein staining.

The diagnosis can often be made on the basis of typical physical findings that appear after the application of a known sensitizer, such as an ocular antibiotic or anesthetic. In cases of unclear origin, patch testing can help identify the allergen.[19] Treatment of contact allergy of the eye is to remove the inciting agent and to prevent future exposure to the allergen. Cool compresses can provide relief from mild or moderate swelling and itching, and short-term use of a mild topical corticosteroid agent (Table 5-2) or a short course of oral prednisone helps speed recovery in more severely affected individuals. Corticosteroid therapy is contraindicated if herpes infection of the eye is a consideration. For this reason, cases involving vesiculation of the eyelids, preauricular adenopathy, or corneal inflammation should be referred to an ophthalmologist for evaluation and treatment.

Vernal Keratoconjunctivitis

Vernal keratoconjunctivitis is a severe allergic eye disease that occurs primarily in young boys with allergic backgrounds.[16] As with hay fever conjunctivitis and atopic dermatitis, serum and local IgE levels are elevated, and conjunctival scrapings reveal increased numbers of activated T cells, eosinophils, and mast cells.[16,20] Specific respiratory allergies have been implicated in some cases.[16] The disorder typically appears in the preteen years and is active for 5 to 10 years before gradually resolving. The distinguishing feature of vernal keratoconjunctivitis is the development of severe allergic eye symptoms accompanied by a 'cobblestone' inflammation of the tarsal conjunctiva, consisting of many giant flat-topped papillae. These papillae can produce significant traumatic damage to the cornea, consisting of erosions or plaquelike deposits of epithelial cells in the anterior cornea.[21]

Treatment consists of providing symptomatic relief because the disease is self-limited and has a good prognosis if corneal complications can be avoided.[16,20] Allergen avoidance may be helpful if specific allergies are present. Medical therapy includes the use of mast-cell stabilizing agents such as cromolyn or lodoxamide or dual-action topical antihistamines such as olopatadine or ketotifen (Zaditor®).[9] Long-term use of corticosteroids should be avoided. Topical cyclosporine (Sandimmune®) has been helpful in some refractory cases.[22] The use of lubricating ointments (petrolatum) at night can help protect the cornea from traumatic damage.

Giant Papillary Conjunctivitis

Giant papillary conjunctivitis (GPC), a disorder found in wearers of soft contact lenses and in patients with ocular prostheses, has physical findings that resemble vernal conjunctivitis.[23] Although the mechanism underlying GPC is unknown, it is thought to be an immunologic reaction to the contact lens or prosthesis, or to a protein deposit on these materials.[24] Risk factors for developing GPC due to contact lenses include a personal history of allergy and infrequent changing of lenses.[25] Gradual loss of meibomian glands is also observed in GPC, although it is not clear whether this is a cause or an effect of the disease.[26] Symptoms usually include redness, burning, itching, and discharge, which are relieved by removing the contacts for several days. Physical findings consist of redness of the conjunctiva, accompanied by a fine papillary response on the tarsal conjunctiva or large individual papillae in more chronic cases.

The most effective treatment for GPC is to discontinue wearing the contact lenses. For patients who desire to continue to wear contact lenses, disposable, daily-wear lenses are often well tolerated. The lens polymer is an important factor because nonionic lenses with a low water content generally cause less inflammation.[25] Topical mast cell stabilizers or dual-action antihistamines may also be helpful for patients with GPC who wish to continue wearing contact lenses.[16]

Summary

Because of the presence of immunologically active tissue in the eye and the large degree of exposure to the environment, ocular allergy is one of the most frequently encountered complaints in a general office practice. Familiarity with the common forms of ocular allergy and their treatment enables the physician to provide effective therapy for these common diseases and to refer cases with potentially severe ocular complications to an ophthalmologist for further treatment.

References

1. Broide DH: The pathophysiology of allergic rhinoconjunctivitis. *Allergy Asthma Proc* 2007;28:398-403.

2. Bielory L: Differential diagnoses of conjunctivitis for clinical allergist-immunologists. *Ann Allergy Asthma Immunol* 2007;98: 105-114.

3. Sohoel P, Freng BA, Kramer J, et al: Topical levocabastine compared with orally administered terfenadine for the prophylaxis and treatment of seasonal rhinoconjunctivitis. *J Allergy Clin Immunol* 1993;92(1 pt 1):73-81.

4.   Schultz BL: Pharmacology of ocular allergy. *Curr Opin Allergy Clin Immunol* 2006;6:383-389.

5.   Ventura MT, Giuliano G, Di Corato R, et al: Modulation of eosinophilic chemotaxis with azelastine and budesonide in allergic patients. *Immunopharmacol Immunotoxicol* 1998;20: 383-398.

6.   Kato M, Hattori T, Takahashi M, et al: Eosinophil cationic protein and prophylactic treatment in pollinosis in natural allergen provocation. *Br J Clin Pract* 1994;48:299-301.

7.   Ketorolac for seasonal allergic conjunctivitis. *Med Lett Drugs Ther* 1993;35:88-89.

8.   Blumenthal M, Casale T, Dockhorn R, et al: Efficacy and safety of nedocromil sodium ophthalmic solution in the treatment of seasonal allergic conjunctivitis. *Am J Ophthalmol* 1992;113:56-63.

9.   Lodoxamide for vernal keratoconjunctivitis. *Med Lett Drugs Ther* 1994;36:26.

10.   Juniper EF, Guyatt GH, Ferrie PJ, et al: Sodium cromoglycate eye drops: regular versus "as needed" use in the treatment of seasonal allergic conjunctivitis. *J Allergy Clin Immunol* 1994;94: 36-43.

11.   Friedlaender MH: Corticosteroid therapy of ocular allergy. *Int Ophthalmol Clin* 1983;23:175-182.

12.   Durham SR, Walker SM, Varga EM, et al: Long-term clinical efficacy of grass pollen immunotherapy. *N Engl J Med* 1999; 341:468-475.

13.   Bielory L: Allergic and immunologic disorders of the eye. Part II: ocular allergy. *J Allergy Clin Immunol* 2000;106:1019-1032.

14.   Tuft SJ, Kemeny DM, Dart JK, et al: Clinical features of atopic keratoconjunctivitis. *Ophthalmology* 1991;98:150-158.

15.   Ono SJ, Abelson MB: Allergic conjunctivitis: update on pathophysiology and prospects for future treatment. *J Allergy Clin Immunol* 2005;115:118-122.

16.   Barney NP, Graziano FM: Allergic and Immunologic Disorders of the Eye. In: Adkinson NF Jr, Yunginger JW, Busse WW, et al, eds: *Middleton's Allergy: Principles and Practice,* 6th ed. St. Louis, MO, Mosby, 2003, pp 1599-1617.

17.   Akpek EK, Dart JK, Watson S, et al: A randomized trial of topical cyclosporin 0.05% in topical steroid-resistant atopic keratoconjunctivitis. *Ophthalmology* 2004;111:476-482.

18. Fyhrquist-Vanni N, Alenius H, Lauerma A: Contact dermatitis. *Dermatol Clin* 2007;25:613-623.

19. Oshima H, Kawahara D, Hashimoto Y, et al: An approach to evaluating patch test results. *Contact Dermatitis* 1994;31:189-191.

20. Bonini S, Coassin M, Aronni S, et al: Vernal keratoconjunctivitis. *Eye* 2004;18:345-351.

21. Cameron JA: Shield ulcers and plaques of the cornea in vernal keratoconjunctivitis. *Ophthalmology* 1995;102:985-993.

22. Spadavecchia L, Fanelli P, Tesse R, et al: Efficacy of 1.25% and 1% topical cyclosporine in the treatment of severe vernal keratoconjunctivitis in childhood. *Pediatr Allergy Immunol* 2006; 17:527-532.

23. Donshik PC: Giant papillary conjunctivitis. *Trans Am Ophthalmol Soc* 1994;92:687-744.

24. Meisler DM, Keller WB: Contact lens type, material, and deposits and giant papillary conjunctivitis. *CLAO J* 1995;21:77-80.

25. Donshik PC, Porazinski AD: Giant papillary conjunctivitis in frequent-replacement contact lens wearers: a retrospective study. *Trans Am Ophthalmol Soc* 1999;97:205-216.

26. Mathers WD, Billborough M: Meibomian gland function and giant papillary conjunctivitis. *Am J Ophthalmol* 1992;114: 188-192.

Chapter **6**

Allergic Rhinitis

A llergic rhinitis is the most common form of respiratory allergy, with an estimated prevalence of 9% to 42% in the United States, and, like asthma, its prevalence is increasing for reasons that are unclear.[1,2] Allergic rhinitis is primarily an affliction of children and young adults. Symptoms can appear as early as infancy; prevalence is greatest during the teenage years and the early 20s and gradually decreases thereafter.[1] Although symptoms can be mild, allergic rhinitis can cause severe symptoms that curtail daytime activities, reduce productivity at work, and disturb sleep. Despite the availability of safe and effective remedies, a large segment of the population is undertreated and continues to suffer through the allergy seasons with only marginally effective over-the-counter remedies.[3]

Diagnosis

The signs and symptoms of allergic rhinitis are well known to most health-care providers (Table 6-1), and making the diagnosis of seasonal allergic rhinitis or hay fever is usually straightforward. Symptoms such as nasal congestion, rhinorrhea, nasal itching, and sneezing that occur seasonally strongly support the diagnosis of allergic rhinitis. Associated problems can include allergic conjunctivitis, otitis media, sinusitis, loss of taste or smell, sleep distur-

Table 6-1: Clinical Presentation of Allergic Rhinitis

Symptoms	Signs	Complications
• Nasal congestion	• Swollen nasal mucosa: pale, bluish, or red	• Allergic conjunctivitis
• Rhinorrhea	• Rhinorrhea	• Otitis media
• Nasal itching	• Lymphoid aggregates on mucous membranes	• Sinusitis
• Loss of taste and smell		• Sleep disturbances
• Itching of the soft palate	• Dennie's lines	
• Sneezing	• Allergic salute	
• Headache	• Nasal crease	
	• Serous middle ear effusion	

bances, and headache. Physical findings can include puffy, red eyes; swollen nasal mucosa that may be pale, bluish, or even red, nasal discharge that is usually clear and thin; serous effusion in the middle ears; and lymphoid aggregates on the soft palate and posterior pharynx. Other telltale signs of allergic rhinitis include extra skin folds under the lower eyelids (Dennie's lines) and a crease on the anterior third of the nose from frequent nasal itching.

These stereotypical signs and symptoms of allergic rhinitis are usually sufficient to arrive at the correct diagnosis. However, laboratory testing to confirm the clinical suspicion may be useful when symptoms are perennial instead of seasonal or when patients do not respond favorably to standard treatment regimens. Allergy testing also provides important preventive information that can be used to guide recom-

Table 6-2: Testing for Allergic Rhinitis

- Allergen-specific IgE
  - RAST
  - Skin tests (prick or intradermal)
- Total serum IgE–poor sensitivity and specificity
- Nasal smear for eosinophils

RAST=radioallergosorbent test

mendations about allergen avoidance (see Chapter 16). This is especially important in the case of sensitization to indoor allergens such as animals, house dust mites, and mold.[4] In general, comprehensive efforts at allergen reduction are needed for clinical benefits to be achieved.[5]

Testing for respiratory allergy is based on the detection of allergen-specific immunoglobulin E (IgE) (Table 6-2). Both immediate hypersensitivity skin tests and in vitro tests (eg, radioallergosorbent test [RAST], or fluoroenzyme immunoassay [FEIA]) for allergen-specific IgE provide information that is clinically useful, and the choice of which test to use depends on several considerations.[6] Skin tests yield information within a few minutes and are relatively inexpensive, and a wide variety of allergenic extracts are available. Skin testing can be difficult to interpret if there is a generalized skin rash, and medications, such as antihistamines and tricyclic antidepressants (TCAs) blunt the response to skin testing. On the other hand, in vitro tests for allergen-specific IgE are relatively expensive but are widely available, and results are not influenced by medications such as antihistamines. In contrast to the clinical utility of measuring allergen-specific IgE, total serum IgE is not useful in evaluating patients with suspected allergic rhinitis because of the large degree of overlap between total serum IgE levels in allergic and nonallergic individuals.[7]

Finally, examining nasal secretions for eosinophilia can help in evaluating patients with chronic rhinitis. A nasal smear is prepared by having the patient blow his or her nose into a sheet of plastic wrap, transferring the secretions to a microscope slide, allowing it to air dry, and then staining the slide with either Hansel's or Giemsa stain. The presence of >25% eosinophils suggests either respiratory allergy or non-allergic rhinitis with eosinophilia (NARES).[8]

Treatment

Three modes of therapy are effective for treating allergic rhinitis: allergen avoidance, medical therapy, and immuno-therapy/allergen desensitization (Figure 6-1).

Allergen avoidance is an effective means of preventing symptoms triggered by indoor allergies, such as house dust mite, animals, or mold (see Chapter 16).[9] However, it is difficult to avoid airborne pollens during warm-weather months. Symptoms that persist despite allergen avoidance are treated with medical therapy, which is directed at the underlying inflammation of the nasal mucosa and at inhibition of mediators, such as histamine and leukotrienes.[10] The combination of a topical corticosteroid nasal spray and an oral antihistamine produces a good clinical response in most patients, although patients with mild symptoms may do well with an antihistamine alone.

Second-generation antihistamines are commonly pre-scribed for symptoms of allergy, and exert their effects by binding to the H_1-histamine receptor and stabilizing the receptor in an inactive conformation.[11] Histamine is only one of many mediators causing allergic rhinitis symptoms,[10] and consequently antihistamines provide only partial symptom relief for most patients. In general, antihistamines are effective for treatment of sneezing, itching, and rhinorrhea, but have relatively little effect on congestion, which is one of the most troublesome symptoms of allergic rhinitis.[12] First-generation antihistamines are effective histamine blockers but produce clinically apparent sedation in about

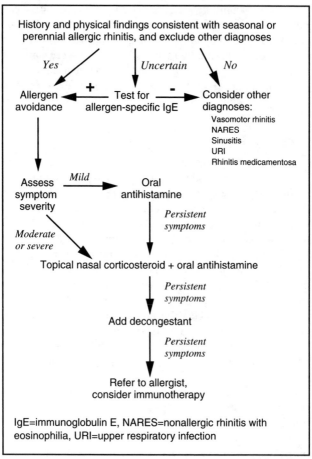

Figure 6-1: Overview of the diagnosis and treatment of allergic rhinitis.

one third of users. Recent studies using neuropsychologic testing or electroencephalographic monitoring have demonstrated that first-generation antihistamines produce subtle central nervous system (CNS) effects in most patients.[13]

In addition, tests conducted in a driving simulator indicate that therapeutic doses of diphenhydramine (Benadryl®) impair driving performance and that effects were comparable to a blood alcohol level of 0.01% (legal definition of intoxication).[14] The sedative effects of antihistamines can be especially pronounced in the elderly, and others with some degree of baseline cognitive impairment.[15]

The second-generation antihistamines (Table 6-3) are lipophobic, and most do not cross the blood-brain barrier.[11] As a result, the incidence of sedation for loratadine (Claritin®), fexofenadine (Allegra®), levocetirizine (Xyzal®), and desloratidine (Clarinex®) is no greater than placebo,[11,16] while cetirizine (Zyrtec®) causes sedation in 10% to 15% of patients. The second-generation antihistamines also have relatively long half-lives and retain potent antihistaminic effects. Some antihistamines, such as loratadine/pseudoephedrine (Claritin-D®), fexofenadine/pseudoephedrine (Allegra-D®), desloratadine/pseudoephedrine (Clarinex-D®), cetirizine/pseudoephedrine (Zyrtec-D 12 Hour®), and acrivastine/pseudoephedrine (Semprex-D®) have added decongestants. Several of the second-generation antihistamines are now available over the counter and as 12- or 24-hour preparations. Finally, azelastine (Astelin®), a potent H_1 antihistamine and mast-cell stabilizer, is available as a nasal spray. This topical antihistamine provides prompt relief of sneezing and nasal itching, has a low incidence (11.5%) of sedation, and can be used in children ≥5 years of age.[17] Antihistamines can be used either intermittently for symptom relief or prophylactically in anticipation of allergen exposure.[11]

Although they are generally safe, some antihistamines may cause cardiac arrhythmias when taken in overdose, used in standard doses by patients with liver disease or prolonged corrected QT (QTc) interval, or taken in conjunction with medications such as erythromycin and ketoconazole (Nizoral®) that interfere with the P450 microsomal system.[10,11] Fexofenadine, loratadine, cetirizine, and levocetiri-

Table 6-3: Second-Generation Antihistamines

Medication	Brand Name	Recommended Dose
cetirizine	Zyrtec®	5-10 mg PO q.d. (≥6 yrs) 2.5 mg PO b.i.d. (2-5 yrs)
cetirizine/pseudoephedrine	Zyrtec-D 12-Hour®	5 mg/120 mg PO b.i.d.
desloratadine	Clarinex®	5 mg PO q.d.
fexofenadine	Allegra®	30 mg PO b.i.d. (2-11 yrs) 60 mg PO b.i.d. (≥12 yrs) 180 mg PO q.d. (≥12 yrs)
fexofenadine/pseudoephedrine	Allegra-D®	60 mg/120 mg PO b.i.d. (≥12 years)

zine do not produce cardiac side effects because they do not prolong the QTc interval.[10,11]

One common misconception is that antihistamines should not be used in patients with asthma, and this error has been reinforced by long-standing, but mistaken, warnings on package inserts. In fact, good control of allergic rhinitis with antihistamines and topical nasal corticosteroids can actually improve control of lower airway symptoms in patients with asthma. Antihistamines are often combined in drug mixtures with decongestants that may counteract the sedative effect of antihistamines to some degree and potentiate the decongestive effects of the antihistamine.[18] Oral decongestants are

How Supplied	Comments
5 mg, 10 mg tablets 5 mg/5 mL syrup	• Metabolite of hydroxyzine • Incidence of sedation (11% to 14%)
5 mg cetirizine/ 120 mg pseudoephedrine tablets	• Metabolite of hydroxyzine • Incidence of sedation (11% to 14%)
5 mg tablets	• Incidence of sedation similar to placebo
60 mg capsules 30, 60, and 180 mg tablets 30 mg/5 mL suspension	• Metabolite of terfenadine • Incidence of sedation similar to placebo
60 mg fexofenadine/ 120 mg pseudoephedrine tablets	• Metabolite of terfenadine • Incidence of sedation similar to placebo

(continued on next page)

α-adrenergic agonists that act by constricting blood vessels in the nasal mucosa but can also cause side effects, such as tremor, insomnia, and nervousness.[19] Oral decongestants can also aggravate certain other medical conditions, such as hypertension and urinary retention, and they are contraindicated in patients with hypertension or glaucoma.[19]

Another class of mediators that has been implicated in allergic rhinitis is the leukotrienes. Leukotrienes are overproduced in the nasal airways of allergic subjects (but not normal subjects) after allergen exposure.[20] Several double-blind, placebo-controlled studies have demonstrated that treatment with montelukast (Singulair®), a leukotriene-re-

Table 6-3: Second-Generation Antihistamines *(continued)*

Medication	Brand Name	Recommended Dose
loratadine	Claritin®	5 mg PO q.d. (2-6 yrs) 10 mg PO q.d. (≥6 yrs)
loratadine/ pseudoephedrine	Claritin-D® 12 Hour	5 mg/120 mg PO b.i.d.
	Claritin-D® 24 Hour	10 mg/240 mg PO q.d.
levocetirizine	Xyzal®	5 mg PO q.d. 2.5 mg PO q.d. (6-11 yrs)

ceptor blocker, can reduce the severity of a variety of symptoms associated with seasonal allergic rhinitis,[21-23] and these effects may be more pronounced during periods of high pollen exposure.[21]

Topical corticosteroid nasal sprays are the single most effective treatment for allergic rhinitis symptoms (Table 6-4). These medications relieve a wide range of symptoms and have a low incidence of side effects. Local side effects, such as mucosal atrophy and nosebleeds, occur in <5% of patients. In children treated with beclomethasone nasal spray or a metered-dose inhaler (Beconase AQ®), small but measurable effects on growth have been noted. Beclomethasone topical therapy appears to reduce the rate of growth by 1 to 1.5 cm in the first year.[24,25] Because studies suggest that the eventual attained height of children treated with topical corticosteroids is normal, it is assumed that the ef-

How Supplied	Comments
10 mg tablets 5 mg/5 mL syrup 10 mg rapidly disintegrating tablets	• Incidence of sedation similar to placebo • Freeze-dried tablet that dissolves on the tongue and can be taken without water
5 mg loratadine/120 mg pseudoephedrine tablets 10 mg loratadine/240 mg pseudoephedrine tablets	• Only once-daily combination agent (Claritin-D® 24 Hour) • Low incidence of insomnia (5%)
5 mg scored tablets	• Incidence of sedation similar to placebo

fect on growth is temporary and that catch-up growth does occur.[26] Even so, low-dose topical therapy with mometasone (Nasonex®) or fluticasone (Flonase®), which are more rapidly metabolized, has not been associated with growth delay,[27,28] and these may be the preferred medications for treating allergic rhinitis in children. In addition to allergic rhinitis, studies have shown that fluticasone nasal spray (Flonase®, Veramyst™) is effective in treating ocular allergies.[29]

Because few studies compare the different corticosteroid medications head to head, the choice of which spray to prescribe for a particular patient is largely one of personal preference. Differentiating features include dry vs wet sprays and scented vs unscented formulations. Several of the topical corticosteroids are particularly easy to use because they can be administered once daily. Regardless of which preparation is selected, corticosteroid sprays are

Table 6-4: Topical Nasal Corticosteroid Preparations

Medication	Brand Name	µg/puff
beclomethasone	Beconase AQ®	42
budesonide	Rhinocort Aqua®	32
ciclesonide	Alvesco®, Omnaris™	50
flunisolide	Nasarel®	25
fluticasone	Flonase®	50
	Veramyst™	27.5
mometasone	Nasonex®	50
triamcinolone	Nasacort AQ®	55

*If a positive clinical response occurs, titrate the dose downward to determine the lowest daily dose that provides adequate relief of symptoms.

Recommended Dose*				
Pediatric**		Adult		
Spray(s) per nostril	μg/d	Spray(s) per nostril	μg/d	Comments
1 b.i.d. (1-2 b.i.d.)	168-336	**1 b.i.d.** (1-2 b.i.d.)	168-336	Scented spray
1 q.d. (1-2 q.d.)	64-128	**1 q.d.** (1-4 q.d.)	64-256	Unscented aqueous spray
2 q.d.		**2 q.d.**	200	Aqueous spray
2 b.i.d. or **1 t.i.d.**	150-200	**2 b.i.d.**	200-400	Unscented aqueous spray
		(2 b.i.d.- q.i.d.)	200-400	
1 q.d. (1-2 q.d.)	100-200	**2 q.d.** (1-2 q.d.)	100-200	Scented aqueous spray approved for patients ≥4 years of age
1 q.d.	55	**2 q.d.**	110	Low-volume suspension approved for children ≥2 years
1 q.d.	100	**2 q.d.**	200	Scented aqueous spray approved for patients ≥2 years
1 q.d. (1-2 q.d.)	110-220	**2 q.d.**	220	Unscented aqueous spray

**≥6 years unless otherwise noted.
Boldface: Recommended starting dose.
Dosage range shown in parentheses.

most effective when used prophylactically, and using them intermittently may produce suboptimal clinical responses.[30] To derive maximum benefit, it is best to start topical nasal corticosteroid therapy 1 or 2 weeks before the start of an allergy season. Although these medications have an excellent safety record, patients who use nasal corticosteroid preparations daily should have a nasal examination performed every 6 to 12 months because atrophy or ulceration of the nasal mucosa can occur with overuse or improper administration technique.

Topical cromolyn (Intal®) also has anti-inflammatory properties and an excellent safety record and is now available without a prescription. However, topical cromolyn is less effective than nasal corticosteroids,[31] has the disadvantage of high cost, and requires frequent administration (3 to 4 times/day).

Two other classes of medications may also be useful in treating chronic rhinitis. Anticholinergic nasal sprays such as ipratropium bromide (Atrovent®) act directly on the secretory glands of the nose to decrease the production of nasal secretions. These medications represent a major advance in the treatment of vasomotor rhinitis,[32] but they are used less for allergic rhinitis because rhinorrhea is selectively inhibited, while there is little or no effect on other symptoms such as nasal congestion and sneezing.

When prescribing nasal inhalers, it is important to review with the patient the instructions for proper medication administration (Table 6-5). Moreover, the patient must demonstrate proper technique during the clinic visit. Do not assume that patients will learn the proper method for administration by reading the package insert. Improper use of topical corticosteroids can reduce the efficacy of these medications and also increase the frequency of side effects such as nosebleeds.

Patients who suffer severe nasal symptoms during the pollen allergy season, especially those who present with completely occluded nasal passageways, may benefit sig-

Table 6-5: Technique for Administering Topical Nasal Spray

- Shake canister and remove the cover.
  Pump sprays must be 'primed' before the first use of a new bottle by pumping the sprayer 2-4 times until a uniform spray is produced.

- Blow your nose to clear the airway.

- Insert the nosepiece of the inhaler just inside one nostril. Aim the tip away from the nasal septum and toward the ipsilateral earlobe.

- Activate inhaler while gently inspiring through the nose.

- Spray the other nostril, and repeat as directed.

nificantly by taking a short course of an oral corticosteroid (eg, prednisone 20 mg PO b.i.d. x 5 days in adolescents or adults). This accomplishes two goals: prompt and dramatic clinical relief and opening of the airway so that topical nasal sprays can reach the target tissues. The patient's overall health should always be considered when prescribing a systemic corticosteriod. Although short courses of oral corticosteroids rarely cause serious side effects, corticosteroid therapy may cause problems in patients with complicating health problems, such as hypertension or diabetes.

Topical vasoconstrictors, such as oxymetazoline and phenylephrine, are advertised for the treatment of upper respiratory infections (URIs) and allergic symptoms. Because of the possibility of rebound congestion that occurs after only a few days of continuous use in some patients, topical vasoconstrictors are not suitable for use in allergic rhinitis patients, whose symptoms may last several weeks or months.

Finally, immunotherapy is another allergic rhinitis treatment with proven efficacy. Although allergy specialists have different opinions about when to recommend immunotherapy, it is probably best used in patients who do not respond favorably to the combination of allergen avoidance and medications. Double-blind, placebo-controlled trials have shown that immunotherapy can produce long-lasting relief of allergic rhinitis symptoms triggered by pollens, house dust mites, molds, and, in some cases, pets.[33,34]

Summary

Because allergic rhinitis is one of the most common symptoms prompting outpatient clinic visits, health-care providers of every specialty need to be familiar with the presenting signs, symptoms, and therapy for this bothersome disorder. Topical corticosteroid preparations and the newer antihistamines provide effective relief of rhinitis symptoms, with low instances of side effects and a good safety record. Patients who do not respond to the combination of allergen avoidance and medical therapy should be referred to an allergist for further evaluation and to consider the possibility of treatment with immunotherapy.

References

1.   Blaiss MS: Allergic rhinoconjunctivitis: burden of disease. *Allergy Asthma Proc* 2007;28:393-397.

2.   Schaub B, Lauener R, von Mutius E: The many faces of the hygiene hypothesis. *J Allergy Clin Immunol* 2006;117:969-977.

3.   Richards S, Thornhill D, Roberts H, et al: How many people think they have hay fever, and what they do about it. *Br J Gen Pract* 1992;42:284-286.

4.   Platts-Mills T, Leung DY, Schatz M: The role of allergens in asthma. *Am Fam Physician* 2007;76:675-680.

5.   Sheikh A, Hurwitz B, Shehata Y: House dust mite avoidance measures for perennial allergic rhinitis. *Cochrane Database Syst Rev* 2007;(1):CD001563.

6.   Bush RK, Gern JE: Allergy evaluation: who, what and how. In: Schidlow DV, Smith DS, eds: *A Practical Guide to Pediatric*

Respiratory Diseases. Philadelphia, PA, Hanley & Belfus, 1994, pp 261-270.

7. Klink M, Cline MG, Halonen M, et al: Problems in defining normal limits for serum IgE. *J Allergy Clin Immunol* 1990; 85:440-444.

8. Mullarkey MF, Hill JS, Webb DR: Allergic and nonallergic rhinitis: their characterization with attention to the meaning of nasal eosinophilia. *J Allergy Clin Immunol* 1980;65:122-126.

9. Platts-Mills TA, Vaughan JW, Carter MC, et al: The role of intervention in established allergy: avoidance of indoor allergens in the treatment of chronic allergic disease. *J Allergy Clin Immunol* 2000;106:787-804.

10. Howarth PH: Allergic and nonallergic rhinitis. In: Adkinson NF, Jr., Yunginger JW, Busse WW, et al, eds: *Middleton's Allergy: Principles and Practice*, 6th ed. St. Louis, MO, Mosby, 2003, pp 1391-1406.

11. Simons FE: Advances in H1-antihistamines. *N Engl J Med* 2004; 351:2203-2217.

12. Weiner JM, Abramson MJ, Puy RM: Intranasal corticosteroids versus oral H1 receptor antagonists in allergic rhinitis: systematic review of randomised controlled trials. *BMJ* 1998;317:1624-1629.

13. Bender B, Milgrom H: Neuropsychiatric effects of medications for allergic diseases. *J Allergy Clin Immunol* 1995;95:523-528.

14. Weiler JM, Bloomfield JR, Woodworth GG, et al: Effects of fexofenadine, diphenhydramine, and alcohol on driving performance. A randomized, placebo-controlled trial in the Iowa driving simulator. *Ann Intern Med* 2000;132:354-363.

15. Simons FE, Fraser TG, Maher J, et al: Central nervous system effects of H1-receptor antagonists in the elderly. *Ann Allergy Asthma Immunol* 1999;82:157-160.

16. Hindmarch I, Johnson S, Meadows R, et al: The acute and subchronic effects of levocetirizine, cetirizine, loratadine, promethazine and placebo on cognitive function, psychomotor performance, and weal and flare. *Curr Med Res Opin* 2001;17:241-255.

17. Azelastine nasal spray for allergic rhinitis. *Med Lett Drugs Ther* 1997;39:45-47.

18. Falliers CJ, Redding MA: Controlled comparison of a new antihistamine-decongestant combination to its individual components. *Ann Allergy* 1980;45:75-80.

19. Calderon-Zapata MA, Davis RJ: Antiallergic and vasoactive drugs for rhinitis (Chapter 108). In: Busse WW, Holgate ST, eds: *Asthma and Rhinitis*. Oxford, England, Blackwell Science, 2000, pp 1660-1668.

20. Creticos PS, Peters SP, Adkinson NF Jr, et al: Peptide leukotriene release after antigen challenge in patients sensitive to ragweed. *N Engl J Med* 1984;310:1626-1630.

21. Chervinsky P, Philip G, Malice MP, et al: Montelukast for treating fall allergic rhinitis: effect of pollen exposure in 3 studies. *Ann Allergy Asthma Immunol* 2004;92:367-373.

22. van Adelsberg J, Philip G, Pedinoff AJ, et al: Montelukast improves symptoms of seasonal allergic rhintis over a 4-week treatment period. *Allergy* 2003;58:1268-1276.

23. Nayak AS, Philip G, Lu S, et al, and the Montelukast Fall Rhinitis Investigator Group: Efficacy and tolerability of montelukast alone or in combination with loratadine in seasonal allergic rhinitis: a multicenter, randomized, double-blind, placebo-controlled trial performed in the fall. *Ann Allergy Asthma Immunol* 2002;88:592-600.

24. Skoner DP, Rachelefsky GS, Meltzer EO, et al: Detection of growth suppression in children during treatment with intranasal beclomethasone dipropionate. *Pediatrics* 2000;105:E23.

25. Simons FE: A comparison of beclomethasone, salmeterol, and placebo in children with asthma. Canadian Beclomethasone Dipropionate-Salmeterol Xinafoate Study Group. *N Engl J Med* 1997;337:1659-1665.

26. Agertoft L, Pedersen S: Effect of long-term treatment with inhaled budesonide on adult height in children with asthma. *N Engl J Med* 2000;343:1064-1069.

27. Allen DB: Do intranasal corticosteroids affect childhood growth? *Allergy* 2000;55(suppl 62):15-18.

28. Schenkel EJ, Skoner DP, Bronsky EA, et al: Absence of growth retardation in children with perennial allergic rhinitis after one year of treatment with mometasone furoate aqueous nasal spray. *Pediatrics* 2000;105:E22.

29. Kaiser HB, Naclerio RM, Given J, et al: Fluticasone furoate nasal spray: a single treatment option for the symptoms of seasonal allergic rhinitis. *J Allergy Clin Immunol* 2007;119:1430-1437.

30. Juniper EF, Guyatt GH, Archer B, et al: Aqueous beclometha-sone dipropionate in the treatment of ragweed pollen-induced rhini-tis: further exploration of "as needed" use. *J Allergy Clin Immunol* 1993;92(1 pt 1):66-72.

31. Welsh PW, Stricker WE, Chu CP, et al: Efficacy of beclo-methasone nasal solution, flunisolide, and cromolyn in relieving symptoms of ragweed allergy. *Mayo Clin Proc* 1987;62:125-134.

32. Grossman J, Banov C, Boggs P, et al: Use of ipratropium bromide nasal spray in chronic treatment of nonallergic peren-nial rhinitis, alone and in combination with other perennial rhinitis medications. *J Allergy Clin Immunol* 1995;95(5 pt 2):1123-1127.

33. Frew AJ: Immunotherapy of allergic disease. *J Allergy Clin Immunol* 2003;111(2 suppl):S712-S719.

34. Durham SR, Walker SM, Varga EM, et al: Long-term clin-ical efficacy of grass-pollen immunotherapy. *N Engl J Med* 1999; 341:468-475.

Chapter 7

Asthma:
Adolescents and Adults

Although asthma has always been a common medical problem, its prevalence and severity have increased worldwide over the past 20 years. This trend has coincided with an explosion of knowledge about the pathogenesis of asthma, which has led to the development of new and more effective treatment strategies. In this chapter, we will outline the diagnostic evaluation of asthma and the development of treatment regimens that are individualized according to specific triggers of acute symptoms and to the severity of disease. Much of the information in this chapter is based on the new National Asthma Education and Prevention Program (NAEPP), 3rd ed.,[1] and the executive summary of that document.[2]

Definition and Pathopysiology

Asthma is a disorder of recurrent airway obstruction and respiratory symptoms, caused by chronic airway inflammation, airway hyperresponsiveness, and structural remodeling. As a result of these abnormalities, common clinical symptoms include episodic bouts of cough, wheeze, and shortness of breath (Figure 7-1). Airway hyperresponsiveness is an increased susceptibility to bronchoconstriction that may be triggered by physical stimuli (exercise, cold air), irritants

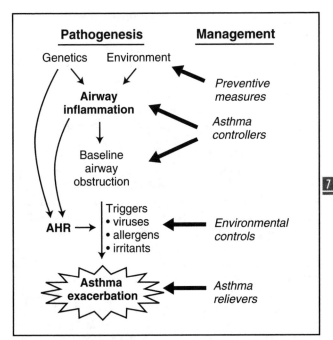

Figure 7-1: Overview of the pathogenesis of asthma. AHR=airway hyperresponsiveness.

(methacholine, tobacco smoke), or allergens.[3] Studies involving direct sampling of lower airway cells or secretions by flexible bronchoscopy have helped to characterize the inflammatory and structural changes associated with asthma.[1,2] Pathologic findings in asthma include infiltration of the lower airway mucosa and secretions with inflammatory cells such as eosinophils, mast cells, and activated T lymphocytes.[3] The mediators and cytokines secreted by these cells cause many of the hallmark features of asthma, including damage to airway epithelial cells, edema of the airway mucosa, hypersecretion of mucus, and increased airway responsiveness. In addition, asthma is associatedwith structural changes in the

103

airway, including thickening of the basement membrane and deposition of collagen in the bronchial wall.[4] This 'airway remodeling' contributes to chronic small airway obstruction in asthma and, if progressive, may eventually lead to irreversible chronic obstructive pulmonary disease (COPD).

Genetic and epidemiologic studies have provided additional insights regarding the underlying causes of asthma. For example, asthma has been linked to polymorphisms in specific genes, including immunoregulatory genes (eg, interleukin 13 [IL-13], human leukocyte antigen (HLA)-G molecule, and genes related to airway structure (eg, filaggrin, ADAM-33).[5,6] Studies of epithelial cells in tissue culture suggest that asthma may be associated with reduced antiviral responses, which could contribute to the propensity of infections with common cold viruses to cause exacerbations of asthma.[7] Epidemiologic studies have demonstrated an uneven distribution of asthma throughout the world, even among populations with similar ethnic backgrounds, implying that environmental factors are important.[8] Furthermore, elements of a rural lifestyle appear to be protective against asthma and other allergic diseases.[9] Outdoor pollutants and exposure to tobacco smoke clearly exacerbate asthma, and may also promote asthma incidence.[10]

Diagnosing Asthma

The diagnosis of asthma is based on the patient's medical history and physical examination, and objective measurements of pulmonary function (Figure 7-2). The medical history should include a description of the character and pattern of respiratory symptoms, triggers for symptoms, and any medications (over-the-counter or prescribed) used to treat symptoms (Table 7-1). Cough, wheezing, or dyspnea that worsen in the middle of the night and early morning hours or with exercise are typical complaints. Triggers for acute asthma symptoms often include exercise, common colds, and exposure to specific allergens on pollutants. In addition, it is important to determine whether asthma limits

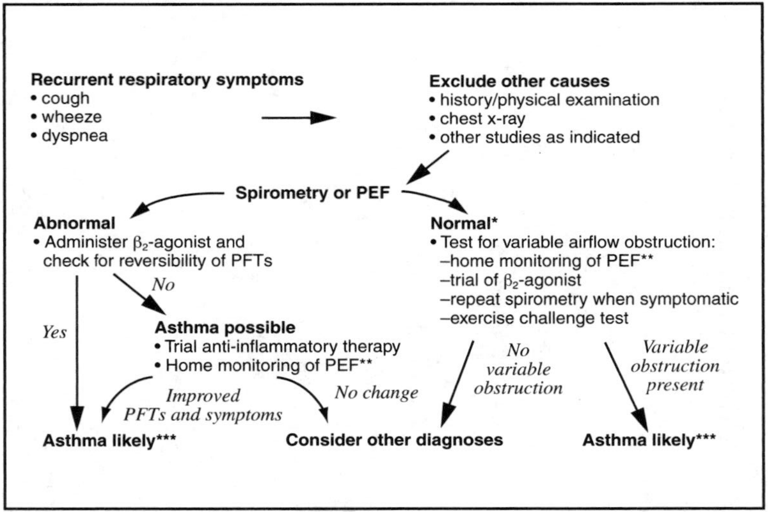

Figure 7-2: Diagnostic evaluation of asthma.

*Peak expiratory flow (PEF) in the 'normal' range may in fact be low for an individual whose lung function is usually above average. Spirometry provides additional information (eg, FEV_1/FVC ratio) that can be helpful in recognizing airway obstruction. If PEF is 'normal' and spirometry is not available, consider testing for improvement of PEF after administration of a β_2-agonist.

**Monitor PEF during asymptomatic and symptomatic periods for 1 to 2 weeks. If the PEF is low, document the response of PEF and symptoms to inhaled β_2-agonist.

***Institute therapy and re-evaluate in 1 month.

FEV_1=forced expiratory volume in 1 second, FVC=forced vital capacity, PFTs=pulmonary function tests

Recurrent respiratory symptoms
• cough
• wheeze
• dyspnea

↓

Spirometry or PEF

Abnormal
• Administer β_2-agonist and check for reversibility of PFTs

— Yes → **Asthma likely***

— No →

Asthma possible
• Trial anti-inflammatory therapy
• Home monitoring of PEF**

— *Improved PFTs and symptoms* → **Asthma likely***

— *No change* → **Consider other diagnoses**

Normal*
• Test for variable airflow obstruction:
  –home monitoring of PEF**
  –trial of β_2-agonist
  –repeat spirometry when symptomatic
  –exercise challenge test

— *No variable obstruction* → **Consider other diagnoses**

— *Variable obstruction present* → **Asthma likely***

Exclude other causes
• history/physical examination
• chest x-ray
• other studies as indicated

Table 7-1: Asthma: Important Aspects of the Medical History

Symptoms
- Coughing, wheezing, shortness of breath, modest sputum production
- Often worse at night
- Response to bronchodilators

Triggers
- Upper respiratory infection
- Allergen exposure (pets, house dust, pollens)
- Work-related exposures
- Irritants (tobacco smoke)
- Exercise
- Cold air
- Emotions

Disease course
- Age at onset and diagnosis
- Response to previous treatments
- Hospitalizations, intensive care unit (ICU) or emergency department visits

Impact of disease on patient or family
- School or workdays missed
- Limitation of exercise
- Nocturnal awakenings
- Psychological effects

exercise or affects school or job performance. For example, someone who consistently wheezes with exercise may consciously or unconsciously decide to stop exercising.

Family and social histories are relevant to the diagnosis and treatment of asthma. Most asthmatic patients have relatives with asthma, respiratory allergies, or eczema. Previous family experiences with asthma may strongly influence a patient's own attitude toward treatment. Exposure to environmental factors associated with asthma, such as pets, molds, tobacco smoke, and occupational irritants or allergens, should also be elicited. Risk factors for particularly severe exacerbations should be identified. These risk factors may reflect severe asthma, socioeconomic hindrances, or a combination of these factors (Table 7-2) and will identify patients with special treatment needs.[1]

If the medical history suggests the possibility of asthma, particular attention should be focused on the examination of the chest, upper respiratory tract, and skin. Wheezing of the chest is one of the primary characteristics of asthma, but because airway obstruction in asthma is often erratic, examination of the chest during regular visits is often normal. It is important to note that wheezing may be absent even with moderate (up to 25% reduction in peak expiratory flow [PEF]) airway obstruction[11] and during severe exacerbations of asthma when airflow is severely limited. Other physical findings associated with asthma are the use of accessory muscles during tidal breathing, a prolonged expiratory phase, and a barrel-chested appearance. Physical examination may also reveal signs of coexistent atopic diseases, such as allergic rhinitis, allergic conjunctivitis, or atopic dermatitis. The presence of nasal polyps suggests aspirin hypersensitivity[12] or cystic fibrosis.[13] Clubbing of the fingers is not characteristic of asthma and suggests either heart disease or other chronic respiratory conditions such as bronchiectasis or cystic fibrosis.

Patients whose history and physical findings suggest asthma should be further evaluated with objective mea-

Table 7-2: Risk Factors for Asthma Mortality

Age
- Elderly
- Teenagers

Ethnicity
- Blacks

Hospital admissions
- Intubation
- ICU admission

Underestimation of asthma severity
- Poor recognition of asthma symptoms
- Inadequate treatment
- Overuse of inhaled bronchodilators

Psychological factors
- Depression

Low socioeconomic status
- Lack of access to medical care

Alternaria *allergy*

surements of pulmonary function. A spirometer is a wise investment for any health-care practitioner who regularly cares for patients with asthma. Measurements that suggest obstruction of the small airways include reduction in forced expiratory volume in 1 second (FEV_1), in PEF, in the FEV_1/FVC ratio, or in the midexpiratory forced expiratory flow rate ($FEF_{25\%-75\%}$).[1,2] For patients with evidence of airway obstruction, a β_2-adrenergic agonist should be administered either via metered-dose inhaler (MDI) or nebulizer, and pulmonary function tests (PFTs) should be repeated 15 to 30 minutes later to determine whether the abnormalities are reversible. An increase in PEF or FEV_1 of >12% and 200 mL from baseline values strongly supports the diagnosis of asthma.[14] Some patients with asthma, however, have suboptimal responses to bronchodilator administration, and this may be related to airway edema and inflammation.[15] In these patients, a short course (1 to 3 weeks) of oral corticosteroids (20 mg PO twice daily in adults or 1 mg/kg/day in divided doses for children) produces significant improvement in pulmonary function if asthma exists.

Because there is considerable overlap between values of PFTs in normal and asthmatic individuals, patients with a suggestive history and 'normal' PEF or FEV_1 should also be tested for reversibility of pulmonary function after β-adrenergic agonist administration. The results of the PFTs should be evaluated using the criteria outlined above. Ninety-five percent of normal individuals have a <10% increase in FEV_1 after bronchodilator use.[14]

If peak flow measurements are used in the office instead of spirometry, it is strongly recommended that every patient with suspected asthma be referred for a more complete PFT at least once, to exclude other respiratory disorders that can mimic asthma. Once the diagnosis of asthma has been established, it is then reasonable to follow PEF as a longitudinal indicator of pulmonary function.

Chest radiographs are usually not helpful in the evaluation or management of acute exacerbations of asthma.[1,16] Indications for a chest film include asthma presenting in a very young child or a high clinical suspicion of pneumonia, pneumothorax, pneumomediastinum, or foreign-body aspiration. Allergy skin tests or a radioallergosorbent test (RAST) is also recommended in the initial evaluation of asthma because more than half of adults with asthma are sensitized to respiratory allergens, and control of environmental allergens can improve asthma control.[1,17] Food allergies, however, are rarely implicated as the cause of asthma in the absence of skin or gastrointestinal (GI) symptoms.[18]

Additional studies may be indicated in patients who have findings that suggest other disorders, and in patients who do not seem to respond to asthma treatment programs. These studies may include sinus radiographs or rhinoscopies to rule out chronic sinusitis, esophageal pH monitoring to detect gastroesophageal reflux, or direct visualization of the larynx to diagnose vocal cord paralysis or dysfunction.[19] Patients with equivocal clinical data or with incomplete responses to standard asthma therapy should be referred to an asthma specialist for additional evaluation.

Asthma Management

The goals of asthma management include restoring normal levels of activity and pulmonary function, preventing acute and chronic asthma symptoms, and avoiding adverse effects from asthma medication.[1,2] Three components of asthma care are recommended to achieve these goals. The first component is to assess and monitor asthma severity and control. Secondly, patient education and partnership in establishing individualized treatment goals, promoting self-management techniques and encouraging adherence to prescribed therapy should be encouraged. Third, the initial assessment of asthma should include identification of environmental triggers of asthma and comorbid conditions that can complicate asthma management. Environmental factors that contribute to symptoms include exposure to allergens or irritants such as tobacco smoke. Conditions that can impede the management of asthma include allergic rhinitis, sinusitis, smoking, gastroesophageal reflux, obesity, and depression. Accordingly, allergen avoidance, management of comorbid conditions, and patient education are all important components of the asthma treatment plan.

The fourth component of asthma therapy is pharmacotherapy, guided by assessments of asthma severity (Figure 7-3) and asthma control (Figure 7-4). Severity is defined as the intrinsic intensity of the disease process, and is easiest to classify in the untreated patient. If treatment is ongoing, the amount of medication that is required to maintain control of asthma can be used to estimate severity. Asthma control is the degree to which symptoms and manifestations of asthma are minimized.[1,2]

The concepts of impairment and risk (Table 7-3) should be considered when assessing both asthma severity and control. Impairment consists of the day-to-day symptoms of asthma, and the effects of asthma on daytime activities (work, school, exercise) and the quality of sleep. In addition, lung function tests and validated questionnaires such as the Asthma Control Test™ (ACT) can be used to measure impairment.[20] In contrast, the risk domain refers to the likelihood of developing acute exacerbations of asthma, progressive impairment of lung function, or side effects from asthma medications. Although risk is more difficult to measure than impairment, a history of recent visits to the emergency department, hospitalizations, and ICU admission are all indicators of increased risk.

Estimating the severity of asthma is helpful in determining the initial treatment regimen.[1,2] Asthma pharmacotherapy includes quick-relief medications (Table 7-4) to treat acute symptoms, and asthma controllers (Table 7-5) to treat chronic inflammation and airway obstruction. Once therapy is initiated, periodic monitoring of asthma control is used to guide adjustments in the treatment regimen in a stepwise fashion (Figure 7-5). The recently released National Asthma Education and Prevention Program (NAEPP) Guidelines for the Diagnosis and Management of Asthma refer to treatment options as *preferred* or *alternative* based upon an evidence-based review of group mean responses in clinical trials.[1,2] If one regimen does not provide asthma control, it is recommended to consider other regimens in the same step before proceeding to the next step. It is important to remember that asthma is a heterogeneous disease, both in terms of disease characteristics and in its response to treatment.[21]

Classification of Asthma Severity (≥12 years of age)

Components of Severity		Intermittent	Persistent		
			Mild	Moderate	Severe
Impairment Normal FEV₁/FVC: 8-19 yr 85% 20-39 yr 80% 40-59 yr 75% 60-80 yr 70%	Symptoms	≤2 days/week	>2 days/week but not daily	Daily	Throughout the day
	Nighttime awakenings	≤2 times/month	3-4 times/month	>1 time/week but not nightly	Often 7 times/week
	Short-acting β₂-agonist use for symptom control (not prevention of EIB)	≤2 days/week	>2 days/week but not daily, and not more than 1 time on any day	Daily	Several times per day
	Interference with normal activity	None	Minor limitation	Some limitation	Extremely limited
	Lung function	• Normal FEV₁ between exacerbations • FEV₁ >80% predicted • FEV₁/FVC normal	• FEV₁ >80% predicted • FEV₁/FVC normal	• FEV₁ >60% <80% predicted • FEV₁/FVC reduced 5%	• FEV₁ <60% predicted • FEV₁/FVC reduced >5%

		0-1/year (see note)	≥2/year (see note)
Risk	Exacerbations requiring oral systemic corticosteroids	Consider severity and interval since last exacerbation. Frequency and severity may fluctuate over time for patients in any severity category. Relative annual risk of exacerbations may be related to FEV_1.	
Recommend Step for Initiating Treatment See "Stepwise Approach for Managing Asthma" for treatment steps.)		Step 1	Step 2
			Step 3 and consider short course of oral systemic corticosteroids
			Step 4 or 5
		In 2–6 weeks, evaluate level of asthma control that is achieved and adjust therapy accordingly.	

Figure 7-3: Classifying asthma severity and initiating treatment in youths 12 years of age of adults who are not currently taking long-term control medications.[2] Level of severity is determined by assessment of both impairment and risk. Assess impairment domain by patient's/caregiver's recall of previous 2–4 weeks and spirometry. Assign severity to the most severe category in which any feature occurs. EIB=exercise-induced bronchospasm, FEV_1=forced expiratory volume in 1 second, FVC=forced vital capacity, ICU=intensive care unit

Classification of Asthma Control (≥12 years of age)

Components of Control		Well Controlled	Not Well Controlled	Very Poorly Controlled
Impairment	Symptoms	≤2 days/week	>2 days/week	Throughout the day
	Nighttime awakenings	≤2 days/month	1-3 times/week	≥4 times/week
	Interference with normal activity	None	Some limitation	Extremely limited
	Short-acting β₂-agonist use for symptom control (not prevention of EIB)	≤2 days/week	>2 days/week	Several times per day
	• FEV₁ or peak flow	>80% predicted/personal best	>60-80% predicted/personal best	<60% predicted/personal best
	• Validated questionnaires ATAQ ACQ ACT	0 ≤0.75* ≥20	1-2 ≥1.5 16-19	3-4 N/A ≤15

Risk		0-1/year	≥2/year (see note)
	Exacerbations requiring oral systemic corticosteroids	Consider severity and interval since last exacerbation	
	Progress loss of lung function	Evaluation requires long-term follow-up care.	
	Treatment-related adverse effects	Mediation side effects can vary in intensity from none to very troublesome and worrisome. The level of intensity does not correlate to specific levels of control but should be considered in the overall assessment of risk.	
Recommend Action for Treatment See "Stepwise Approach for Managing Asthma" for treatment steps.)		• Maintain current step. • Regular follow-up at every 1-6 months to maintain control. • Consider step down if well controlled for at least 3 months.	• Step up one step. • Re-evaluate in 2-6 weeks. • For side effects, consider alternative treatment options.	• Consider short course of oral systemic corticosteroids. • Step up 1-2 steps. • Re-evaluate in 2 weeks. • For side effects, consider alternative treatment options.

Figure 7-4: Assessing asthma control and adjusting therapy in youths ≥12 years of age and adults. The level of control is based on the most severe impairment or risk category. Assess impairment domain by patient's recall of previous 2-4 weeks and by spirometry/or peak flow measures. Symptom assessment for longer periods should reflect a global assessment, such as inquiring whether the patient's asthma is better or worse since the last visit. Minimal important difference: 1.0 for the ATAQ; 0.5 for the ACQ; not determined for the ACT. Before step up in therapy: review adherence to medication, inhaler technique, environmental control, and comorbid conditions; if an alternative treatment option was used in a step, discontinue and use the preferred treatment for that step. *=ACQ values of 0.76-1.4 are indeterminate regarding well-controlled asthma. ACQ=Asthma Control Questionnaire, ACT=Asthma Control Test, ATAQ=Asthma Therapy Assessment Questionnaire, EIB=exercise-induced bronchospasm, ICU=intensive care unit. Modified from NAEPP guidelines[2]

Table 7-3: Goal of Therapy: Control of Asthma

Reduce impairment

- Prevent chronic and troublesome symptoms (eg, coughing or breathlessness in the daytime, during the night, or after exertion).
- Require infrequent use (≤2 d/wk) of inhaled SABA for quick relief of symptoms (not including prevention of EIB).
- Maintain (near) normal pulmonary function.
- Maintain normal activity levels (including exercise and other physical activity and attendance at school or work).
- Meet patient and family expectations of, and satisfaction with, asthma care.

Reduce risk

- Prevent recurrent exacerbations of asthma and minimize the need for ED visits or hospitalizations.
- Prevent loss of lung function; for children, prevent reduced lung growth.
- Provide optimal pharmacotherapy with minimal or no adverse effects of therapy.

ED=emergency department, EIB=exercise-induced bronchospasm, SABA=short-acting β_2-agonist
Modified from NAEPP guidelines[2]

Many patients have intermittent asthma, characterized by infrequent daytime (≤2 days/week) and nighttime (≤2 nights/month) symptoms and normal activity and pulmonary function between episodes of asthma. For these patients, step 1 therapy (Figure 7-5) is recommended, which consists of an inhaled β_2-adrenergic agonist, such as albuterol (ProAir®, Ventolin®), levalbuterol (Xopenex®), or pirbuterol (Maxair® Autohaler®) used up to twice weekly as needed to relieve episodic symptoms. These medications can also be used before strenuous activity to prevent exercise-induced bronchospasm (EIB). As alternatives to β_2-adrenergic agonists, leukotriene-receptor antagonists attenuate EIB in about 50% of patients, and prophylactic use of cromolyn (Intal®) can also be effective.

In contrast to intermittent asthma, patients with mild persistent asthma have symptoms that occur more than twice weekly but less than daily, and these symptoms may occasionally disturb sleep or interfere with daytime activity. Although PFTs may be within the normal range between exacerbations, studies using bronchoscopy have revealed that persistent asthma symptoms, even when mild, are usually accompanied by lower airway inflammation. Consequently, daily preventive medications, such as low-dose inhaled corticosteroids, leukotriene modifiers, cromolyn, nedocromil, or oral theophylline, are recommended to control mild persistent asthma (step 2). Inhaled corticosteroids are the most potent and effective anti-inflammatory medications,[1,19] and, consequently, low-dose inhaled corticosteroids are preferred for the treatment of mild persistent asthma. Data from clinical trials has been used to estimate the relative potency of various inhaled corticosteroids (Table 7-6).

The leukotriene modifiers, including receptor antagonists (montelukast [Singulair®], zafirlukast [Accolate®]) and synthesis inhibitors (zileuton [Zyflo®, Zyflo CR™]) produce long-lasting bronchodilation and reduce blood eosinophil counts and antigen-induced eosinophil recruitment.[22] These medications have the advantage of oral administration, and they can be used instead of inhaled corticosteroid medications in selected patients. Zileuton is used less often because it occasionally causes liver inflammation, and liver enzymes should be monitored periodically. Cromolyn and

Table 7-4: Usual Dosages for Quick-Relief Medications in Youths ≥12 Years and Adults

Medication	Dosage Form	Adult Dose
Short-Acting Inhaled β₂-Agonists (SABAs)		
Metered-dose inhaler (MDI)		
albuterol CFC (Ventolin®)	90 μg/puff, 200 puffs	2 puffs 5 min before exercise 2 puffs q4-6h as needed for symptoms
albuterol HFA (ProAir® HFA, Proventil® HFA, Ventolin® HFA)	90 μg/puff, 200 puffs	2 puffs 5 min before exercise 2 puffs q4-6h as needed for symptoms
levalbuterol HFA (Xopenex® HFA)	45 μg/puff, 200 puffs	2 puffs 5 min before exercise 2 puffs q4-6h as needed for symptoms
pirbuterol CFC autohaler (Maxair® Autohaler®)	200 μg/puff, 400 puffs	2 puffs 5 min before exercise 2 puffs q4-6h as needed for symptoms
Nebulizer solution		
albuterol	0.63 mg/3 mL 1.25 mg/3 mL 2.5 mg/3 mL 5 mg/mL	1.25-5 mg in 3 mL of saline q4-8h, as needed for symptoms
	0.083% (unit dose vials)	3 mL (2.5 mg) q4-8h
levalbuterol (R-albuterol)	0.31 mg/3 mL, 0.63 mg/ 3 mL, 1.25 mg/0.5 mL, 1.25 mg/3 mL	0.63-1.25 mg q8h as needed for symptoms

Dosages for this table are provided for those products that have been approved by the US Food and Drug Administration or have sufficient clinical trial safety and efficacy data in the appropriate age ranges to support their use.

Modified from NAEPP guidelines[2]

Potential
Adverse Effects

Comments

(Apply to all SABAs listed on page 118)

- Tachycardia, skeletal muscle tremor, hypokalemia, increased lactic acid, headache, hyperglycemia. Inhaled route, in general, causes few systemic adverse effects. Patients with pre-existing cardiovascular disease (CVD), especially the elderly, may have adverse cardiovascular reactions with inhaled therapy.

- Drugs of choice for acute bronchospasm.
- Differences in potencies exist, but all products are essential comparable on a puff-per-puff basis.
- An increasing use or lack of expected effect indicates diminished control of asthma.
- Not recommended for long-term daily treatment. Regular use exceeding 2 d/wk for symptom control (not prevention of EIB) indicates the need for additional long-term control therapy.
- May double usual dose for mild exacerbations.
- For levalbuterol, prime the inhaler by releasing 4 actuations prior to use.
- For HFA: periodically clean HFA actuator, as drug may plug orifice.

7

- Same as with MDI

- Nonselective agents (ie, epinephrine, isoproterenol, metoprolol) are not recommended due to their potential for excessive cardiac stimulation, especially in high doses.

- Same as with MDI

- May mix with cromolyn solution, budesonide, inhalant suspension, or ipratropium solution for nebulization. May double dose for severe exacerbations.
- Compatible with budesonide inhalant suspension. The product is a sterile-filled, preservative-free unit dose vial.

CFC=chlorofluorocarbon, ED=emergency department, EIB=exercise-induced bronchospasm, HFA=hydrofluoroalkane, IM=intramuscular, MDI=metered-dose inhaler, PEF=peak expiratory flow, SABA=short-acting β_2-agonist

(continued on next page)

Table 7-4: Usual Dosages for Quick-Relief Medications in Youths ≥12 Years and Adults *(continued)*

Medication	Dosage Form	Adult Dose
Anticholinergics		
Metered-dose inhaler (MDI)		
ipratropium HFA (Atrovent® HFA)	17 µg/puff, 200 puffs	2-3 puffs q6h
ipratropium/albuterol (Combivent®, Duoneb®)	18 µg/puff of ipratropium and 90 µg/puff of albuterol, 200 puffs	2-3 puffs q4-6h
Nebulizer solution		
ipratropium HFA (Atrovent® HFA)	0.25 mg/mL (0.025%)	0.25 mg q6h
ipratropium/albuterol (Combivent®, Duoneb®)	0.5 mg/3 mL ipratropium and 2.5 mg/3 mL albuterol	3 mL q4-6h

oral theophylline are other alternatives that are not often used because of concerns related to frequent administration (cromolyn) and a narrow therapeutic window (theophylline), respectively. In addition to controller medications, inhaled β_2-adrenergic agonists can be used every 4 to 6 hours as needed to relieve acute symptoms of asthma. Frequent use

Potential Adverse Effects | Comments

(Apply to all anticholinergics listed on page 120)

- Drying of mouth and respiratory secretions, increased wheezing in some individuals, blurred vision if sprayed in eyes. If used in the ED, produces less cardiac stimulation than SABAs.

- Multiple doses in the ED (not hospital) setting provide additive benefit to SABA.
- Treatment of choice for bronchospasm due to β-blocker medication.
- Does not block EIB.
- Reverses only cholinergically mediated bronchospasm; does not modify reaction to antigen.
- May be an alternative for patients who cannot tolerate SABA.
- Has not proven to be efficacious as long-term control therapy for asthma.

- Contains EDTA to prevent discoloration of the solution. The additive does not induce bronchospasm.

(continued on next page)

of a β_2-adrenergic agonist is a good indicator of suboptimal asthma control, signaling the need to re-evaluate asthma triggers and the preventive medication regimen.

Moderate persistent asthma is usually accompanied by daily symptoms (before treatment is initiated), disturbance of sleep or daytime activities more than once weekly, and

Table 7-4: Usual Dosages for Quick-Relief Medications in Youths ≥12 Years and Adults *(continued)*

Medication	Dosage Form	Adult Dose
Systemic Corticosteroids		
methylprednisolone (Medrol®)	2, 4, 8, 16, 32 mg tablets	Short-course 'burst': 40-60 mg/d as single or two divided doses for 3-10 days
prednisolone	10, 15 mg disintegrating tabs, 5 mg/ 5 mL 15 mg/5 mL	Same as for methylprednisolone
prednisone	1, 2.5, 5, 10, 20, 50 mg tabs; 5 mg/mL, 5 mg/5 mL	Same as for methylprednisolone
methylprednisolone acetate (Depo-Medrol®)	40 mg/mL, 80 mg/mL respository injection	240 mg IM once

occasionally, more severe exacerbations requiring acute-care visits to the doctor's office or emergency department. Pulmonary function tests (PFTs) often show signs of airway obstruction, at least before anti-inflammatory therapy has been instituted. For patients with moderate persistent asthma, or symptoms that are inadequately controlled with low-dose

Potential Adverse Effects

Comments

(Apply to all corticosteroids listed on page 122)

- Short term: reversible abnormalities in glucose metabolism, increased appetite, fluid retention, weight gain, facial flushing, mood alteration, hypertension, peptic ulcer, and rarely aseptic necrosis.

- Consideration should be given to coexisting conditions that could be worsened by systemic corticosteroids, such as herpes virus infection, varicella, tuberculosis, hypertension, peptic ulcer, diabetes, osteoporosis, and *Strongyloides*.

- Short courses or 'bursts' are effective for establishing control when initiating therapy or during a period of gradual deterioration. Action may begin within 1 hour.

- The burst should be continued until patient achieves 80% PEF personal best or symptoms resolve. This usually requires 3-10 days, but may require longer. There is no evidence that tapering the dose after improvement prevents relapse in asthma exacerbations.

- Other systemic corticosteroids such as hydrocortisone and dexamethasone, given in equipotent daily doses are likely to be as effective as prednisolone.

- Repository injection of methylprednisolone acetate may be used in place of a short burst of oral steroids in patients who are vomiting or if adherence is a problem.

inhaled corticosteroids alone, there are two preferred options for step 3 therapy. For moderate asthma, two regimens should be considered for preferred therapy: either a medium-dose inhaled corticosteroid alone, or a combination of low-dose inhaled corticosteroid together with a long-acting inhaled β-agonist (fluticasone/salmeterol [Advair Diskus®]

Table 7-5: Usual Dosages for Long-Term Control Medications

Medication	Dosage Form	Adult Dose
Inhaled Corticosteroids (see Table 7-6)		
Oral Systemic Corticosteroids		
methylprednisolone	2, 4, 8, 16, 32 mg tablets	• 7.5 to 60 mg/d in a single dose in the morning or q.o.d. as needed for control
prednisolone	5 mg tabs, 5 mg/5 mL, 15 mg/5 mL	• Short-course 'burst' to achieve control: 40 to 60 mg/d as single dose or two divided doses for 3-10 d
prednisone	1, 2.5, 5, 10, 20, 50 mg tablets; 5 mg/mL, 5 mg/5 mL	

Dosages for this table are provided for those products that have been approved by the US Food and Drug Administration or have sufficient clinical trial safety and efficacy data in the appropriate age ranges to support their use.

Modified from NAEPP guidelines[2]

or budesonide/formoterol [Symbicort®]). The choice of budesonide/formoterol provides improved symptom relief, lung function, and protection from asthma exacerbations compared with higher doses of an inhaled corticosteroid alone.[23,24] However, there is clinical evidence that treatment

Potential Adverse Effects	Comments
• Short term: reversible abnormalities in glucose metabolism, increased appetite, fluid retention, weight gain, facial flushing, mood alteration, hypertension, peptic ulcer, and rarely aseptic necrosis. • Long term: adrenal axis suppression, growth suppression, dermal thinning, hypertension, diabetes, Cushing's syndrome, cataracts, muscle weakness, and, in rare instances, impaired immune function. • Consider co-existing conditions that could be worsened by systemic corticosteroids, ie, herpes virus infections, varicella, tuberculosis, hypertension, peptic ulcer, diabetes, osteoporosis, and *Strongyloides*.	• For long-term treatment of severe persistent asthma, administer single dose in the morning either daily or alternate days (alternate-day therapy may produce less adrenal suppression). • Short courses or 'bursts' are effective for establishing control when initiating therapy or during a period of gradual deterioration. • There is no evidence that tapering the dose following improvement in symptom control and pulmonary function prevents relapse. • For patients unable to tolerate liquid preparations, dexamethasone syrup at 0.4 mg/kg/d may be an alternative. Studies are limited, however, and the longer duration of activity increases the risk of adrenal suppression.

(continued on next page)

with a long-acting β_2-agonist alone (without the concomitant use of an inhaled corticosteroid) masks the symptoms of worsening asthma, and may increase the risk of severe exacerbations and even death.[25,26] These findings prompted the FDA to put a black box warning label on all products

Table 7-5: Usual Dosages for Long-Term Control Medications
(continued)

Medication	Dosage Form	Adult Dose
Long-acting Inhaled β_2-agonists		
salmeterol (Serevent®)	DPI 50 µg/blister	1 blister q12h
formoterol (Foradil®, Performist™)	DPI 12 µg/single-use capsule	1 capsule q12h
Combined Medication		
fluticasone/salmeterol (Advair Diskus®)	DPI 100, 250, or 500 µg/50 µg HFA 45 µg, 115 µg, 230 µg/21 µg	1 inhalation b.i.d.; dose depends on level of severity or control
budesonide/formoterol (Symbicort®)	HFA MDI 80 or 160 µg/4.5 µg	2 puffs b.i.d; dose depends on level of severity or control

DPI=dry powder inhaler, EIB=exercise-induced bronchospasm, HFA=hydrofluoroalkane, ICS=inhaled corticosteroids, IgE=immunoglobulin E, LABA=long-acting β_2-agonist, MDI=metered-dose inhaler, QTc=corrected QT, SABA=short-acting β_2-agonist, SVT=supraventricular tachycardia

Potential Adverse Effects	Comments
• Tachycardia, skeletal muscle tremor, hypokalemia, prolongation of QTc interval in overdose.	• **Should not be used for symptom relief or for exacerbations. Use only with ICS.**
• A diminished broncho-protective effect may occur within 1 wk of chronic therapy. Clinical significance has not been established.	• Decreased duration of protection against EIB may occur with regular use.
	• Do not blow into inhaler after dose is activated.
• Potential risk of uncommon, severe, life-threatening, or fatal exacerbation; see text for additional discussion regarding safety of LABAs.	• Each capsule is for single use only; additional doses should not be administered for at least 12 hrs.
	• Capsules should be used only with the inhaler and should not be taken orally.
See notes for ICS and LABA	• Do not blow into inhaler after dose is activated.
	• 100/50 DPI or 45/21 HFA for patients who have uncontrolled asthma on low-to-medium dose ICS.
	• 250/50 DPI or 115/21 HFA for patients who have uncontrolled asthma on medium-to-high dose ICS.
See notes for ICS and LABA	• 80/4.5 for patients who have uncontrolled asthma on low-to-medium dose ICS.
	• 160/4.5 for patients who have uncontrolled asthma on medium-to-high dose ICS.

(continued on next page)

7

Table 7-5: Usual Dosages for Long-Term Control Medications
(continued)

Medication	Dosage Form	Adult Dose
Cromolyn and Nedocromil		
cromolyn (Intal®)	MDI 0.8 mg/puff	2 puffs q.i.d.
	Nebulizer 20 mg/ampule	1 ampule q.i.d.
nedocromil (Tilade®)	MDI 1.75 mg/puff	2 puffs q.i.d.
Immunomodulators		
omalizumab (anti-IgE) (Xolair®)	SC injection, 150 mg/1.2 mL following reconstitution with 1.4 mL sterile water for injection	150-375 SC q 2-4 weeks, depending on body weight and pretreatment serum IgE level (see Table 7-7)

containing long-acting β_2-agonists, and in fact long-acting β_2-agonists alone should not be used to treat persistent asthma. In choosing a treatment regimen, this information needs to be weighed against the considerable body of evidence indicating

Potential Adverse Effects

- Cough and irritation
- 15%-20% of patients complain of an unpleasant taste from nedocromil.
- Safety is the primary advantage of cromolyn and nedocromil.

Comments

- One dose of cromolyn before exercise or allergen exposure provides effective prophylaxis for 1-2 hrs. Not as effective as inhaled β_2-agonists for EIB as SABA.
- 4-6 wk trial of cromolyn or nedocromil may be needed to determine maximum benefit.
- Dose by MDI may be inadequate to affect hyperresponsiveness.
- Once control is achieved, the frequency of dosing may be reduced.

- Pain and bruising of injection sites in 5%-20% of patients.
- Anaphylaxis has been reported in 0.2% of treated patients.
- Malignant neoplasms were reported in 0.5% of patients compared with 0.2% receiving placebo; relationship to drug is unclear.

- Do not administer >150 μg/injection site.
- Monitor patients following injections; be prepared and equipped to identify and treat anaphylaxis that may occur.
- Whether patients will develop significant antibody titers to the drug with long-term administration is unknown.

(continued on next page)

that combination medications are both safe and effective.[1,27] Finally, as alternatives to long-acting β_2-agonists, the leukotriene modifiers or theophylline can also be used as an adjunct to inhaled corticosteroids in patients with moderate asthma.

Table 7-5: Usual Dosages for Long-Term Control Medications
(continued)

Medication	Dosage Form	Adult Dose
Leukotriene Modifiers		
leukotriene-receptor antagonists		
montelukast (Singulair®)	4 or 5 mg chewable tablet, 4 mg oral granules, 10 mg tablet	10 mg q.h.s
zafirlukast (Accolate®)	10 or 20 mg tablet	40 mg daily (20 mg tablet b.i.d.)
5-lipoxygenase inhibitor		
zileuton (Zyflo®, Zyflo CR™)	600 mg tablet	2,400 mg daily (give tablets q.i.d.)

Potential Adverse Effects

Comments

- No specific adverse effects have been identified.
- Rare cases of Churg-Strauss syndrome have occurred, but the association is unclear.

- Postmarketing surveillance has reported cases of reversible hepatitis and, rarely, irreversible hepatic failure resulting in death or liver transplantation.
- Elevation of liver enzymes has been reported. Limited case reports of reversible hepatitis and hyperbilirubinemia.

- Montelukast exhibits a flat dose-response curve. Doses >10 mg will not produce a greater response in adults.
- Long-term therapy may attenuate EIB in some patients, but less effective than ICS therapy.

- For zafirlukast, administration with meals decreases bioavailability; take at least 1 hr before or 2 hrs after meals.
- Zafirlukast is a microsomal P450 enzyme inhibitor that can inhibit the metabolism of warfarin. Doses of these drugs should be monitored accordingly.
- Monitor hepatic enzymes (ALT). Warn patients to discontinue use if they experience signs and symptoms of liver dysfunction.

- For zileuton, monitor hepatic enzymes (ALT).
- Zileuton is a microsomal P450 enzyme inhibitor that can inhibit the metabolism of warfarin and theophylline. Doses of these drugs should be monitored accordingly.

(continued on next page)

Table 7-5: Usual Dosages for Long-Term Control Medications
(continued)

Medication	Dosage Form	Adult Dose
Methylxanthines		
theophylline	Liquids, sustained-release tablets, and capsules	Starting dose 10 mg/kg/d up to 300 mg max dose; usual daily max 800 mg/d

It is especially important to identify patients who have severe asthma so that aggressive intervention (steps 4 to 6) can prevent serious morbidity or even fatal attacks. Severe asthma is usually accompanied by daily wheezing and frequent exacerbations. These patients typically have a history of frequent visits to emergency departments or acute outpatient visits for asthma. Hospitalization is common in this group, and the occurrence of respiratory failure with intubation should be a 'red flag' for the identification of patients at increased risk for additional severe asthma exacerbations. These patients typically have poor exercise tolerance that limits their physical activities, and they also experience frequent night awakening. PFTs reveal significant airway ob-

Potential Adverse Effects	Comments
• Dose-related acute toxicities include tachycardia, nausea and vomiting, tachyarrhythmias (SVT), central nervous system (CNS) stimulation, headache, seizures, hematemesis, hyperglycemia, and hypokalemia.	• Adjust dosage to achieve serum concentration of 5-15 µg/mL at steady state (at least 48 hrs on the same dosage).
	• Due to wide interpatient variability in theophylline metabolic clearance, routine serum theophylline level monitoring is essential.
• Adverse effects at usual therapeutic doses include insomnia, gastric upset, aggravation of ulcer or reflux, difficulty in urination in elderly males who have prostatism.	• Patients should be told to discontinue if they experience toxicity.
	• Various factors (diet, food, febrile illness, age, smoking, and other medications) can affect serum concentrations. See package inserts for details.

struction that often does not completely reverse with bronchodilator use. Medical therapy is more intensive for these patients and includes medium- to high-dose inhaled corticosteroids with a long-acting β_2-agonist, and may be supplemented by daily or every-other-day oral corticosteroids. Adjunctive therapy to provide greater control of symptoms and minimize the required dose of oral corticosteroid may include long-acting β_2-agonists, sustained-release theophylline, a leukotriene-receptor antagonist or synthesis inhibitor, or omalizumab (Xolair®).[1]

Omalizumab is a humanized mouse monoclonal antibody that is approved for the treatment of moderate-to-severe persistent allergic asthma that is incompletely controlled with

Persistent Asthma: Daily Medication

Consult with asthma specialist if step 4 care or higher is required.
Consider consultation at step 3.

Intermittent Asthma

Step 1
Preferred:
SABA PRN

Step 2
Preferred:
Low-dose ICS
Alternative:
Cromolyn, LTRA, Nedocromil, or Theophylline

Step 3
Preferred:
Low-dose ICS + LABA
OR
Medium-dose ICS
Alternative:
Low-dose ICS + either LTRA, Theophylline, or Zileuton

Step 4
Preferred:
Medium-dose ICS + LABA
Alternative:
Medium-dose ICS + either LTRA, Theophylline, or Zileuton

Step 5
Preferred:
High-dose ICS + LABA
AND
Consider Omalizumab for patients who have allergies

Step 6
Preferred:
High-dose ICS + LABA + oral corticosteroid
AND
Consider Omalizumab for patients who have allergies

Step up if needed
(first check adherence, environmental control, and comorbid conditions)

Assess control

Step down if possible

Each step: Patient education, environmental control, and management of comorbidities.
Steps 2-4: Consider subcutaneous allergen immunotherapy for patients who have allergic asthma (see notes).

(and asthma is well controlled at least 3 months)

→

Quick-Relief Medication for All Patients

- SABA as needed for symptoms. Intensity of treatment depends on severity of symptoms: up to 3 treatments at 20-minute intervals as needed. Short course of oral systemic corticosteroids may be needed.
- Use of SABA >2 days a week for symptom relief (not prevention of EIB) generally indicates inadequate control and the need to step up treatment.

7

Figure 7-5: Stepwise approach for managing asthma in youths ≥12 years of age and adults. The stepwise approach is meant to assist, not replace, the clinical decision-making required to meet individual patient needs. If alternative treatment is used and response is inadequate, discontinue that treatment and use the preferred treatment before stepping up. In step 6, before oral corticosteroids are introduced, a trial of high-dose ICS + LABA + either LTRA, theophylline, or zileuton may be considered, although this approach has not been studied in clinical trials. Clinicians who administer immunotherapy or omalizumab should be prepared and equipped to identify and treat anaphylaxis that may occur. Alphabetical order is used when more than one treatment option is listed within either preferred or alternative therapy. ICS=inhaled corticosteroid, LABA=long-acting β_2-agonist, LTRA=leukotriene-receptor antagonist, SABA=short-acting β_2-agonist. Modified from NAEPP guidelines[2]

Table 7-6: Estimated Comparative Daily Dosages for Inhaled Corticosteroids, for Patients ≥12 Years

Drug	Low Daily Dose
beclomethasone HFA 40 or 80 µg/puff	80-240 µg
budesonide DPI 90, 180, or 200 µg/ suspension	180-600 µg
budesonide suspension for nebulization	N/A
flunisolide (Aerobid®) 250 µg/puff	500-1,000 µg
flunisolide HFA 80 µg/puff	320 µg
fluticasone HFA/MDI (Flovent®) 44, 110, or 220 µg/puff	88-264 µg
fluticasone DPI (Flovent® Diskus®) 50, 100, or 250 µg/ inhalation	100-300 µg
mometasone DPI 220 µg/inhalation	220 µg
triamcinolone acetonide 100 µg/puff	600-800 µg

DPI=dry powder inhaler, HFA=hydrofluoroalkane, MDI=metered-dose inhaler, N/A=not available (either not approved, no data available, or safety and efficacy not established for this age group).
Modified from NAEPP guidelines[2]

Medium Daily Dose	High Daily Dose
>240-480 µg	>480 µg
>600-1,200 µg	>1,200 µg
N/A	N/A
>1,000-2,000 µg	>2,000 µg
>320-640 µg	>640 µg
>264-440 µg	>440 µg
>300-500 µg	>500 µg
220-440 µg	>440 µg
>800-1600 µg	>1,600 µg

7

(continued on next page)

Therapeutic issues:

- The most important determinant of appropriate dosing is the clinician's judgment of the patient's response to therapy. The clinician must monitor the patient's response on several clinical parameters and adjust the dose accordingly. Once control of asthma is achieved, the dose should be carefully titrated to the minimum dose required to maintain control.

- Preparations are not interchangeable on a μg or per-puff basis. This table presents estimated comparable daily doses.

- Some doses may be outside package labeling, especially in the high-dose range.

Potential adverse effects of inhaled corticosteroids:

- Cough, dysphonia, oral thrush (candidiasis)

- Spacer or valved holding chamber with nonbreath-actu-ated MDIs and mouthwashing and spitting after inhalation decrease local side effects.

inhaled corticosteroids in adults and adolescents ≥12 years. This molecule binds to the Fc receptor of IgE, thereby preventing the IgE molecule from binding to its receptor on mast cells or other inflammatory cells.[27] Omalizumab is administered subcutaneously every 2 or 4 weeks and dosing is based on weight and total serum IgE levels (Table 7-7). Benefits that have been seen in clinical trials involving adults with moderate-to-severe asthma include significant reductions in the dose of maintenance corticosteroid; reductions in symptoms, exacerbations, and asthma-related

***Potential adverse effects
of inhaled corticosteroids:*** *(continued)*

- A number of ICS, including budesonide, fluticasone, and mometasone (Nasonex®), are metabolized in the gastrointestinal (GI) tract and liver by CYP 3A4 isoenzymes, Potent inhibitors of CYP 3A4, such as ritonavir (Norvir®) and ketoconazole (Nizoral®), have the potential for increasing systemic concentrations of these ICS by increasing oral availability and decreasing systemic clearance. Some cases of clinically significant Cushing's syndrome and secondary adrenal insufficiency have been reported.

- In high doses, systemic effects may occur, although studies are not conclusive, and the clinical significance of these effects has not been established (eg, adrenal suppression, osteoporosis, dermal thinning, easy bruising).

Modified from NAEPP guidelines[2]

hospitalizations; and improved quality of life.[28-31] Adverse effects associated with omalizumab include mild irritant reactions at the site of injection and, less commonly, allergic reactions. Clinicians prescribing omalizumab need to be equipped and trained to treat anaphylaxis, and guidelines for office procedures have recently been published.[32]

Adherence to medical therapy should be carefully assessed in patients with moderate-to-severe asthma because poor control of asthma can signal underuse of asthma controller medications.[1] Unfortunately, estimating adher-

Table 7-7: Omalizumab Dosage in Adults and Adolescents With Asthma*

Pretreatment Serum IgE (IU/mL)	Body Weight (kg)	
	30-60	>60-70
≥30-100	150 mg q 4 wk	150 mg q 4 wk
>100-200	300 mg q 4 wk	300 mg q 4 wk
>200-300	300 mg q 4 wk	225 mg q 2 wk
>300-400	225 mg q 2 wk	225 mg q 2 wk
>400-500	300 mg q 2 wk	300 mg q 2 wk
>500-600	300 mg q 2 wk	375 mg q 2 wk
>600-700	375 mg q 2 wk	**

*Administered by subcutaneous injection in adults and adolescents 12 years of age and older.
**Do not dose omalizumab in these patients.
IgE=immunoglobulin E, IU=international units

ence can be difficult and there is no correlation between adherence and income, gender, ethnicity, or physician assessment. Helpful information can be obtained from the pharmacist to determine if prescriptions are being filled. In addition, prescription dates can be checked at office visits or the physician can choose a product that allows them to monitor use, ie, Ventolin®, which includes a dose counter.

Body Weight (kg)	
>70-90	>90-150
150 mg q 4 wk	300 mg q 4 wk
300 mg q 4 wk	225 mg q 2 wk
225 mg q 2 wk	300 mg q 2 wk
300 mg q 2 wk	**
375 mg q 2 wk	**
**	**
**	**

Data from Xolair® (omalizumab) for subcutaneous use. San Francisco, CA, Genentech Inc., 2003.

Furthermore, it is important to ask how the patient perceives prescribed medications, especially in terms of side effects, efficacy, cost, and 'steroid phobia.' Finally, the regimen should be as simple as possible and always include a written treatment plan (Table 7-8) so that the patient has a clear understanding of the prescribed therapy. Many fine educational materials can be obtained from the NAEPP (PO Box 30105,

Table 7-8: Suggested Content for a Written Asthma Control Plan

- Instructions to control exposure to environmental allergens and irritants
- Guidelines for monitoring PEF:
  - Establish personal best value
  - Establish green, yellow, and red zones
- Provide written instructions regarding medication use:
  - Maintenance medications
  - Prophylaxis for exercise, allergen exposure, etc.
  - Rescue medications
- Provide contact telephone numbers to report acute asthma symptoms:
  - Clinic
  - Emergency services

PEF=peak expiratory flow

Bethesda, MD 20824-0105; telephone 301-592-8573; Web site http://www.nhlbi.nih.gov/about/naepp).

The recent trend toward reliance on inhaled medication for treating asthma is well supported by data proving the efficacy and relative safety of these products. However, improper use of a metered-dose inhaler is a common problem leading to suboptimal responses to asthma treatment regimens. Technique should always be reviewed with the patient after prescribing an inhaled medication (Table 7-9), and it is most helpful to have the patient demonstrate his or her inhaler technique at each outpatient visit. Spacer devices (Aerochamber®, Inspirease®, and others) can increase inhaler effectiveness and reduce side effects, especially in patients with suboptimal inhaler technique.[33] Selection of the spacer is determined by many factors, including the age of

Table 7-9: Proper Inhaler Technique*

- Remove cap and hold inhaler upright.
- Shake the inhaler.
- Tilt head back slightly and breathe out.
- Use a spacer device, or open mouth** and place inhaler 1-2 inches away.
- Press down on inhaler to release medication as you start to breathe in slowly.
- Breathe in slowly (over 3-5 seconds) and hold breath for 5-10 seconds.
- Repeat puffs as directed. Wait 1 minute between puffs.

*Spacer devices are especially recommended for children and the elderly.
For dry powder inhalers, see package insert.
**For breath-activated inhalers, the inhaler opening must be held in the mouth with lips closed.
Adapted from NAEPP guidelines.[1]

the patient, the type of metered-dose inhaler or medication, and the cost. Use of a spacer device with an inhaler does not eliminate the need to carefully review proper administration technique with the patient or parent, preferably during the clinic visit.

Monitoring of pulmonary function at home with a peak flow meter can increase awareness of asthma and encourage self-management skills.[1] PEF, which is the greatest flow velocity (L/min) that is generated during forced expiration, correlates reasonably well with FEV_1. Home monitoring of PEF can be especially helpful for patients with moderate or severe asthma, or in patients who have poor perception of their lung function. Use of a peak flow meter may also have psychological benefits by allowing patients to effectively manage most asthmatic exacerbations and by providing positive feedback for the asthma treatment plan. It should be emphasized to patients that PEF meters are not infallible, and falsely low PEF readings can occur if instruments are dirty or broken. Treatment plans based on symptoms can be equally effective, and the key is to ensure that patients are comfortable with their own monitoring plan.

A useful protocol for using peak flow meters in managing asthma is outlined in the *Guidelines for the Diagnosis and Management of Asthma,* published by the US Department of Health and Human Services.[1,2] The first goal is to ascertain the patient's personal best peak flow rate, which requires the appropriate use of medications to maximize pulmonary function. Once this value has been established, the calculation of green (80% to 100% of personal best), yellow (50% to 80% of personal best), and red (<50% of personal best) zones can be accomplished. Peak flow rates in the green zone indicate stable disease activity, provided no other warning signs are present (eg, nocturnal awakenings due to asthma, exercise intolerance). If the peak flow rate is in the yellow zone, a short-acting β-agonist should be administered. If the patient does not improve or if peak flow rates drop into the red zone, oral corticosteroid therapy (prednisone 20 mg PO twice daily administered for 5 to 10 days) should be initiated, and the patient should contact a physician as soon as possible. Although prednisone given over short periods has relatively few side effects, extra caution must be used in prescribing oral corticosteroid therapy to patients with significant health problems such as diabetes, hypertension, or glaucoma. In addition, patients who develop varicella within 30 days of receiving a course of oral corticosteroids may require specific antiviral therapy, although patients receiving standard doses of inhaled corticosteroids do not appear to be at increased risk.[34]

For milder exacerbations or for patients who do not tolerate oral corticosteroids, high-dose inhaled corticosteroids have been used as a yellow zone therapy, although optimal doses and regimens have not yet been determined.[35]

Summary

Accurate diagnosis of asthma requires the use of an objective measurement of pulmonary function in addition to careful evaluation of medical history and physical findings. Treatment should be tailored to the individual patient, based upon identification of triggers for acute symptoms and classification of disease severity. Optimal control of asthma symptoms is achieved using a combination of patient education, environmental modifications, and medical therapy, which should include topical anti-inflammatory drugs for all but mild disease. Goals of therapy should include restoring normal pulmonary function and controlling symptoms while avoiding side effects from asthma medications.

References

1. National Asthma Education and Prevention Program, National Heart, Lung, and Blood Institute, National Institutes of Health: Expert Panel Report 3: *Guidelines for the Diagnosis and Management of Asthma (Full Report 2007)*. Bethesda, MD, US Department of Health and Human Services, 2007, NIH publication number 08-5846. Available at: http://www.nhlbi.nih.gov/guidelines/asthma/asthgdln.htm. Accessed January 21, 2008.

2. National Asthma Education and Prevention Program: Expert Panel Report EPR-3: Guidelines for the Diagnosis and Management of Asthma—Summary Report 2007. Available at: http://nhlbi.nih.gov/guidelines/archives. Accessed January 21, 2008.

3. Busse WW, Lemanske RF Jr: Asthma. *N Engl J Med* 2001;344: 350-362.

4. Mauad T, Bel EH, Sterk PJ: Asthma therapy and airway remodeling. *J Allergy Clin Immunol* 2007;120:997-1009.

5. Ober C: Perspectives on the past decade of asthma genetics. *J Allergy Clin Immunol* 2005;116:274-278.

6. Palmer CN, Irvine AD, Terron-Kwiatkowski A, et al: Common loss-of-function variants of the epidermal barrier protein filaggrin are a major predisposing factor for atopic dermatitis. *Nat Genet* 2006;38:441-446.

7.   Contoli M, Message SD, Laza-Stanca V, et al: Role of deficient type III interferon-lambda production in asthma exacerbations. *Nat Med* 2006;12:1023-1026.

8.   Pearce N, Ait-Khaled N, Beasley R, et al: Worldwide trends in the prevalence of asthma symptoms: phase III of the International Study of Asthma and Allergies in Childhood (ISAAC). *Thorax* 2007;62:758-766.

9.   von Mutius E: Allergies, infections and the hygiene hypothesis—the epidemiological evidence. *Immunobiology* 2007;212: 433-439.

10. Peden DB: The epidemiology and genetics of asthma risk associated with air pollution. *J Allergy Clin Immunol* 2005;115:213-219.

11. Shim CS, Williams MH Jr: Relationship of wheezing to the severity of obstruction in asthma. *Arch Intern Med* 1983;143: 890-892.

12. Bush RK, Asbury D: Aspirin-sensitive asthma. In: Busse WW, Holgate ST, eds: *Asthma and Rhinitis*. Oxford, England, Blackwell Scientific, 2000, pp 1315-1325.

13. Daniel S: Infection and inflammation CF: management of the basics upper airway diseases. *Paediatr Respir Rev* 2006;7(suppl 1): S154-S155.

14. Lung function testing: selection of reference values and interpretative strategies. American Thoracic Society. *Am Rev Respir Dis* 1991;144:1202-1218.

15. Enright PL, Lebowitz MD, Cockroft DW: Physiologic measures: pulmonary function tests. Asthma outcome. *Am J Respir Crit Care Med* 1994;149(2 pt 2):S9-S18.

16. Gershel JC, Goldman HS, Stein RE, et al: The usefulness of chest radiographs in first asthma attacks. *N Engl J Med* 1983; 309:336-339.

17. Platts-Mills T, Leung DY, Schatz M: The role of allergens in asthma. *Am Fam Physician* 2007;76:675-680.

18. James JM, Bernhisel-Broadbent J, Sampson HA: Respiratory reactions provoked by double-blind food challenges in children. *Am J Respir Crit Care Med* 1994;149:59-64.

19. Jarjour NN: Asthma in Adults: Evaluation and Management. In: Adkinson NF, Yunginger JW, Busse WW, et al, eds: *Middleton's Allergy: Principles and Practice*, 6th ed. St. Louis, MO, Mosby, 2003, pp 1257-1282.

20. Schatz M, Sorkness CA, Li JT, et al: Asthma Control Test: reliability, validity, and responsiveness in patients not previously followed by asthma specialists. *J Allergy Clin Immunol* 2006;117:549-556.

21. Tantisira KG, Weiss ST: The pharmacogenetics of asthma therapy. *Curr Drug Targets* 2006;7:1697-1708.

22. Bisgaard H: Pathophysiology of the cysteinyl leukotrienes and effects of leukotriene receptor antagonists in asthma. *Allergy* 2001;56(suppl 66):7-11.

23. Bateman ED, Boushey HA, Bousquet J, et al, and GOAL Investigators Group: Can guideline-defined asthma control be achieved? The Gaining Optimal Asthma ControL study. *Am J Respir Crit Care Med* 2004;170:836-844.

24. Kuna P, Creemers JP, Vondra V, et al: Once-daily dosing with budesonide/formoterol compared with twice-daily budesonide/formoterol and once-daily budesonide in adults with mild to moderate asthma. *Respir Med* 2006;100:2151-2159.

25. Nelson HS, Weiss ST, Bleecker ER, et al: The Salmeterol Multicenter Asthma Research Trial: a comparison of usual pharmacotherapy for asthma or usual pharmacotherapy plus salmeterol. *Chest* 2006;129:15-26.

26. Mann M, Chowdhury B, Sullivan E, et al: Serious asthma exacerbations in asthmatics treated with high-dose formoterol. *Chest* 2003;124:70-74.

27. Nelson HS: Is there a problem with inhaled long-acting beta-adrenergic agonists? *J Allergy Clin Immunol* 2006;117:3-16.

28. Holgate ST, Chuchalin AG, Hebert J, et al, and Omalizumab 011 International Study Group: Efficacy and safety of a recombinant anti-immunoglobulin E antibody (omalizumab) in severe allergic asthma. *Clin Exp Allergy* 2004;34:632-638.

29. Finn A, Gross G, van Bavel J, et al: Omalizumab improves asthma-related quality of life in patients with severe allergic asthma. *J Allergy Clin Immunol* 2003;111:278-284.

30. Corren J, Casale T, Deniz Y, et al: Omalizumab, a recombinant humanized anti-IgE antibody, reduces asthma-related emergency room visits and hospitalizations in patients with allergic asthma. *J Allergy Clin Immunol* 2003;111:87-90.

31. Busse W, Corren J, Lanier BQ, et al: Omalizumab, anti-IgE recombinant humanized monoclonal antibody, for the treatment of severe allergic asthma. *J Allergy Clin Immunol* 2001;108:184-190.

32. Cox L, Platts-Mills TA, Finegold I, et al: American Academy of Allergy, Asthma & Immunology/American College of Allergy, Asthma and Immunology Joint Task Force Report on omalizumab-associated anaphylaxis. *J Allergy Clin Immunol* 2007;120:1373-1377.

33. McFadden ER Jr: Improper patient techniques with metered dose inhalers: clinical consequences and solutions to misuse. *J Allergy Clin Immunol* 1995;96:278-283.

34. Inhaled corticosteroids and severe viral infections. Executive Committee. American Academy of Allergy and Immunology. *J Allergy Clin Immunol* 1993;92:223-228.

35. Foresi A, Morelli MC, Catena E: Low-dose budesonide with the addition of an increased dose during exacerbations is effective in long-term asthma control. On behalf of the Italian Study Group. *Chest* 2000;117:440-446.

Chapter 8

Asthma in Children

Asthma is a heterogenous disease, and this is especially true in childhood. Several phenotypes of childhood wheezing have been described, and these include transient wheezing, persistent wheezing, late-onset wheezing, and nonatopic virus-induced wheezing.[1,2] For most children, wheezing begins in infancy, and viruses such as respiratory syncytial virus (RSV), rhinoviruses, parainfluenza viruses, and coronaviruses are common causes of infantile wheezing.[3,4] Some infants develop recurrent wheezing with viruses, and of this group, 'transient wheezers' stop wheezing between ages 3 and 6, while 'persistent wheezers' continue to wheeze with viruses, and eventually, other stimuli such as exercise and allergens. Late onset wheezing typically starts after the age of 3, and is associated with the development of allergic sensitization and other atopic problems. Of these early wheezing phenotypes, children with either persistent or late onset wheezing are most likely to develop chronic asthma. Nonatopic viral wheezing is characterized by virus-induced wheezing in a school-aged child, and these children are often asymptomatic between infections. These early wheezing illnesses and asthma are more common in boys until puberty, and then the incidence of asthma becomes higher in girls.

Clinical studies have demonstrated that many of the features of asthma, such as airway remodeling, eosinophilic inflammation of the airways, and airway hyperresponsiveness, can be established in infancy.[5-7] Furthermore, airflow limitation can begin at an early age, and persistent wheezing in infancy can be associated with loss of lung function in the preschool years.[8] These findings have prompted studies to determine whether starting therapy early in the disease process can interrupt the progression of asthma pathology; however, so far this approach has not been successful.[9,10]

Risk Factors

Wheezing infants can present a diagnostic challenge, especially since objective measures of lung function are not readily available in this age group. Prospective studies have identified risk factors for the development of asthma after virus-induced wheezing in the first few years, and an asthma predictive index has been developed that is useful to estimate the risk of developing asthma (Table 8-1).[2,11,12] Infectious risk factors for the development of asthma include severe (eg, requiring hospitalization) or recurrent virus-induced wheezing episodes, and wheezing due to common cold viruses such as rhinoviruses.[4,13,14] Host factors that increase the development of asthma include a personal history of allergy or atopic dermatitis and a family history of asthma. Environmental and lifestyle factors also influence asthma: contact with farm animals in early life is protective, and overweight and perhaps lack of exercise increases asthma risk.[15,16]

Diagnosis

The diagnosis of asthma in young children depends on assessment of the frequency, pattern, and severity of signs and symptoms of airway obstruction such as cough, wheezing, and shortness of breath. The general approach to asthma diagnosis is outlined in Chapter 7. In the initial assessment of asthma in young children, it is also important to consider the age-specific differential diagnosis

Table 8-1: Asthma Predictive Index

Children <3 years who had four or more episodes of wheezing in the past year that affected sleep are significantly likely to have asthma after the age of 5 years if they also have either:

(1) One of the following:

- Parental history of asthma

- Atopic dermatitis

- Evidence of sensitization to aeroallergens

or

(2) Two of the following:

- Sensitization to foods

- ≥4 percent peripheral blood eosinophilia

- Wheezing apart from colds

Adapted from NAEPP guidelines,[2] Guilbert et al,[11] Castro-Rodriguez et al[12]

of asthma (see Chapter 1). Congenital anomalies, foreign body ingestion, cystic fibrosis, and gastroesophageal reflux and aspiration can all mimic the signs and symptoms of asthma in infants and young children. Congenital anomalies such as tracheal web and compression of the airway by an anomalous blood vessel tend to produce wheezing at an early age, and wheezing is often present continuously, with increases during upper respiratory infections (URIs) and crying. Cystic fibrosis can be associated with poor growth or chronic diarrhea, in addition to pulmonary manifestations of the disease. Foreign body aspiration is especially likely in toddlers, and often presents with an acute coughing or choking episode. After the initial episode, there is an abrupt onset of chronic cough and/or wheezing. If this condition is suspected, consultation with a pediatric pulmonologist or otorhinolaryngologist is recommended.[17,18]

Clinical manifestations of asthma generally consist of coughing, wheezing, and shortness of breath. Young children with 'cough variant asthma' have coughing as the main symptom, with little or no wheezing. In some cases, this clinical presentation persists, while in others, wheezing and shortness of breath will develop over time. Physical signs of airway obstruction in infants can include mild tachypnea, substernal and intercostal retractions, and wheezing. Evidence of other atopic disorders such as atopic dermatitis or allergic rhinoconjunctivitis is often present. In older children, signs and symptoms are similar to those of asthma in adults (see Chapter 7).

The pattern of symptoms is also important. Symptoms of asthma tend to increase at night, particularly in the early morning hours, with exercise, during upper respiratory infections, and upon exposure to tobacco smoke or other irritants. In addition, children with allergies can develop acute cough, wheezing, and dyspnea after relevant exposures.

Pulmonary function tests can be performed by most children after age 4 to 5 years, and the results can prove valuable for the diagnostic process.[2] The forced expiratory volume in 1 second (FEV_1), peak expiratory flow (PEF), and mid-expiratory flow rate can all be decreased in moderate-to-severe asthma, or in mild asthma during symptomatic periods. Furthermore, the forced vital capacity (FVC) is normal or near normal. Collectively, this pattern of lung function indicates an obstructive airway pattern. The FEV_1/FVC ratio may be the most sensitive indicator of asthma in childhood. If these abnormalities are present, it is helpful to administer a bronchodilator (eg, 2 puffs of albuterol metered-dose inhaler [MDI]) and repeat spirometry or PEF. A 12% increase in FEV_1 post bronchodilator is strong evidence of asthma. If should be emphasized, however, that children with asthma are more likely than adults to have normal pulmonary function in between acute episodes of asthma.

Table 8-2: Four Components of Asthma Management

I. Measures of assessment and monitoring
- Objective tests
- Physical examination
- Patient history

II. Education for partnership in asthma care

III. Control of conditions that affect asthma
- Environmental factors
- Comorbidities

IV. Pharmacologic therapy
- Control medications
- Quick-relief medications

Adapted from NAEPP guidelines,[2] EPR-3[19]

Management of Childhood Asthma

The most recent National Asthma Education Program (NAEPP) Guidelines for the Management of Asthma lists four components to asthma management in children and adults (Table 8-2).[2,19] These components are discussed in the following sections.

Measures of assessment and monitoring

As in adults, asthma can be characterized in terms of two key concepts: impairment and risk (see Chapter 7, Table 7-3). Both of these domains are useful in the initial assessment of asthma severity in a newly diagnosed patient, and also to estimate asthma control once therapy has been initiated.

Education

Providing education related to key areas of asthma pathogenesis and management will help to promote self-management skills, adherence to medical therapy, and improve out-comes. Helpful educational components include discussion of the basics of asthma pathogenesis, the difference between asthma control medications and quick-relief medications, and proper technique for the use of inhaled medications. Providing written instructions and an asthma care plan will help to reinforce instructions and educational information.

Environmental triggers and comorbid conditions

The patient and/or parent should be asked about activi-ties of exposures that tend to provoke symptoms of asthma. Examples include exposure to pets, tobacco smoke (active or passive), and exercise. If the history or allergy testing indicate allergy to indoor allergens, multifaceted efforts to control exposure to allergens such as house dust mites, pets, or cockroaches can lead to improvements in asthma control.

Several medical conditions are known to aggravate asthma, and identification and treatment of these condi-tions can improve asthma control. These conditions include gastroesophageal reflux, sinusitis, respiratory allergies, and vocal cord dysfunction. Gastroesophageal reflux can lead to coughing and wheezing, particularly at night.[20] The symptoms of sinusitis in children differ from those in adults, and prolonged cough and rhinitis following a viral URI is a typical story.[21] There is evidence that effective control of respiratory allergies helps to promote asthma control as well. Finally, vocal cord dysfunction is an abnormal reflex in which the vocal cords constrict rather than open dur-ing inhalation. Symptoms include hoarseness of the voice, and wheezing that occurs mainly during inspiration, and is worsened by strenuous exercise or stress. The hallmarks on pulmonary function testing is a flattened inspiratory flow loop, and visualization of the vocal cords by laryngoscopy during symptomatic periods is diagnostic.[22]

Pharmacologic treatment

Pharmacotherapy of asthma should be guided by assess-ment of asthma severity (Figure 8-1) and asthma control (Figure 8-2). Severity is defined as the intrinsic intensity of the disease process, and is easiest to classify in the untreated patient. If treatment is ongoing, the amount of medication that is required to maintain control of asthma can be used to estimate severity. Asthma control is the degree to which symptoms and manifestations of asthma are minimized.[1,2]

Asthma pharmacotherapy includes quick-relief medications (Table 8-3) to treat acute symptoms and asthma controllers (Table 8-4) to treat chronic inflammation and airway obstruction. Use of asthma control medications can reduce both impairment and the rate of asthma exacerbations in children, resulting in improved quality of life. However, current clinical studies have not been able to demonstrate that use of inhaled corticosteroids moderates the underlying severity or slows progression of disease.[9]

The recently released NAEPP Guidelines for the Diagnosis and Management of Asthma refer to treatment options as preferred or alternative based on an evidence based review of group mean responses in clinical trials.[1,2] Once therapy is initiated, periodic monitoring of asthma control is used to guide adjustments in the treatment regimen in a stepwise fashion (Figure 8-3), and separate sets of recommendations have been developed for children ≤4 years, and for children ≥5 years. It is important to remember that asthma is a heterogeneous disease, both in terms of disease characteristics, and in the response to treatment.[21] If one regimen does not provide asthma control, other regimens in the same step should be considered before proceeding to the next step.

Many children have intermittent asthma (Figure 8-1), characterized by infrequent daytime and nighttime symptoms and normal activity and pulmonary function between episodes of asthma. For these patients, step 1 therapy (Figure 8-2) is recommended, which consists of an inhaled β_2-adrenergic agonist, ie, albuterol (ProAir® HFA, Proventil® HFA, Ventolin® HFA), levalbuterol (Xopenex®), or pirbuterol (Maxair® Autohaler®) used up to twice weekly as needed

(continued on page 162)

Components of Severity		Intermittent	
		Ages 0-4	Ages 5-11
Impairment	Symptoms	≤2 days/week	
	Nighttime awakenings	0	≤2 times/ month
	Short-acting β₂-agonist use for symptom control	≤2 days/week	
	Interference with normal activity	None	
	Lung Function	N/A	Normal FEV$_1$ between exacerbations
	• FEV$_1$ (predicted) or peak flow (personal best)		>80%
	• FEV$_1$/FVC		>0.85
Risk	Exacerbations requiring oral systemic corticosteroids (consider severity and interval since last exacerbation)	0-1/year (see notes)	
Recommended Step for Initiating Therapy (See "Stepwise Approach for Managing Asthma" for treatment steps.) The stepwise approach is meant to assist, not replace, the clinical decision making required to meet individual patient needs.		Step 1 (for both age groups)	

Figure 8-1: Classifying asthma severity and initiating therapy in children. Level of severity is determined by both impairment and risk. Assess impairment domain by caregiver's recall of previous 2 to 4 weeks. Assign severity to the

Persistent					
Mild		**Moderate**		**Severe**	
Ages 0-4	Ages 5-11	Ages 0-4	Ages 5-11	Ages 0-4	Ages 5-11
>2 days/week but not daily		Daily		Throughout the day	
>2 times/month	3-4 times/month	3-4 times/month	>1 time/week but not nightly	>1 time/week	Often 7 times/week
>2 days/week but not daily		Daily		Several times per day	
Minor limitation		Some limitation		Extremely limited	
N/A	>80%	N/A	60-80%	N/A	<60%
	>0.85		0.75-0.85		<0.75
≥2 exacerbations in 6 months requiring oral systemic corticosteroids, or ≥4 wheezing episodes/1 year lasting >1 day AND risk factors for persistent asthma	≤2 days/year (see notes) Relative annual risk may be related to FEV_1		→		→
Step 2 (for both age groups)		Step 3 and consider short course of oral systemic corticosteroids	Step 3: medium-dose ICS option and consider short course of oral systemic corticosteroids	Step 3 and consider short course of oral systemic corticosteroids	Step 3: medium-dose ICS OR step 4 and consider short course of oral systemic corticosteroids

In 2-6 weeks, depending on severity, evaluate level of asthma control that is achieved.
- Children 0-4 years old: If no clear benefit is observed in 4-6 weeks, stop treatment and consider alternative diagnoses or adjusting therapy.
  Children 5-6 years old: Adjust therapy accordingly.

most severe category in which any feature occurs. FEV_1= forced expiratory volume in 1 second, FVC=forced vital capacity, ICS=inhaled corticosteroids, ICU=intensive care unit, N/A=not applicable. Modified from NAEPP guidelines[2]

Components of Control		Well Controlled	
		Ages 0-4	Ages 5-11
Impairment	Symptoms	≤2 days/week but not more than once on each day	
	Nighttime awakenings	≤1 time/month	
	Interference with normal activity	None	
	Short-acting β_2-agonist use for symptom control (not prevention of EIB)	≤2 days/week	
	Lung function • FEV_1 (predicted) or peak flow (personal best) • FEV_1 FVC	N/A	>80% >0.80
Risk	Exacerbations requiring oral systemic corticosteroids	0-1 time/year	
	Reduction in lung growth	N/A	Requires long-term follow-up
	Treatment-related adverse effects	Medication side effects can vary in worrisome. The level of intensity does not but should be considered in the overall	
Recommended Action for Treatment (See "Stepwise Approach for Managing Asthma" for treatment steps.) The stepwise approach is meant to assist, not replace, the clinical decision making required to meet individual patient needs.		• Maintain current step. • Regular follow-up every 1-6 months. • Consider step down if well controlled for at least 3 months.	

Figure 8-2: Assessing asthma control and adjusting therapy in children. The level of control is based on the most severe impairment or risk category. Assess impairment domain by patient's or caregiver's recall of previous 2 to 4 weeks. Symptom assessment for longer periods should reflect a

Not Well Controlled		Very Poorly Controlled	
Ages 0-4	Ages 5-11	Ages 0-4	Ages 5-11
>2 days/week or multiple times on ≤2 days/week		Throughout the day	
>1 time/month	≥2 times/month	>1 time/week	≥2 times/week
Some limitation		Extremely limited	
>2 days/week		Several times per day	
N/A	60-80%	N/A	<60%
	0.75-0.80		<0.75
2-3 times/year	≥2 times/year	>3 times/year	≥2 times/year
N/A		N/A	
intensity from none to very troublesome and correlate to specific levels of control assessment of risk.			
Step up 1 step	Step up at least 1 step	• Consider short course of oral systemic corticosteroids, • Step up 1-2 steps	

8

• Before step up:
  Review adherence to medication, inhaler technique, and environmental control.
  If alternative treatment was used, discontinue it and use preferred treatment for that step.
• Re-evaluate the level of asthma control in 2-6 weeks to achieve control; every 1-6 months to maintain control.
  Children 0-4: If no clear benefit is observed in 4-6 weeks, consider alternative diagnoses or adjusting therapy.
  Children 5-11 years old: Adjust therapy accordingly.
• For side effects, consider alternative treatment options.

global assessment, such as whether the patient's asthma is better or worse since the last visit. EIB=exercise-induced bronchospasm, FEV1=forced expiratory volume in 1 second, FVC=forced vital capacity, ICU=intensive care unit, N/A=not applicable. Modified from NAEPP guidelines[2]

Table 8-3: Usual Dosages for Quick-Relief Medications*

Medication	<5 Years	5-11 Years
Inhaled Short-Acting β_2-Agonists (SABAs)		
Metered-dose inhaler (MDI)		
Albuterol CFC 90 µg/puff, 200 puffs/ canister	1-2 puffs 5 min before exercise, 2 puffs every 4-6 hrs, as needed for symptoms	2 puffs 5 min before exercise, 2 puffs every 4-6 hrs, as needed for symptoms
Albuterol HFA 90 µg/puff, 200 puffs/ canister	1-2 puffs 5 min before exercise, 2 puffs every 4-6 hrs, as needed for symptoms	2 puffs 5 min before exercise, 2 puffs every 4-6 hrs, as needed for symptoms
Levalbuterol HFA 45 µg/puff, 200 puffs/ canister	NA <4 years of age	2 puffs 5 min before exercise, 2 puffs every 4-6 hrs, as needed for symptoms

*Note: Dosages are provided for those products that have been approved by the US Food and Drug Administration (FDA) or have sufficient clinical trial safety and efficacy data in the appropriate age ranges to support their use.
Modified from NAEPP guidelines[2]

Potential Adverse Effects	Comments (not all inclusive)
(Apply to all three SABAs)	

- Tachycardia, skeletal muscle tremor, hypokalemia, increased lactic acid, headache, hyperglycemia. Inhaled route, in general, causes few systemic adverse effects. Patients with preexisting cardiovascular disease (CVD), especially the elderly, may have adverse cardiovascular reactions with inhaled therapy.

- Drugs of choice for acute bronchospasm.
- Differences in potencies exist, but all products are essentially comparable on a puff-per-puff basis.
- An increasing use or lack of expected effect indicates diminished control of asthma.
- Not recommended for long-term daily treatment. Regular use exceeding 2 d/wk for symptom control (not prevention of EIB) indicates the need for additional long-term control therapy.
- May double usual dose for mild exacerbations.
- For levalbuterol, prime the inhaler by releasing 4 actuations prior to use.
- For HFA: periodically clean HFA actuator, as drug may plug orifice.

(continued on next page)

**Table 8-3: Usual Dosages
for Quick-Relief Medications***
(continued)

Medication	<5 Years	5-11 Years
Inhaled Short-Acting β₂-Agonists (SABAs) (continued)		
Nebulizer solution		
Albuterol 0.63,1.25, 2.5 mg/3 mL, 5 mg/mL (0.5%)	0.63-2.5 mg in 3 mL of saline q4-6h, as needed	1.25-5 mg in 3 mL of saline q4-8h, as needed
Levalbuterol (R-albuterol) 0.31, 0.63, 1.25 mg/3 mL, 1.25 mg/0.5 mL	0.31-1.25 mg in 3 mL q4-6h, as needed for symptoms	0.31-0.63 mg, q8h, as needed for symptoms

DPI=dry powder inhaler, EIB=exercise-induced broncho-spasm, HFA=hydrofluoroalkane, ICS=inhaled corticosteroids, IgE=immunoglobulin E, MDI=metered-dose inhaler, NA=not available (either not approved, no data available, or safety and efficacy not established for this age group), SABA=short-acting β₂-agonist

to relieve episodic symptoms. These medications can also be used before strenuous activity to prevent exercise-induced bronchospasm (EIB). As alternatives to β₂-adrenergic agonists, leukotriene-receptor antagonists attenuate EIB in about half of patients, and prophylactic use of cromolyn (Intal®) can also be effective.

Potential Adverse Effects	Comments (not all inclusive) *(continued from page 161)*
(Same as with MDI)	• Nonselective agents (ie, epinephrine, isoproterenol, metaproterenol [Alupent®]) are not recommended due to their potential for excessive cardiac stimulation, especially in high doses.
(Same as with MDI)	• May mix with cromolyn solution, budesonide inhalant suspension, or ipratropium solution for nebulization. May double dose for severe exacerbations.
	• Does not have FDA-approved labeling for children <6 years.
	• Compatible with budesonide inhalant suspension. The product is a sterile-filled preservative-free unit dose vial.

8

(continued on next page)

Some children have intermittent asthma exacerbations that can be quite severe, and yet experience no impairment between episodes.[23] These exacerbations are often initiated by an acute viral respiratory infection. Options to treat these episodes include initiation of oral corticosteroids therapy with the onset of cold symptoms, or use of an inhaled corti-

Table 8-3: Usual Dosages for Quick-Relief Medications*
(continued)

Medication	<5 Years	5-11 Years
Systemic Corticosteroids		
Methylprednisolone 2, 4, 8, 16, 32 mg tablets	Short course 'burst:' 1-2 mg/kg/d, max 30 mg/d, for 3-10 d	Short course 'burst': 1-2 mg/kg/d, max 60 mg/d, for 3-10 d
Prednisolone 10, 15 mg tablets, 5 mg/5 mL, 15 mg/5 mL	Short course 'burst:' 1-2 mg/kg/d, max 30 mg/d, for 3-10 d	Short course 'burst': 1-2 mg/kg/d, max 60 mg/d, for 3-10 d
Prednisone 1, 2.5, 5, 10, 20, 50 mg tablets; 5 mg/mL, 5 mg/5 mL	Short course 'burst:' 1-2 mg/kg/d, max 30 mg/d, for 3-10 d	Short course 'burst': 1-2 mg/kg/d, max 60 mg/d, for 3-10 d

costeroid in an attempt to reduce the frequency and severity of these episodes.

In contrast to intermittent asthma, patients with mild persistent asthma have symptoms that occur more than twice weekly but less than daily, and these symptoms may occa-

Potential Adverse Effects

Comments (not all inclusive)
(continued)

(Apply to all three corticosteroids)

- Short term: reversible abnormalities in glucose metabolism, increased appetite, fluid retention, weight gain, facial flushing, mood alteration, hypertension, peptic ulcer, aseptic necrosis (rare).

- Consider co-existing conditions that could be worsened by systemic corticosteroids, ie, herpes virus infections, varicella, tuberculosis, hypertension, peptic ulcer, diabetes, osteoporosis, and *Strongyloides*

- Short courses or 'bursts' are effective for establishing control when initiating therapy or during a period of gradual deterioration. Action may begin within 1 hr.

- The burst should be continued until patient achieves 80% PEF personal best or symptoms resolve. This usually requires 3-10 d, but may require longer. There is no evidence that tapering the dose following improvement prevents relapse in asthma exacerbations.

- Other systemic corticosteroids, ie, hydrocortisone, dexamethasone, given in equipotent daily doses are likely to be as effective as prednisolone.

(continued on next page)

sionally disturb sleep or interfere with daytime activity. Although pulmonary function tests (PFTs) may be within the normal range between exacerbations, studies using bronchoscopy have revealed that persistent asthma symptoms, even when mild, are usually accompanied by lower airway

**Table 8-3: Usual Dosages
for Quick-Relief Medications***
(continued)

Medication	<5 Years	5-11 Years
Methylprednisolone acetate 40 mg/mL, 80 mg/mL repository injection	7.5 mg/kg IM once	7.5 mg/kg IM once, max 240 mg

inflammation. Consequently, daily preventive medications, such as low-dose inhaled corticosteroids, leukotriene modifiers, cromolyn, nedocromil, or oral theophylline, are recommended to control mild persistent asthma (step 2). Inhaled corticosteroids are the most potent and effective anti-inflammatory medications, and consequently low-dose inhaled corticosteroids are preferred for the treatment of mild persistent asthma. Data from clinical trials has been used to estimate the relative potency of various inhaled corticosteroids (Table 8-5).

The leukotriene modifiers, including receptor antagonists (montelukast [Singulair®], and for children 7 years and older, zafirlukast [Accolate®],) reduce blood eosinophil counts and antigen-induced eosinophil recruitment.[2,24] These medications have the advantage of oral administration, and can be used instead of inhaled corticosteroid medications in selected patients. Other alternative treatments that are used less often for mild persistent asthma in children include cromolyn and theophylline. Cromolyn is quite safe, but has limited efficacy and requires frequent administration, while theophylline has a narrow therapeutic window, and is not recommended for children <5 years. In addition to controller medications, inhaled β_2-adrenergic agonists can be used

Potential Adverse Effects	Comments (not all inclusive) *(continued)*
	• May be used in place of a short burst of oral steroids in patients who are vomiting or if adherence is a problem.

every 4 to 6 hours as needed to relieve acute symptoms. Frequent use of a β_2-adrenergic agonist is a good indicator of suboptimal asthma control, signaling the need to re-evaluate asthma triggers and the preventive medication regimen.

Decisions to start controller therapy can be especially difficult in young children. Many children who wheeze in infancy do not go on to develop asthma, and in these children treatment has little effect on either the acute illness or prognosis, which is favorable. On the other hand, children who have at least four episodes of wheezing in early childhood that disturb sleep are likely to develop asthma by age 5 if they have a positive asthma predictive index (Table 8-1).[2,11,12] Asthma control medications should be considered for children in this category.

Moderate persistent asthma is usually accompanied by daily symptoms (before treatment is initiated), periodic disturbance of sleep or daytime activities, and occasional exacerbations requiring acute care visits to the doctor's office or hospital emergency department. PFTs in older children typically show signs of airway obstruction, at least before anti-inflammatory therapy has been instituted. For children newly diagnosed with moderate persistent asthma, or symptoms that are inadequately controlled with low dose inhaled

Table 8-4: Usual Dosages for Long-Term Control Medications*

Medication	<5 Years	5-11 Years
Oral Systemic Corticosteroids		
Methylprednisolone 2, 4, 8, 16, 32 mg tablets	0.25-2 mg/kg daily in single dose in AM or q.o.d. as needed for control Short-course 'burst': 1-2 mg/kg/d, max 30 mg/d for 3-10 d	0.25-2 mg/kg daily in single dose in AM or q.o.d. as needed for control Short-course 'burst': 1-2 mg/kg/d, max 60 mg/d for 3-10 d
Prednisolone 5 mg tablets, 5 mg/5 mL, 15 mg/5 mL	Same as for methylprednisolone	Same as for methylprednisolone
Prednisone 1, 2.5, 5, 10, 20, 50 mg tablets; 5 mg/mL, 5 mg/5 mL	Same as for methylprednisolone	Same as for methylprednisolone

*Note: Dosages are provided for those products that have been approved by the US Food and Drug Administration or have sufficient clinical trial safety and efficacy data in the appropriate age ranges to support their use.
Modified from NAEPP guidelines[2]

Potential Adverse Effects	Comments (not all inclusive)
(Apply to all three corticosteroids)	

(Apply to all three corticosteroids)

- Short term: reversible abnormalities in glucose metabolism, increased appetite, fluid retention, weight gain, mood alteration, hypertension, peptic ulcer, aseptic necrosis (rare)
- Long term: adrenal axis suppression, growth suppression, dermal thinning, hypertension, diabetes, Cushing's syndrome, cataracts, muscle weakness, and impaired immune function (rare).
- Consider co-existing conditions that could be worsened by systemic corticosteroids, ie, herpes virus infections, varicella, tuberculosis, hypertension, peptic ulcer, diabetes, osteoporosis, and *Strongyloides*.

- Long-term treatment of severe persistent asthma: single dose in AM daily or on alternate days (alternate-day therapy may produce less adrenal suppression).
- Short course 'bursts' are effective for establishing control when initiating therapy or during a period of gradual deterioration.
- No evidence that tapering the dose following improvement in symptom control and pulmonary function prevents relapse.
- Children receiving the lower dose (1 mg/kg/d) experience fewer behavioral side effects, and it appears to be equally efficacious.
- For patients unable to tolerate the liquid form, dexamethasone syrup 0.4 mg/kg/d may be an option. Studies are limited and the longer duration of activity increases the risk of adrenal suppression.

(continued on next page)

8

Table 8-4: Usual Dosages for Long-Term Control Medications* *(continued)*

Medication	<5 Years	5-11 Years
Inhaled Long-Acting β₂-Agonists (LABAs)		
Salmeterol DPI 50 µg/ blister	NA	1 blister q12h
Formoterol DPI 12 µg/ single-use capsule	NA	1 capsule q12h

DPI=dry powder inhaler, EIB=exercise-induced bronchospasm, HFA=hydrofluoroalkane, ICS=inhaled corticosteroids, IgE= immunoglobulin E, MDI=metered-dose inhaler, NA=not available (either not approved, no data available, or safety and efficacy not established for this age group), SABA=short-acting β₂-agonist

corticosteroids alone, step 3 therapy is recommended. For younger children, moderate doses of inhaled corticosteroids are recommended, and for children ≥5 years, there are two regimens that are considered preferred therapy: either a medium dose corticosteroid alone, or combination therapy.

Potential Adverse Effects	Comments (not all inclusive)
(Apply to both LABAs)	
• Tachycardia, skeletal muscle tremor, hypokalemia, prolongation of corrected QT (QTc) interval in overdose.	• Should not be used for acute symptom relief or exacerbations. Use only with ICS.
• A diminished broncho-protective effect may occur within 1 wk of chronic therapy. Clinical significance has not been established.	• Decreased duration of protection against EIB may occur with regular use.
	• Most children <4 years cannot provide sufficient inspiratory flow for adequate lung delivery. Do not blow into inhaler after dose is activated.
• Potential risk of uncommon, severe, life-threatening or fatal exacerbation; see text for additional discussion regarding safety of LABAs.	• Each capsule is for single use only; additional doses should not be administered for at least 12 hrs.
	• Capsules should be used only with the inhaler and should not be taken orally.

(continued on next page)

Choices for combination therapy include an inhaled corticosteroid together with an inhaled long-acting β_2-agonist (fluticasone/salmeterol [Advair Diskus®] or budesonide/formoterol [Symbicort®]), a leukotriene modifier, or theophylline. There is currently insufficient clinical data in this age group

Table 8-4: Usual Dosages for Long-Term Control Medications* *(continued)*

Medication	<5 Years	5-11 Years
Combined Medication		
Fluticasone/ Salmeterol DPI 100, 250, or 500 μg/50 μg	NA	1 inhalation b.i.d., dose depends on level of severity or control
Fluticasone/ Salmeterol HFA 45, 115, 230 μg/21 μg		
Budesonide/ Formoterol HFA/MDI 80, 160 μg/ 4.5 μg	NA	2 puffs b.i.d., dose depends on level of severity or control

to make firm recommendations as to the relative benefits of these three options for adjunctive therapy, and additional clinical studies are needed. However, Advair Diskus® is indicated for children as young as 4 years. Finally, for children presenting with symptoms that are moderate to severe, a short course of oral corticosteroid should be considered in an effort to rapidly gain control of the disease process.[2]

It is especially important to identify patients who have severe asthma so that aggressive intervention (steps 4-6) can prevent serious morbidity or even fatal attacks. Severe

Potential Adverse Effects	Comments (not all inclusive)
• See notes for ICS and LABA.	• There have been no clinical trials in children <4 years of age.
	• Most children <4 years of age cannot provide sufficient inspiratory flow for adequate lung delivery.
	• Do not blow into inhaler after dose is activated.
• See notes for ICS and LABA.	• There have been no clinical trials in children <4 years.
	• Currently approved for use in youths ≥12 years. Dose for children 5-12 years based on clinical trials using DPI with slightly different delivery characteristics.

(continued on next page)

asthma is usually accompanied by daily wheezing and frequent exacerbations. These patients typically have a history of frequent visits to emergency departments or acute outpatient visits for asthma. Hospitalization is common in this group, and the occurrence of respiratory failure with intubation should be a 'red flag' for the identification of patients at increased risk for additional severe asthma exacerbations. These patients also typically have poor exercise tolerance that limits their physical activities, and they experience frequent night awakening. PFTs in older children reveal sig-

Table 8-4: Usual Dosages for Long-Term Control Medications* *(continued)*

Medication	<5 Years	5-11 Years
Cromolyn and Nedocromil		
Cromolyn MDI 0.8 mg/puff	NA	2 puffs q.i.d.
Cromolyn nebulizer 20 mg/ampule	1 ampule q.i.d. NA <2 years of age	1 ampule q.i.d.
Nedocromil MDI 1.75 mg/puff	NA <6 years of age	2 puffs q.i.d.

nificant airway obstruction that often does not completely reverse with bronchodilator use. Medical therapy is more intensive for these patients and includes medium to high-dose inhaled corticosteroids with a long-acting β_2-agonist, and may be supplemented by daily or every-other-day oral corticosteroids. Adjunctive therapy to provide greater control of symptoms and miminize the required dose of oral corticosteroid may include long-acting β_2-agonists, sustained-release theophylline, and/or a leukotriene-receptor antagonist.[2] For children with severe asthma symptoms that are not responding to therapy, it is especially important to re-evaluate the

Potential Adverse Effects	Comments (not all inclusive)
• Cough and irritation • 15%-20% of patients complain of an unpleasant taste from nedocromil. • Safety is the primary advantage of these medications.	• One dose of cromolyn before exercise or allergen exposure provides effective prophylaxis for 1-2 hrs. Not as effective as inhaled β_2-agonists for EIB as SABA. • 4- to 6-wk trial of cromolyn or nedocromil may be needed to determine maximum benefit. • Dose by MDI may be inadequate to affect airway hyperresponsiveness. • Once control is achieved, the frequency of dosing may be reduced.

8

(continued on next page)

diagnosis, and to consider comorbidities, and environmental exposures that may be aggravating asthma.

Adherence with medical therapy should be carefully assessed in patients with moderate-to-severe asthma because poor control of asthma can signal underuse of asthma-controlling medications. Unfortunately, estimating adherence can be difficult, and there is no correlation between adherence and income, gender, ethnicity, or physician assessment. Helpful information can be obtained from the pharmacist to determine if prescriptions are being filled. In addition, prescription dates can be checked at office visits,

Table 8-4: Usual Dosages for Long-Term Control Medications* *(continued)*

Medication	<5 Years	5-11 Years
Leukotriene Modifiers		
Leukotriene-Receptor Antagonists (LTRAs)		
Montelukast 4 mg or 5 mg chewable tablet, 4 mg granule packets, 10 mg tablet	4 mg q.h.s. (1-5 yrs of age)	5 mg q.h.s. (6-14 yrs of age)
Zafirlukast 10 mg tablet, 20 mg tablet	NA	10 mg b.i.d. (7-11 yrs of age)

Potential Adverse Effects	**Comments (not all inclusive)**
• No specific adverse effects have been identified. • Rare cases of Churg-Strauss syndrome have occurred, but the association is unclear.	• Montelukast exhibits a flat dose-response curve. Doses >10 mg will not produce a greater response in adults. • No more efficacious than placebo in infants ages 6-24 months. • As long-term therapy may attenuate EIB in some patients, but less effective than ICS therapy.
• Postmarketing surveillance has reported cases of reversible hepatitis and, rarely, irreversible hepatic failure resulting in death and liver transplantation.	• For zafirlukast, administration with meals decreases bioavailability; take at least 1 hr before or 2 hrs after meals. • Zarfirlukast is a microsomal P450 enzyme inhibitor that can inhibit the metabolism of warfarin. Doses of these drugs should be monitored accordingly. • Monitor hepatic enzymes (alanine transaminase [ALT]). Warn patients to discontinue use if they experience signs and symptoms of liver dysfunction.

(continued on next page)

Table 8-4: Usual Dosages for Long-Term Control Medications* *(continued)*

Medication	<5 Years	5-11 Years
Methylxanthines		
Theophylline liquids, sustained-release tablets, and capsules	Starting dose 10 g/kg/d; usual max: • <1 yr of age: 0.2 (age in wks) + 5 = mg/kg/d • ≥1 yr of age: 16 mg/kg/d	Starting dose 10 mg/kg/d; usual max=16 mg/kg/d

or the physician can choose a product that allows them to monitor use, ie, Ventolin®, which includes a dose counter. Furthermore, it is important to ask how the parent how he/she and the patient perceive prescribed medications, especially in terms of side effects, efficacy, cost, and 'steroid phobia.' Finally, the regimen should be as simple as possible and always include a written treatment plan (see Chapter 7,

Potential Adverse Effects	Comments (not all inclusive)
• Dose-related acute toxicities include tachycardia, nausea and vomiting, tachyarrhythmias (SVT), central nervous system stimulation, headache, seizures, hematemesis, hyperglycemia, and hypokalemia.	• Adjust dosage to achieve serum concentration of 5-15 µg/mL at steady state (at least 48 hours on same dosage).
	• Routine serum-theophylline level monitoring is essential.
	• Patients should be told to discontinue if they experience toxicity.
• Adverse effects at usual therapeutic doses include insomnia, gastric upset, aggravation of ulcer or reflux, increase in hyperactivity in some children, difficulty in urination in elderly males who have prostatism.	• Various factors (diet, food, febrile illness, age, smoking, and other medications) can affect serum concentrations. See package inserts for details.

Table 7-8) so that the patient has a clear understanding of the prescribed therapy. Many fine educational materials can be obtained from the National Asthma Education and Prevention Program (NAEPP, PO Box 30105, Bethesda, MD 20824-0105; telephone 301-951-3260; Web site http://www.nhlbi.nih.gov/about/naepp).

(continued on page 186)

Children 0–4 Years of Age

Step up if needed (first check inhaler technique, adherence, environmental control, and comorbid conditions)

Assess control

Step down if possible (and asthma is well controlled at least 3 months)

	Step 1	Step 2	Step 3	Step 4	Step 5	Step 6
	Intermittent Asthma	Persistent Asthma: Daily Medication				
		Consult with asthma specialist if step 3 care or higher is required. Consider consultation at step 2.				
Preferred	SABA PRN	Low-dose ICS	Medium-dose ICS	Medium-dose ICS + LABA or Montelukast	High-dose ICS + LABA or Montelukast	High-dose ICS + Oral systemic corticosteroids ICS + LABA or Montelukast
Alternative		Cromolyn or Montelukast				

Each Step: Patient Education and Environmental Control

- SABA as needed for symptoms. Intensity of treatment depends on severity of symptoms.
- With viral respiratory symptoms: SABA q 4-6 hours up to 24 hours (longer with physician consult). Consider short course of oral systemic corticosteroids if exacerbation is severe or patient has history of previous severe exacerbations.

Caution: Frequent use of SABA may indicate the need to step up treatment. See text for recommendations on initiating daily long-term-control therapy

Quick-Relief Medication

Children 5-11 Years of Age

	Intermittent Asthma	Persistent Asthma: Daily Medication				
		Consult with asthma specialist if step 3 care or higher is required. Consider consultation at step 2.				
Preferred	SABA PRN	Low-dose ICS	Low-dose ICS + LABA, LTRA, or Theophylline OR Medium-dose ICS	Medium-dose ICS + LABA	High-dose ICS + LABA	High-dose ICS + LABA + Oral systemic corticosteroids
Alternative		Cromolyn, LTRA, Nedocromil, or Theophylline	Medium-dose ICS	Medium-dose ICS + LTRA or Theophylline	High-dose ICS + LTRA or Theophylline	High-dose ICS + LTRA or Theophylline + oral systemic corticosteroids
Each Step: Patient Education and Environmental Control and Management of Comorbidities						
Steps 2–4: Consider subcutaneous allergen immunotherapy for patients who have persistent, allergic asthma.						
Quick-Relief Medication	• SABA as needed for symptoms. Intensity of treatment depends on severity of symptoms: up to 3 treatments at 20-minute intervals as needed. Short course of oral systemic corticosteroids may be needed.					
	Caution: Frequent use of SABA or use >2 days/week for symptom relief (not prevention of EIB) generally indicates inadequate control and the need to step up treatment.					

8

Figure 8-3: Stepwise approach for managing asthma long term in children 0-4 and 5-11 years. The stepwise approach is meant to assist, not replace, the clinical decision making required to meet individual patient needs. If an alternative treatment is used and response is inadequate, discontinue that treatment and use the preferred treatment before stepping up. If clear benefit is not observed within 4-6 weeks, and patient's/family's medication technique and adherence are satisfactory, consider adjusting therapy or an alternative diagnosis. For children 5-11 years, theophylline is a less desirable alternative due to the need to monitor serum concentration levels. Alphabetical listing is used when more than one treatment option is listed within either preferred or alternative therapy. ICS=inhaled corticosteroid, LABA=inhaled long-acting β_2-agonist, LTRA=leukotriene-receptor agonist, SABA=inhaled short-acting β_2-agonist. Modified from NAEPP guidelines[2]

181

Table 8-5: Estimated Comparative Daily Dosages for Inhaled Corticosteroids

Drug	Low Daily Dose	
	Child 0-4	Child 5-11
beclomethasone HFA 40 or 80 μg/puff	NA	80-160 μg
budesonide DPI 90, 180, or 200 μg/inhalation	NA	180-400 μg
budesonide suspension for nebulization	0.25-0.5 mg	0.5 mg
flunisolide 250 μg/puff	NA	500-700 μg
flunisolide HFA 80 μg/puff	NA	160 μg
fluticasone HFA/MDI (Flovent®) 44, 110, or 220 μg/puff	176 μg	88-176 μg
fluticasone DPI (Flovent® Diskus®) 50, 100, or 250 μg/inhalation	NA	100-200 μg
triamcinolone acetonide 75 μg/puff	NA	300-600 μg

DPI=dry powder inhaler, HFA=hydrofluoroalkane, MDI=metered-dose inhaler, N/A=not available (either not approved, no data available, or safety and efficacy not established for this age group).

Modified from NAEPP guidelines[2]

Medium Daily Dose		High Daily Dose	
Child 0-4	Child 5-11	Child 0-4	Child 5-11
NA	>160-320 µg	NA	>320 µg
NA	>400-800 µg	NA	>800 µg
>0.5-1 mg	1 mg	>1 mg	2 mg
NA	1,000-1,250 µg	NA	>1,250 µg
NA	320 µg	NA	≥640 µg
>176-352 µg	>176-352 µg	>352 µg	>352 µg
NA	>200-400 µg	NA	>400 µg
NA	>600-900 µg	NA	>900 µg

8

(continued on next page)

Table 8-5: Estimated Comparative Daily Dosages for Inhaled Corticosteroids (continued)

Therapeutic Issues:

- The most important determinant of appropriate dosing is the clinician's judgment of the patient's response to therapy. The clinician must monitor the patient's response on several clinical parameters and adjust the dose accordingly. Once control of asthma is achieved, the dose should be carefully titrated to the minimum dose required to maintain control.

- Preparations are not interchangeable on a μg or per-puff basis. This figure presents estimated comparable daily doses.

- Some doses may be outside package labeling, especially in the high-dose range.

- For children <4 years: the safety and efficacy of ICS in children <1 year has not been established. Children <4 years generally require delivery of an ICS (budesonide and fluticasone HFA) through a face mask that should fit snugly over nose and mouth and avoid nebulizing in the eyes. Wash face after each treatment to prevent local corticosteroid side effects. For budesonide, the dose may be administered 1-3 times daily. Budesonide inhalant suspension is compatible with albuterol, ipratropium, and levalbuterol nebulizer solutions in the same nebulizer. Use only jet nebulizers, as ultrasonic nebulizers are ineffective for suspensions. For fluticasone HFA, the dose should be divided 2 times daily; the low dose for children <4 years is higher than for children 5-11 years due to lower dose delivered with face mask and data on efficacy in young children.

Potential Adverse Effects of Inhaled Corticosteroids:

- Cough, dysphonia, oral thrush (candidiasis).

- Spacer or valved holding chamber with nonbreath-actuated MDI and mouthwashing and spitting after inhalation decrease local side effects.

- A number of the ICS, including budesonide, fluticasone, and mometasone, are metabolized in the gastrointestinal (GI) tract and liver by CYP 3A4 isoenzymes. Potent inhibitors of CYP 3A4, such as ritonavir and ketoconazole, have the potential for increasing systemic concentrations of these ICS by increasing oral availability and decreasing systemic clearance. Some cases of clinically significant Cushing's syndrome and secondary adrenal insufficiency have been reported.

- In high doses, systemic effects may occur, although studies are not conclusive, and clinical significance of these effects has not been established (eg, adrenal suppression, osteoporosis, dermal thinning, and easy bruising). In low-to-medium doses, suppression of growth velocity has been observed in children, but this effect may be transient, and the clinical significance has not been established.

Modified from NAEPP guidelines[2]

The recent trend toward reliance on inhaled medication for treating asthma is well supported by data proving the efficacy and relative safety of these products. However, improper use of an MDI is a common problem leading to suboptimal responses to asthma treatment regimens, particularly in children. Technique should always be reviewed with the patient after prescribing an inhaled medication (see Chapter 7, Table 7-9), and it is most helpful to have the patient demonstrate his or her inhaler technique at each outpatient visit. Spacer devices (Aerochamber®, Inspirease®, and others) can increase inhaler effectiveness and reduce side effects, especially in patients with suboptimal inhaler technique.[25] Selection of the spacer is determined by many factors, including the age of the patient, the type of MDI or medication, and the cost. Use of a spacer device with an inhaler does not eliminate the need to carefully review proper administration technique with the patient or parent, preferably during the clinic visit.

Monitoring of pulmonary function at home with a peak flow meter can increase awareness of asthma and encourage self-management skills.[2] PEF, which is the greatest flow velocity (L/min) that is generated during forced expiration, correlates reasonably well with FEV_1. Home monitoring of PEF can be especially helpful for patients with moderate or severe asthma, or in patients who have poor perception of their lung function. A useful protocol for using peak flow meters in managing asthma is outlined in the Guidelines for the Diagnosis and Management of Asthma, published by the US Department of Health and Human Services,[2] and this is outlined in Chapter 7. Treatment plans based on symptoms can be equally effective, and the key is to ensure that patients are comfortable with their own monitoring plan.

Summary

Childhood asthma is heterogeneous, and there is an increasing amount of information related to the definition of specific phenotypes, along with corresponding risk factors and prognosis. Age-specific treatment is based on identification of triggers for acute symptoms, and through estimation of impairment and risk, classification of disease severity. Long-term control of asthma is best achieved using a combination of patient education, environmental modifications, and medical therapy, which should include topical anti-inflammatory drugs for all but mild disease. Goals of therapy include restoring normal pulmonary function and controlling symptoms while avoiding side effects from asthma medications.

References

1. Martinez FD, Wright AL, Taussig LM, et al: Asthma and wheezing in the first six years of life. *N Engl J Med* 1995; 332:133-138.

2. National Asthma Education and Prevention Program, National Heart LaBI, National Institutes of Health. Expert Panel Report 3: Guidelines for the Diagnosis and Management of Asthma. 2007. Bethesda, MD, U.S. Department of Health and Human Services.

3. Jartti T, Lehtinen P, Vuorinen T, et al: Respiratory picornaviruses and respiratory syncytial virus as causative agents of acute expiratory wheezing in children. *Emerg Infect Dis* 2004;10:1095-1101.

4. Lemanske RF, Jr., Jackson DJ, Gangnon RE, et al: Rhinovirus illnesses during infancy predict subsequent childhood wheezing. *J Allergy Clin Immunol* 2005;116:571-577.

5. Krawiec ME, Westcott JY, Chu HW, et al: Persistent wheezing in very young children is associated with lower respiratory inflammation. *Am J Respir Crit Care Med* 2001;163:1338-1343.

6. Palmer LJ, Rye PJ, Gibson NA, et al: Airway responsiveness in early infancy predicts asthma, lung function, and respiratory symptoms by school age. *Am J Respir Crit Care Med* 2001;163: 37-42.

7. Kim ES, Kim SH, Kim KW, et al: Basement membrane thickening and clinical features of children with asthma. *Allergy* 2007; 62:635-640.

8. Taussig LM, Wright AL, Holberg CJ, et al: Tucson children's respiratory study: 1980 to present. *J Allergy Clin Immunol* 2003;111: 661-675.

9. Guilbert TW, Morgan WJ, Zeiger RS, et al: Long-term inhaled corticosteroids in preschool children at high risk for asthma. *N Engl J Med* 2006;354:1985-1997.

10. Szefler S, Weiss S, Tonascia A, et al: Long-term effects of budesonide or nedocromil in children with asthma. *N Engl J Med* 2000;343:1054-1063.

11. Guilbert TW, Morgan WJ, Zeiger RS, et al: Atopic characteristics of children with recurrent wheezing at high risk for the development of childhood asthma. *J Allergy Clin Immunol* 2004;114:1282-1287.

12. Castro-Rodriguez JA, Holberg CJ, Wright AL, et al: A clinical index to define risk of asthma in young children with recurrent wheezing. *Am J Respir Crit Care Med* 2000;162:1403-1406.

13. Kusel MM, de Klerk NH, Kebadze T, et al: Early-life respiratory viral infections, atopic sensitization, and risk of subsequent development of persistent asthma. *J Allergy Clin Immunol* 2007;119:1105-1110.

14. Kotaniemi-Syrjanen A, Vainionpaa R, Reijonen TM, et al: Rhinovirus-induced wheezing in infancy--the first sign of childhood asthma? *J Allergy Clin Immunol* 2003;111:66-71.

15. Ege MJ, Frei R, Bieli C, et al: Not all farming environments protect against the development of asthma and wheeze in children. *J Allergy Clin Immunol* 2007;119:1140-1147.

16. Platts-Mills TA, Erwin E, Heymann P, et al: Is the hygiene hypothesis still a viable explanation for the increased prevalence of asthma? *Allergy* 2005;60(suppl 79):25-31.

17. Soysal O, Kuzucu A, Ulutas H: Tracheobronchial foreign body aspiration: a continuing challenge. *Otolaryngol Head Neck Surg* 2006;135:223-226.

18. Even L, Heno N, Talmon Y: Diagnostic evaluation of foreign body aspiration in children: a prospective study. *J Pediatr Surg* 2005; 40:1122-1127.

19. Expert Panel Report 3 (EPR-3): Guidelines for the Diagnosis and Management of Asthma-Summary Report 2007. *J Allergy Clin Immunol* 2007; 20(5 suppl):S94-S138.

20. Gold BD: Asthma and gastroesophageal reflux disease in children: exploring the relationship. *J Pediatr* 2005;146(3 suppl): S13-S20.

21. Slavin RG, Spector SL, Bernstein IL, et al: The diagnosis and management of sinusitis: a practice parameter update. *J Allergy Clin Immunol* 2005;116(6 suppl):S13-S47.

22. Balkissoon R: Vocal cord dysfunction, gastroesophageal reflux disease, and nonallergic rhinitis. *Clin Allergy Immunol* 2007; 19:411-426.

23. Bacharier LB, Phillips BR, Bloomberg GR, et al: Severe intermittent wheezing in preschool children: a distinct phenotype. *J Allergy Clin Immunol* 2007;119:604-610.

24. Storms W: Update on montelukast and its role in the treatment of asthma, allergic rhinitis and exercise-induced bronchoconstriction. *Expert Opin Pharmacother* 2007;8:2173-2187.

25. McFadden ER, Jr: Improper patient techniques with metered dose inhalers: Clinical consequences and solutions to misuse. *J Allergy Clin Immunol* 1995;96:278-283.

8

Chapter 9

Management of Acute Asthma Exacerbations

Asthma is a chronic inflammatory disease of the airways characterized by episodic airway obstruction of variable duration and intensity. Many asthma attacks can be controlled by the use of quick-relief medications such as inhaled β_2-adrenergic agonists or bursts of oral prednisone (Deltasone®). However, symptoms sometimes progressively worsen over minutes, hours, or days, despite the use of inhaled or oral bronchodilators. At the far end of the spectrum is status asthmaticus, which is defined as unremitting asthma symptoms that put the patient at risk for respiratory failure.

The most effective strategy for dealing with status asthmaticus is prevention, achieved by recognition of the first signs and symptoms of progressively worsening asthma and by the early use of oral or high-dose inhaled corticosteroids. This chapter outlines the office or emergency department management of patients who have not received or have not responded favorably to early interventions and have proceeded to develop acute asthma exacerbations.

Clinical Assessment

Patients with severe dyspnea must be identified quickly, and personnel working in the reception area of the emergency department or the doctor's office must be trained to triage patients with severe asthma episodes directly into a treatment area. The patient's medical history provides important clues about the severity of the asthma episode. It is essential to obtain a description of the factors that initiated asthma symptoms, the risk factors for severe asthma exacerbations, and the asthma medications being used. This information guides immediate therapy and can be helpful later in determining the disposition of patients who experience only partial improvement after emergency department therapy.[1,2] Medical history features that indicate a high risk for asthma-associated morbidity and mortality include previous intubation or intensive care unit (ICU) admission, frequent emergency department visits, poor compliance with asthma controllers or overuse of quick-relief medications, underappreciation of airflow obstruction, psychiatric conditions, *Alternaria* allergy, and hospitalization despite the chronic use of oral corticosteroids.[1-3] Asthma that has been building in severity over several days may be particularly difficult to reverse in the emergency department. These high-risk patients require extra attention, including intensive efforts at patient education directed at preventing future episodes of severe asthma.

An initial assessment of respiratory status should be performed to establish baseline values and to identify patients with respiratory failure who need intensive care and possibly intubation (Table 9-1). Useful indicators of asthma severity on physical examination include the respiratory rate, the ability to speak, the use of accessory muscles of respiration, the presence or absence of wheezing, and the degree of air movement with respiration.[1,2] Patients who present with mild-to-moderate symptoms and peak expiratory flow (PEF) >40% usually can be treated in the acute care setting and then be discharged to home. Dyspnea at rest or PEF <40% personal best indicates a high likelihood that hospitalization will be required. Inability to speak or PEF <25% of predicted or personal best indicates an exacerbation that is potentially life threatening, and hospitalization with possible ICU admission is recommended. Cyanosis or impaired consciousness are obvious signs of impending respiratory failure, but restlessness, somnolence, fatigue, and inability to recline also indicate severe respiratory compromise.

Symptoms and physical findings are not always reliable indicators of the degree of airway obstruction,[4,5] and objective measurements of pulmonary function can add additional information. Useful indices in the emergency setting include forced expiratory volume in 1 second (FEV_1), and PEF.[1,2] Results of pulmonary function tests (PFTs) should be compared with the patient's personal best, if this is known, or to standardized norms. Objective measurements of pulmonary function are also used to measure the response to therapy, and can help to guide the decision to hospitalize vs discharge to home. In conjunction with trends in symptoms and physical findings, these measurements are used to guide the immediate treatment of acute asthma, and they influence decisions regarding hospitalization (Figure 9-1).

Measurement of arterial blood gases or oxygen saturation by pulse oximetry is indicated for patients who present with moderate or severe airway obstruction. Hypoxia is common once pulmonary function measurements such as FEV_1 or PEF are <50% of predicted.[6] Hypercapnia occurs most often in patients whose FEV_1 is <25% of predicted.

Therapy for Status Asthmaticus

The initial treatment for status asthmaticus consists of oxygen to maintain oxygen saturation >90%, and repeated or continuous administration of a short-acting β_2-agonist (albuterol HFA [ProAir® HFA, Proventil® HFA, Ventolin® HFA] or levalbuterol [Xopenex®], Table 9-2).[1,2] The recommended regimen is up to three doses of short-acting β_2-agonist spaced 20 minutes apart (Table 9-2). Nebulized acting β_2-agonist and oxygen should be administered even if preparations for intubation are taking place because responses to inhaled medication may sometimes be dramatic and obviate the need for intubation. Although short-acting β_2-agonists are used in higher than standard doses during exacerbations, serious side effects associated with the use of selective agonists, ie, albuterol, levalbuterol, and pirbuterol (Maxair® Autohaler®) are rare. Milder side effects, such as tremor, mild tachycardia, and nervousness, are common. Continuous administration of albuterol may produce greater improvement than intermittent dosing.[7]

Metered-dose inhalers (MDIs) can be just as effective as nebulized medications in treating acute asthma.[8] MDIs have the advantage of delivering medications more quickly and less expensively; however, some patients in severe distress may lack the coordination and breath-holding ability needed for best results.

A systemic corticosteroid should be administered early in the treatment course.[1,2] Oral corticosteroids are superior to high-dose inhaled corticosteroids for acute severe asthma because they provide greater improvements in pulmonary function and reduce the risk for hospitalization.[9] Early corticosteroid use may decrease the need for hospitalization and reduce the frequency of readmissions to the emergency suite.[9,10]

Although short-acting β_2-agonists are the bronchodilators of choice for acute asthma, anticholinergic medications such as ipratropium (Atrovent®) may augment the effect of these medications especially in patients who present with moderate-to-severe airway obstruction.[11] Ipratropium, an atropine-like drug with minimal systemic side effects when administered topically, is available in both an MDI and a nebulizer solution. The usual dose of ipratropium in acute asthma is 0.25 to 0.5 mg delivered via nebulization, or 4 to 8 puffs via MDI with a spacer device (Aerochamber®, Inspirease®), given three times at 20-minute intervals. If clinical improvement is observed, anticholinergic therapy can be continued as needed.

Aminophylline is no longer recommended for treating acute exacerbations of asthma in the emergency department. Several studies, including a meta-analysis, have found no evidence that aminophylline is beneficial in acute asthma that has been treated with inhaled β_2-agonists and systemic corti-

Table 9-1: Classifying Severity of Asthma Exacerbations in the Urgent or Emergency Care Setting*

	Symptoms and Signs	Initial PEF (or FEV$_1$)
Mild	Dyspnea only with activity (assess tachypnea in young children)	PEF ≥70% predicted or personal best
Moderate	Dyspnea interferes with or limits usual activity	PEF 40%-69% predicted or personal best
Severe	Dyspnea at rest; interferes with conversation	PEF <40% predicted or personal best
Subset: life threatening	Too dyspneic to speak; perspiring	PEF <25% predicted or personal best

*Patients are instructed to use quick-relief medications if symptoms occur or if PEF drops below 80% predicted or personal best. If PEF is 50%-79%, the patient should monitor response to quick-relief medication carefully and consider contacting a clinician. If PEF is below 50%, immediate medical care is usually required. In the urgent or emergency care setting, the following parameters describe the severity and likely clinical course of an exacerbation.

Clinical Course

- Usually cared for at home
- Prompt relief with inhaled SABA
- Possible short course of oral systemic corticosteroids

- Usually requires office or ED visit
- Relief from frequent inhaled SABA
- Oral systemic corticosteroids; some symptoms last for 1-2 days after start of treatment

- Usually requires ED visit, and hospitalization likely
- Partial relief from frequent inhaled SABA
- Oral systemic corticosteroids; some symptoms last for >3 days after start of treatment
- Adjunctive therapies are helpful

- Requires ED/hospitalization; possible ICU
- Minimal or no relief from frequent inhaled SABA
- Intravenous corticosteroids
- Adjunctive therapies are helpful

ED=emergency department, FEV_1=forced expiratory volume in 1 second, ICU=intensive care unit, PEF=peak expiratory flow, SABA=short-acting β_2-agonist
Modified from NAEPP guidelines[2]

Initial Assessment
Brief history, physical examination (auscultation, use of accessory muscles, heart rate, respiratory rate). PEF or FEV$_1$, oxygen saturation, and other tests as indicated.

FEV$_1$ or PEF ≥40% (Mild-to-Moderate)
- Oxygen to achieve SaO$_2$ ≥90%
- Inhaled SABA by nebulizer or MDI with valved holding chamber, up to 3 doses in first hour
- Oral systemic corticosteroids if no immediate response or if patient recently took oral systemic corticosteroids

FEV$_1$ or PEF <40% (Severe)
- Oxygen to achieve SaO$_2$ ≥90%
- High-dose inhaled SABA plus ipratropium by nebulizer or MDI plus valved holding chamber, every 20 minutes or continuously for 1 hour
- Oral systemic corticosteroids

Impending or Actual Respiratory Arrest
- Intubation and mechanical ventilation with 100% oxygen
- Nebulized SABA and ipratropium
- Intravenous corticosteroids
- Consider adjunct therapies

Admit to Hospital Intensive Care (see box below)

Repeat Assessment
Symptoms, physical examination, PEF, O$_2$ saturation, other tests as needed

Moderate Exacerbation
FEV$_1$ or PEF 40-69% predicted/personal best
Physical exam: moderate symptoms
- Inhaled SABA every 60 minutes
- Oral systemic corticosteroid
- Continue treatment 1-3 hours, provided there is improvement; make admit decision in <4 hours

Severe Exacerbation
FEV$_1$ or PEF <40% predicted/personal best
Physical exam: severe symptoms at rest, accessory muscle use, chest retraction
History: high-risk patient
No improvement after initial treatment
- Oxygen
- Nebulized SABA plus ipratropium, hourly or continuous
- Oral systemic corticosteroids
- Consider adjunct therapies

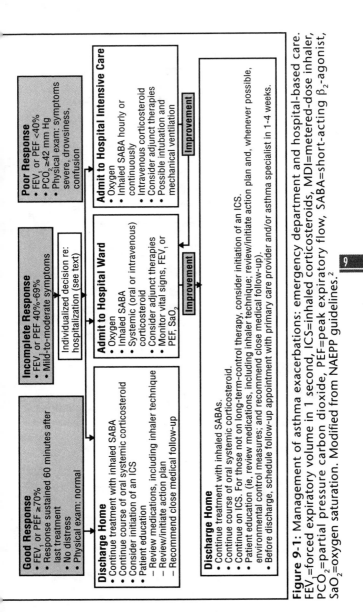

Figure 9-1: Management of asthma exacerbations: emergency department and hospital-based care. FEV_1=forced expiratory volume in 1 second, ICS=inhaled corticosteroids, MDI=metered-dose inhaler, PCO_2=partial pressure carbon dioxide, PEF=peak expiratory flow, SABA=short-acting β_2-agonist, SaO_2=oxygen saturation. Modified from NAEPP guidelines.[2]

Good Response
- FEV_1 or PEF ≥70%
- Response sustained 60 minutes after last treatment
- No distress
- Physical exam: normal

Discharge Home
- Continue treatment with inhaled SABA
- Continue course of oral systemic corticosteroid
- Consider initiation of an ICS
- Patient education
  – Review medications, including inhaler technique
  – Review/initiate action plan
  – Recommend close medical follow-up

Incomplete Response
- FEV_1 or PEF 40%-69%
- Mild-to-moderate symptoms

Individualized decision re: hospitalization (see text)

Admit to Hospital Ward
- Oxygen
- Inhaled SABA
- Systemic (oral or intravenous) corticosteroid
- Consider adjunct therapies
- Monitor vital signs, FEV_1 or PEF, SaO_2

Improvement

Discharge Home
- Continue treatment with inhaled SABAs.
- Continue course of oral systemic corticosteroid.
- Continue on ICS. For those not on long-term-control therapy, consider initiation of an ICS.
- Patient education (ie, review medications, including inhaler technique; review/initiate action plan and, whenever possible, environmental control measures; and recommend close medical follow-up).
- Before discharge, schedule follow-up appointment with primary care provider and/or asthma specialist in 1-4 weeks.

Poor Response
- FEV_1 or PEF <40%
- PCO_2 ≥42 mm Hg
- Physical exam: symptoms severe, drowsiness, confusion

Admit to Hospital Intensive Care
- Oxygen
- Inhaled SABA hourly or continuously
- Intravenous corticosteroid
- Consider adjunct therapies
- Possible intubation and mechanical ventilation

Improvement

9

Table 9-2: Dosages of Drugs for Asthma Exacerbations

Medication	Child Dose (≤12 years)
Inhaled Short-Acting β_2-Agonists (SABAs)	
Albuterol nebulizer solution (0.63, 1.25, 2.5 mg/ 3 mL, 5.0 mg/mL)	0.15 mg/kg (minimum dose=2.5 mg) every 20 min for 3 doses then 0.15-0.3 mg/kg up to 10 mg every 1-4 hrs as needed, or 0.5 mg/kg/hr by continuous nebulization.
Albuterol MDI (90 µg/puff)	4-8 puffs every 20 min for 3 doses,then every 1-4 hrs inhalation maneuver as needed. Use spacer; add mask in children <4 years.
Bitolterol nebulizer solution (2 mg/mL)	See albuterol dose; thought to be half as potent as albuterol on mg basis.
Bitolterol MDI (370 µg/puff)	See albuterol MDI dose.

*Discontinued in the United States

costeroids.[12,13] Intravenous magnesium sulfate has been evaluated for use in acute asthma, and benefits have been observed in some, but not all, studies,[14,15] and it can be considered for severe asthma cases that are resistant to initial therapy.

Adult Dose	Comments (not all inclusive)
2.5-5 mg every 20 min for 3 doses, then 2.5-10 mg every 1-4 hrs as needed, or 10-15 mg/hr continuously.	• Only selective β_2-agonists are recommended. For optimal delivery, dilute aerosols to min. of 3 mL at gas flow of 6-8 L/min. Use large volume nebulizers for continuous administration. May mix with ipratropium nebulizer solution.
4-8 puffs every 20 min up to 4 hrs, then every 1-4 hrs as needed.	• In mild-to-moderate exacerbations, MDI plus spacer is as effective as nebulized therapy with appropriate administration technique and coaching by trained personnel.
See albuterol dose.	• Has not been studied in severe asthma exacerbations. Do not mix with other drugs.
See albuterol MDI dose.	• Has not been studied in severe asthma exacerbations.

9

(continued on next page)

Disposition

The respiratory status of patients presenting with status asthmaticus should be reassessed at frequent intervals. Many emergency departments have developed flow sheets

Table 9-2: Dosages of Drugs for Asthma Exacerbations *(continued)*

Medication	Child Dose (≤12 years)
Inhaled Short-Acting β_2-Agonists (SABAs) *(continued)*	
Levalbuterol (R-albuterol) nebulizer solution (0.63 mg/3 mL, 1.25 mg/0.5 mL 1.25 mg/3 mL)	0.075 mg/kg (min dose 1.25 mg) every 20 min for 3 doses, then 0.075-0.15 mg/kg up to 5 mg every 1-4 hrs as needed.
Levalbuterol (R-albuterol) MDI (45 μg/puff)	See albuterol MDI dose
Pirbuterol MDI (200 μg/puff)	See albuterol MDI dose; thought to be half as potent as albuterol on a mg basis.
Systemic (Injected) β_2-Agonists	
Epinephrine 1:1,000 (1 mg/mL)	0.01 mg/kg up to 0.3-0.5 mg every 20 min for 3 doses SC
Terbutaline (1 mg/mL)	0.01 mg/kg every 20 min for 3 doses then every 2-6 hrs as needed SC

for recording serial measurements of pulmonary function, physical findings, and oxygenation to facilitate monitoring.

Patients who respond well to emergency therapy, with improved pulmonary function and resolved signs and symptoms of asthma, can be discharged to home. Oral or inhaled

Adult Dose	Comments (not all inclusive)
1.25-2.5 mg every 20 min for 3 doses, then 1.25-5 mg every 1-4 hrs as needed.	• Levalbuterol administered in one half the mg dose of albuterol provides comparable efficacy and safety. Has not been evaluated by continuous nebulization.
See albuterol MDI dose.	
See albuterol MDI dose.	• Has not been studied in severe asthma exacerbations.
0.3-0.5 mg every 20 min for 3 doses SC	• No proven advantage of systemic therapy over aerosol.
0.25 mg every 20 min for 3 doses SC	• No proven advantage of systemic therapy over aerosol.

(continued on next page)

9

corticosteroids may be prescribed to reduce the chance of recurrent symptoms and return visits to the emergency department.[16,17] Regardless of the medical therapy prescribed, it is important to maintain close medical follow-up either by telephone or a scheduled clinic appointment. In general, these

Table 9-2: Dosages of Drugs for Asthma Exacerbations (continued)

Medication	Child Dose (≤12 years)
Anticholinergics	
Ipratropium bromide nebulizer solution (0.25 mg/mL)	0.25-0.5 mg every 20 min for 3 doses, then as needed
Ipratropium bromide MDI (18 µg/puff)	4-8 puffs every 20 min as needed up to 3 hrs
Ipratropium with albuterol nebulizer solution (Each 3 mL vial contains 0.5 mg ipratropium bromide and 2.5 mg albuterol)	1.5 mL every 20 min for 3 doses, then as needed
Ipratropium with albuterol MDI (Each puff contains 18 µg ipratropium bromide and 90 µg of albuterol)	4-8 puffs every 20 min as needed up to 3 hrs

Adult Dose	Comments (not all inclusive)
0.5 mg every 20 min for 3 doses, then as needed	• May mix in same nebulizer with albuterol. Should not be used as first-line therapy; should be added to SABA therapy for severe exacerbations. The addition of ipratropium has not been shown to provide further benefit once the patient is hospitalized.
8 puffs every 20 min as needed up to 3 hrs	• Should use with spacer and face mask for children <4 years. Studies have examined ipratropium bromide MDI for up to 3 hrs.
3 mL every 20 min for 3 doses, then as needed	• May be used for up to 3 hrs in the initial management of severe exacerbations. The addition of ipratropium to albuterol has not been shown to provide further benefit once the patient is hospitalized.
8 puffs every 20 min as needed up to 3 hrs	• Should use with spacer and face mask for children <4 years.

9

(continued on next page)

Table 9-2: Dosages of Drugs for Asthma Exacerbations *(continued)*

Medication	Child Dose (≤12 years)
Systemic Corticosteroids	
Prednisone	1 mg/kg in 2 divided doses (max=60 mg/d) until PEF is 70% of predicted or personal best
Methylprednisolone	
Prednisolone	

Notes:

- There is no known advantage for higher doses of corticosteroids in severe asthma exacerbations, nor is there any advantage for intravenous administration over oral therapy provided gastrointestinal transit time or absorption is not impaired.

- The total course of systemic corticosteroids for an asthma exacerbation requiring an ED visit of hospitalization may last from 3 to 10 days. For corticosteroid courses of <1 week, there is no need to taper the dose. For slightly longer courses (eg, up to 10 days), there probably is no need to taper, especially if patients are concurrently taking ICS.

patients should be seen within 1 week of any emergency department visit to reassess their respiratory status and to adjust maintenance therapy to minimize the chance of future exacerbations of asthma.

Patients who have an incomplete response to therapy may require continued treatment with bronchodilators and corticosteroids in the emergency department, but the disposition should be determined within 4 hours after initiating treatment. Most patients who experience partial improvement after emergency treatment may be discharged home with

	Comments
	(not all inclusive)
Adult Dose	

40-80 mg/d in 1 or 2
divided doses until PEF
reaches 70% of predicted
or personal best

- For outpatient 'burst,' use
  40-60 mg in single or 2
  divided doses for total of
  5-10 d in adults (children:
  1-2 mg/kg/d max 60 mg/d
  for 3-10 d).

- ICS can be started at any point in the treatment of an asthma
  exacerbation.

ED=emergency department, MDI=metered-dose inhaler,
PEF=peak expiratory flow, SABA=short-acting β_2-agonist,
SC=subcutaneous

close medical follow-up. However, hospital admission may
be the best course for patients with prolonged episodes of airway obstruction, for those with a history of previous hospital
admissions (especially those associated with respiratory failure), or for those with psychosocial factors that may impede
the successful treatment of asthma.[1,2]

Patients with a poor response to emergency department
treatment of asthma should be admitted to the hospital for close
observation and continued medical therapy. Indications for
hospital admission include hypoxia, hypercapnia, or persistent

severe airway obstruction (PEF <40% of predicted).[1,2] ICU consultation should be made early for those patients at risk for respiratory failure as indicated by extreme dyspnea, poor objective measurements of pulmonary function, or hypercapnia.

We recommend that all patients be observed for at least 30 minutes after their last dose of β_2-agonist to ensure that they are stable before being discharged from the emergency department. All patients discharged from the emergency department should be given a written asthma treatment plan and contingency instructions to be followed if their symptoms worsen.

Hospital Therapy of Asthma

Cooperation and communication between the emergency department or clinic and the inpatient ward are crucial to ensure uninterrupted monitoring and therapy. Because lung function is intrinsically unstable during an asthma attack, severe respiratory distress can develop even in patients who appear to be improving. Pulmonary function before and after β_2-agonist therapy can be serially monitored in the hospital with a bedside peak flow meter. Monitoring of oxygenation with pulse oximetry or arterial blood gases is required in patients who are unstable or who have more severe disease. Chest radiographs should be considered for patients with severe dyspnea or unequal breath sounds, but radiographs contribute little to the management of patients in the absence of these findings.[1]

Inpatient medical therapy should include frequent or continuous administration of short-acting inhaled β_2-agonists. Oxygen should be given to hypoxic patients and to those with unstable pulmonary function. Oral or intravenous corticosteroids should be used to treat underlying airway inflammation. Inhaled ipratropium can be helpful in the emergency department, but does not appear to influence the course of asthma once a patient has been hospitalized.[18] Intravenous aminophylline also has little or no benefit for either children or adults hospitalized with asthma.[19,20]

ICU admission is required for patients who are at risk for respiratory failure, as indicated by clinical evidence of fatigue or progressively worsening dyspnea, FEV_1 or PEF <30% of predicted, or hypercapnia.[1,2] Short-acting β_2-agonists should be administered every 30 to 60 minutes or by constant nebulization. Heliox in combination with nebulized albuterol has been used with some success to increase gas exchange.[1] Patients on high doses of β_2-agonists should have cardiac monitoring to detect cardiac arrhythmias. Corticosteroids should generally be administered intravenously every 6 to 8 hours. The decision to intubate and mechanically ventilate is usually based on clinical evidence of progressive respiratory distress and impending respiratory failure, rather than on any set criteria for pulmonary function or arterial blood gas results.

Once a patient is improving, the frequency of inhaled medication can be reduced, and medications that are being delivered intravenously should be changed to oral preparations. Efforts at patient education should begin as soon as this is practical, and should focus on identifying asthma triggers and the appropriate use of anti-inflammatory and bronchodilator medications.[1,2,21] Oral corticosteroids should be prescribed, with a schedule that tapers to zero (or maintenance requirements) within 1 to 2 weeks of discharge. A follow-up outpatient visit should be arranged before the patient leaves the hospital.

Summary

Acute severe asthma is a medical emergency, and, as with all emergencies, a successful outcome depends on the prompt recognition of signs and symptoms, leading to the initiation of appropriate therapy. Every effort should be made to ensure that patients with frequent emergency department visits follow up with their regular health-care provider or an asthma specialist so that maintenance regimens can be designed to minimize the chances of future exacerbations of asthma.

References

1. National Asthma Education and Prevention Program, National Heart, Lung, and Blood Institute, National Institutes of Health: *Expert Panel Report 3: Guidelines for the Diagnosis and Management of Asthma (Full Report 2007)*. Bethesda, MD, NIH publication number 08-5846, US Department of Health and Human Services, 2007 (http://www.nhlbi.nih.gov/guidelines/asthma/asthgdln.htm).

2. National Asthma Education and Prevention Program, National Heart, Lung, and Blood Institute, National Institutes of Health: Expert Panel Report 3: Guidelines for the Diagnosis and Management of Asthma (Summary Report 2007). *J Allergy Clin Immunol* 2007:120(5 suppl);S94-S138.

3. O'Hollaren MT, Yunginger JW, Offord KP, et al: Exposure to an aeroallergen as a possible precipitating factor in respiratory arrest in young patients with asthma. *N Engl J Med* 1991;324:359-363.

4. McFadden ER Jr, Kiser R, DeGroot WJ: Acute bronchial asthma. Relations between clinical and physiologic manifestations. *N Engl J Med* 1973;288:221-225.

5. Shim CS, Williams MH Jr: Relationship of wheezing to the severity of obstruction in asthma. *Arch Intern Med* 1983;143:890-892.

6. Nowak RM, Tomlanovich MC, Sarkar DD, et al: Arterial blood gases and pulmonary function testing in acute bronchial asthma. Predicting patient outcomes. *JAMA* 1983;249:2043-2046.

7. Camargo CA Jr. Spooner CH, Rowe BH: Continuous versus intermittent beta-agonists in the treatment of acute asthma. *Cochrane Database Syst Rev* 2003;(4):CD001115.

8. Dolovich MB, Ahrens RC, Hess DR, et al: Device selection and outcomes of aerosol therapy: Evidence-based guidelines: American College of Chest Physicians/American College of Asthma, Allergy, and Immunology. *Chest* 2005;127:335-371.

9. Schuh S, Reisman J, Alshehri M, et al: A comparison of inhaled fluticasone and oral prednisone for children with severe acute asthma. *N Engl J Med* 2000;343:689-694.

10. Littenberg B, Gluck EH: A controlled trial of methylprednisolone in the emergency treatment of acute asthma. *N Engl J Med* 1986;314:150-152.

11. Qureshi F, Pestian J, Davis P, et al: Effect of nebulized ipratropium on the hospitalization rates of children with asthma. *N Engl J Med* 1998;339:1030-1035.

12. Littenberg B: Aminophylline treatment in severe, acute asthma. A meta-analysis. *JAMA* 1988;259:1678-1684.

13. Rodrigo C, Rodrigo G: Treatment of acute asthma. Lack of therapeutic benefit and increase of the toxicity from aminophylline given in addition to high doses of salbutamol delivered by metered-dose inhaler with a spacer. *Chest* 1994;106:1071-1076.

14. Rowe BH, Bretzlaff JA, Bourdon C, et al: Intravenous magnesium sulfate treatment for acute asthma in the emergency department: a systematic review of the literature. *Ann Emerg Med* 2000;36:181-190.

15. Cheuk DK, Chau TC, Lee SL: A meta-analysis on intravenous magnesium sulphate for treating acute asthma. *Arch Dis Child* 2005;90:74-77.

16. FitzGerald JM, Shragge D, Haddon J, et al: A randomized, controlled trial of high-dose, inhaled budesonide versus oral prednisone in patients discharged from the emergency department following an acute asthma exacerbation. *Can Respir J* 2000;7:61-67.

17. Chapman KR, Verbeek PR, White JG, et al: Effect of a short course of prednisone in the prevention of early relapse after the emergency room treatment of acute asthma. *N Engl J Med* 1991; 324:788-794.

18. Craven D, Kercsmar CM, Myers TR, et al: Ipratropium bromide plus nebulized albuterol for the treatment of hospitalized children with acute asthma. *J Pediatr* 2001;138:51-58.

19. Parameswaran K, Belda J, Rowe BH: Addition of intravenous aminophylline to beta2-agonists in adults with acute asthma. *Cochrane Database Syst Rev* 2000;(4):CD002742.

20. Mitra A, Bassler D, Goodman K, et al: Intravenous aminophylline for acute severe asthma in children over two years receiving inhaled bronchodilators. *Cochrane Database Syst Rev* 2005;(2):CD001276.

21. National Asthma Education and Prevention Program, National Heart, Lung, and Blood Institute, National Institutes of Health: *Teach Your Patients About Asthma: A Clinician's Guide.* Bethesda, MD, US Department of Health and Human Services, 1992.

9

Chapter 10

Urticaria and Angioedema

U rticaria (hives) and angioedema are common disorders, affecting about 25% of people at some point in their lives.[1] The intense itching and rapidly evolving lesions of urticaria can significantly impair quality of life in areas such as emotional distress, disturbed sleep, and impact on social and work-related interactions.[2] Traditionally, urticaria that lasts <6 weeks is considered acute, while urticaria that lasts >6 weeks is designated chronic.[3] Many patients have intermittent episodes of acute urticaria separated by long periods of remission. Acute urticaria is commonly found in children and young adults, and reaches its peak prevalence in the third decade.[1] Chronic urticaria primarily affects middle-aged people, peaks in the fourth decade, and is more common in women than in men.

Mechanisms and Triggers of Urticaria and Angioedema

Urticaria and angioedema, which commonly coexist, are caused by similar pathogenic mechanisms (Table 10-1). The primary difference between these two disorders is in the location of the inflammation: urticaria primarily involves the dermis, while angioedema involves tissues under the skin.[4] Allergy is commonly implicated in acute urticaria, which can be triggered by foods, medications, or insect stings. A significant percentage of acute urticaria is associated with signs and symptoms of recent viral illness, especially in children. In contrast to acute urticaria, no specific trigger is identified in about two thirds of patients with chronic urticaria.[4] Although the stimulus for chronic urticaria is unclear, the pathogenesis is related to infiltration of the skin by mast cells and mononuclear cells.[5,6] T cells constitute most of the mononuclear cell infiltrate and likely secrete histamine-releasing factors that promote mast cell mediator release. In acute allergic reactions, plasma histamine levels are elevated in 50% of cases and correlate with the extent of urticaria.[7] Autoimmune mechanisms have also been implicated in a subset of chronic urticaria patients who demonstrate autoantibodies that bind to the high-affinity immunoglobulin E (IgE) receptor.[2,4,8]

When a specific trigger for chronic urticaria is identified, physical stimuli are most often involved.[2,4] Dermatographism (acute pressure-induced urticaria), cholinergic urticaria (induced by passive heating, sweating, or fever), and cold-induced urticaria are the most common forms of physical urticaria. Chronic urticaria can also be a manifestation of a systemic disease and occasionally is the presenting feature.[9] For example, chronic viral, parasitic, or bacterial infections are sometimes accompanied by generalized urticaria. Urticaria can also be the heralding sign of autoimmune disease such as systemic lupus erythematosus or thyroiditis. Finally, inherited or acquired C1 esterase-inhibitor deficiency produces recurrent angioedema that is often triggered by minor trauma or surgery.[10]

Diagnosis

The most important factor in evaluating a patient with urticaria or angioedema is the medical history. Patients usually recognize food allergy when it triggers urticaria because the lesions typically appear within 30 minutes of ingesting the offending food, and this pattern occurs each time that food

Table 10-1: Etiologic Classification of Urticaria and Angioedema

Idiopathic
- Subgroup with autoantibodies to high-affinity IgE receptor

Allergic
- IgE-mediated
  - Foods, drugs, insect venoms, aeroallergens
- Anaphylactoid
  - Opiates, radiocontrast material
- Nonsteroidal anti-inflammatory drugs (NSAIDs)
- Serum-sickness reactions
- Contact urticaria

Physical stimuli
- Pressure
  - dermatographism
  - delayed pressure urticaria
- Heat
  - active (cholinergic urticaria)
  - passive (heat contact urticaria)
- Cold-induced urticaria
- Exercise

IgE=immunoglobulin E

protein is ingested.[11,12] A similar temporal relationship usually exists when urticaria or angioedema is triggered by other allergic stimuli such as medications, latex, or animals. In the case of serum sickness, however, urticaria and other signs and

Physical stimuli *(continued)*
- Water (aquagenic urticaria)
- Light (solar urticaria)
- Vibration

Manifestation of systemic disease
- Infection
  - Viral, fungal, bacterial, parasitic
- Autoimmune
  - Urticaria vasculitis, systemic lupus erythematosus, thyroiditis, cryoglobulinemia
- Neoplasm
  - Lymphoma, leukemia
- Psychosomatic
- Mastocytosis

Toxic (acute urticaria or angioedema)
- Stinging nettles
- Fire coral

C1 esterase-inhibitor deficiency (angioedema)
- Hereditary
- Acquired

symptoms usually appear 7 to 14 days after a new medication or serum is started,[13] so the relationship is less obvious. Hives from occupational exposure typically flare while the patient is at work and then improve during weekends or vacations.[14]

Table 10-2: Features of Common Types of Chronic Urticaria*

Type of Urticaria	Age Range (years)	Principal Clinical Features
Chronic idiopathic**	20-50	Profuse or sparse, generalized, pink, edematous papules or wheals, often annular, with itching
Symptomatic dermatographism	20-50	Itchy, linear wheals with surrounding bright red flare at sites of scratching or rubbing
Other physical urticarias		
Cold-induced	10-40	Itchy, pale, or red swelling at sites of contact with cold surfaces or fluids
Pressure-induced**	20-50	Large, painful, or itchy red swelling at sites of pressure (soles, palms, or waist) lasting ≥24 hours
Solar	20-50	Itchy, pale, or red swelling at site of exposure to ultraviolet or visible light
Cholinergic	10-50	Itching, monomorphic pale or pink wheals on trunk, neck, and limbs

*Modified from Greaves,[15] used with permission of the *New England Journal of Medicine* and the Massachusetts Medical Society, 1995;332:1767-1772.

Associated Angioedema?	Diagnostic Test
Yes	_____
No	Light stroking of skin causes an immediate wheal with itching.
Yes	Ten-minute application of an ice pack causes a wheal within 5 minutes of the removal of ice.
No	Application of pressure perpendicular to skin produces persistent red swelling after a latent period of 1-4 hours.
Yes	Irradiation by a 2.5-kW solar simulator (290-690 nm) for 30 to 120 seconds causes wheals within 30 minutes.
Yes	Exercise or a hot shower elicits an eruption.

10

**Pressure-induced and spontaneous wheals appear concurrently in 37% of patients with chronic idiopathic urticaria.

The medical history is also the key factor in identifying physical urticaria, although specific tests are available to confirm the diagnosis (Table 10-2).[15,16] Dermatographism results from mast cells triggered by mild pressure, such as at the belt line or in intertrigo. Cholinergic urticaria often occurs when the core body temperature is raised by exercise, hot showers, or anxiety. A distinguishing factor in cholinergic urticaria is the appearance of the lesion, which is usually a punctate hive with surrounding erythema. Cold-induced urticaria typically occurs on body parts exposed to cold weather or after immersion in cold water, which can sometimes produce massive urticaria and even anaphylaxis. Delayed pressure-induced urticaria and angioedema are more challenging to recognize because the onset of the swelling or skin lesions may occur several hours after strenuous physical exercise or application of pressure. The areas most commonly affected are the hands and feet, and pain is reported more often than itching. Less commonly, urticaria or angioedema can result from solar radiation, vibration, or contact with water.

On physical examination, the classic lesion of urticaria is a raised, pale area of dermal edema surrounded by a rim of erythema. In severe cases, the individual lesions coalesce into continuous skin lesions. As mentioned previously, the skin lesions of cholinergic urticaria have a distinct punctate appearance. Present in most forms of urticaria, pruritus is important in distinguishing urticaria from skin disorders such as erythema multiforme that are similar in appearance.

Angioedema causes localized swelling and pallor of the involved subdermal tissues. The edematous tissues are soft and nonpitting and are not associated with lymphangitis. These features help to distinguish angioedema from other causes of dermal swelling such as infection or contact dermatitis. A diagnosis of C1 esterase-inhibitor deficiency should be considered in cases of recurrent angioedema, especially if there is also a history of recurrent abdominal pain, if angioedema is precipitated by trauma, or if the angioedema is not accompanied by urticarial lesions.[10]

Table 10-3: Laboratory Evaluation of Chronic Idiopathic Urticaria

Routine diagnostic tests
- Complete blood count (CBC) with differential
- Platelet count
- Sedimentation rate

Extended diagnostic tests*
- Infectious diseases (ie, *Helicobacter pylori*)
- Type I allergy
- Autoantibodies
- Thyroid hormones
- Physical tests
- Pseudoallergen-free diet for 3 weeks
- Tryptase, biopsy

*Depending on suspected cause
From Zuberbier et al[2]

Another important clinical feature of urticaria and angioedema is that individual lesions tend to evolve and resolve quickly. In addition, urticaria caused by allergy tend to appear within minutes, while lesions of chronic urticaria evolve more slowly.[2,5] In any case, individual urticarial lesions rarely last >24 hours and are not associated with any bruising or purpura; angioedema usually resolves within 24 to 72 hours. Individual urticarial lesions that persist for longer than 24 hours or are associated with purpura strongly suggest urticarial vasculitis, and these circumstances should trigger a more extensive diagnostic evaluation, including biopsy of suspicious lesions.[17,18]

Table 10-4: Treatment of Chronic Urticaria

Avoid triggers
- Allergens, NSAIDs
- Physical stimuli

Antihistamines
- H_1 blockers
- H_2 blockers

Corticosteroids (not for chronic therapy)

Other
- Leukotriene modifiers
- Doxepin
- Nifedipine (Adalat® CC)
- Cyclosporine
- Intravenous immunoglobulin
- Ultraviolet A (UVA) light +/- oral psoralen

NSAIDs=nonsteroidal anti-inflammatory drugs

There are no characteristic laboratory features of urticaria or angioedema. Allergic causes are more common in acute urticaria or angioedema, and using the medical history to select allergen-specific skin tests or radioallergosorbent tests (RASTs) can be helpful in identifying causative factors. In contrast, allergy tests are rarely useful in evaluating chronic urticaria. Because urticaria can be the presenting sign for a variety of systemic illnesses (Table 10-1), it is reasonable to order a complete blood count (CBC) and sedimentation rate on all patients with uticarial lesions for >6 weeks' duration. (Table 10-3). If there are indications of allergy, physical urticarias, or systemic illnesses, more extensive laboratory tests can help to determine the correct diagnosis.[2] A subset

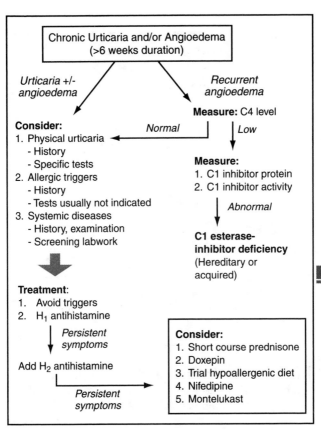

Figure 10-1: Management of chronic urticaria and angioedema.

of patients with chronic urticaria have autoantibodies to the high-affinity IgE receptor. However, the autologous serum skin test, which is the only screening test for this condition, is difficult to standardize and is relatively nonspecific.[2,4]

If angioedema is recurrent, a C4 level should be obtained to screen for hereditary or acquired C1 esterase-inhibitor deficiency. This is addressed in greater detail later in this chapter.

Table 10-5: Complement Profiles With Angioedema

Type	C1-Inh (antigenic)	C1-Inh (functional)	C1
HAE I	↓	↓	N
HAE II	N	↓	N
AAE I	↓	↓	↓
AAE II	N‡	↓	↓
Immune complex vasculitis	N	N	↓
Allergic/ idiopathic	N	N	N

‡Small decrease may be seen.

AAE=acquired angioedema, HAE=hereditary angioedema, Inh=inhibitor, N=normal

Treatment of Urticaria and Angioedema

The treatment of acute and chronic urticaria and angioedema is outlined in Table 10-4. First, any factors that are known to cause the urticaria or angioedema must be avoided, including allergens, alcoholic beverages, and specific physical stimuli. Dietary restrictions are rarely helpful in managing chronic urticaria, and restricted diets should be discouraged unless there is clear evidence of food allergy.

Evidence-based guidelines for pharmacologic management of chronic urticaria have recently been published.[20] The mainstay of medical therapy for angioedema and urticaria is the H_1-receptor antagonist.[19,20] For acute urticaria, first-generation antihistamines, such as diphenhydramine

C4	C3	CH 50/100	Para-protein	Anti-C1-Inh Ab
↓	N	N‡	no	no
↓	N	N‡	no	no
↓	N‡	N‡	yes	no
↓	N‡	N‡	no	yes
↓	↓	↓	no	no
N	N	N	no	no

Used with permission, from Huston et al[21]

10

(Benadryl®) or hydroxyzine (Vistaril®), are used because of rapid onset of action, although sedation is a common side effect. For management of chronic urticaria (Figure 10-1), second-generation antihistamines are preferred because of their long half-lives and because they are either nonsedating (eg, loratadine [Claritin®]) or have a low incidence of sedation (eg, cetirizine [Zyrtec®]). In addition, there is evidence that these medications have some anti-inflammatory properties.[19] For angioedema that is refractory to standard doses of antihistamines, expert opinion favors the use of higher doses of second-generation antihistamines,[2,4] although larger than standard doses are not FDA approved.

Unfortunately, some patients with chronic urticaria do not experience satisfactory relief with H_1 antihistamines alone, which are the only medications approved by the FDA for this indication. Several alternatives have been assessed by randomized controlled trials, although additional studies are needed to clarify specific recommendations. H_2-receptor blockers such as cimetidine (Tagamet®) or ranitidine (Zantac®) are often added to the medical regimen under these circumstances, with evidence of modest clinical benefits.[22,23] There are several trials of leukotriene modifiers, and some show evidence of efficacy.[20,24] Doxepin is a tricyclic antidepressant (TCA) that suppresses urticaria better than traditional antihistamines in some patients, but it frequently produces unpleasant side effects such as sedation and other central nervous system (CNS) effects and drying of the mucous membranes. Nifedipine (Adalat® CC), a calcium-channel blocker (CCB), significantly improved subjective and objective measures of chronic urticaria in one double-blind, placebo-controlled trial.[25] Cyclosporine, intravenous γ-globulin, and ultraviolet A (UVA) light with or without oral psoralen have all been used in a few patients with severe disease, with varying degrees of success.[20] For patients who have an autoantibody directed toward the high-affinity IgE receptor, plasmapheresis can induce clinical remission.[8,9] Oral glucocorticoids can be used to treat acute exacerbations of chronic urticaria, but they are generally not used as maintenance medications because of the severe side effects that can be associated with long-term use.

C1 Esterase-Inhibitor Deficiency

C1 esterase-inhibitor deficiency can be inherited or acquired. Either form leads to unrestrained consumption of C2 and C4 and subsequent activation of the complement and plasma kinin-forming cascades.[10] Both disorders result in acute episodes of nonpruritic angioedema that are usually triggered by trauma, such as dental surgery. The resulting airway obstruction can be life threatening. In addition, edema of the intestines produces episodes of vomiting, severe abdominal pain, and intestinal obstruction. Urticarial lesions are generally not found in patients with hereditary or acquired C1 esterase-inhibitor deficiency.

Hereditary angioedema is transmitted as an autosomal-dominant trait, and two forms have been identified: type 1, where there is an absolute deficiency of the C1 esterase-inhibitor protein; and type 2, where the C1 esterase inhibitor is present but nonfunctional. Acquired C1 inhibitor deficiency is most often associated with B-cell lymphoproliferative disorders. A second form has been described in which serum autoantibodies to C1 inhibitor interfere with its functional activity.

Screening for C1 esterase deficiency is accomplished by performing quantitative measurements of C4, which is decreased even in the absence of angioedema (Table 10-5). It is important to realize that C1 esterase-inhibitor deficiency is associated with angioedema but not urticaria and that C4 levels are generally normal in patients who present with both angioedema and urticaria. The two forms of hereditary angioedema can be distinguished by assaying for C1 esterase-inhibitor protein levels and C1 esterase-inhibitor activity, and these tests can also be helpful for patients who present with suggestive signs and symptoms and have C4 levels in the normal range. Patients with acquired C1 esterase-inhibitor deficiency should be evaluated for a B-cell lymphoproliferative disorder, and serum should be screened for autoantibodies specific for C1 esterase inhibitor.

Treatment of C1 esterase-inhibitor deficiency consists of three separate strategies—long-term prophylaxis, short-term prophylaxis, and treatment of acute attacks.[10] Because the degree of C1 esterase-inhibitor activity varies in affected patients, long-term prophylaxis is not required for all patients. The drugs that are most helpful for prophylaxis are androgens such as danazol or stanozolol, which stimulate C1 esterase-inhibitor synthesis in the liver.[26] Antifibrinolytic drugs such as ε-aminocaproic acid (Amicar®) and tranexamic acid (Cyklokapron®) have also been used for long-term prophylaxis, but their use is limited by side effects, such as thrombosis and myonecrosis.

Short-term prophylaxis is used to prepare a patient for traumatic procedures, such as dental surgery. Purified C1 esterase inhibitor is the most effective treatment agent for short-term prophylaxis or for acute attacks of angioedema,[27] but, if this is not available, fresh frozen plasma can also be used.[28] Some patients with acquired C1 esterase-inhibitor deficiency develop a partial resistance to C1 esterase-inhibitor infusion but usually respond to larger doses.

References

1.   Schafer T, Ring J: Epidemiology of urticaria. *Monogr Allergy* 1993;31:49-60.

2.   Zuberbier T, Bindslev-Jensen C, Canonica W, et al: EAACI/GA2LEN/EDF guideline: definition, classification and diagnosis of urticaria. *Allergy* 2006;61:316-320.

3.   O'Donnell BF, Lawlor F, Simpson J, et al:. The impact of chronic urticaria on the quality of life. *Br J Dermatol* 1997;136:197-201.

4.   Greaves MW, Tan KT. Chronic Urticaria: Recent Advances. *Clin Rev Allergy Immunol* 2007;33:134-143.

5.   Elias J, Boss E, Kaplan AP: Studies of the cellular infiltrate of chronic idiopathic urticaria: prominence of T-lymphocytes, monocytes, and mast cells. *J Allergy Clin Immunol* 1986;78(5 pt 1): 914-918.

6.   Barlow RJ, Ross EL, MacDonald DM, et al: Mast cells and T lymphocytes in chronic urticaria. *Clin Exp Allergy* 1995;25:317-322.

7.   Lin RY, Schwartz LB, Curry A, et al: Histamine and tryptase levels in patients with acute allergic reactions: an emergency department-based study. *J Allergy Clin Immunol* 2000;106(1 pt 1): 65-71.

8.   Hide M, Francis DM, Grattan CE, et al: Autoantibodies against the high-affinity IgE receptor as a cause of histamine release in chronic urticaria. *N Engl J Med* 1993;328:1599-1604.

9.   Stafford CT: Urticaria as a sign of systemic disease. *Ann Allergy* 1990;64:264-270.

10. Frank MM: Hereditary angioedema: the clinical syndrome and its management in the United States. *Immunol Allergy Clin North Am* 2006;26:653-668.

11. Bock SA, Atkins FM: Patterns of food hypersensitivity during sixteen years of double-blind, placebo-controlled food challenges. *J Pediatr* 1990;117:561-567.

12. Sampson HA, McCaskill CC: Food hypersensitivity and atopic dermatitis: evaluation of 113 patients. *J Pediatr* 1985;107:669-675.

13. Lawley TJ, Bielory L, Gascon P, et al: A prospective clinical and immunologic analysis of patients with serum sickness. *N Engl J Med* 1984;311:1407-1413.

14. Slodownik D, Nixon R: Occupational factors in skin diseases. *Curr Probl Dermatol* 2007;35:173-189.

15. Greaves MW: Chronic urticaria. *N Engl J Med* 1995;332:1767-1772.

16. Dice JP: Physical urticaria. *Immunol Allergy Clin North Am* 2004;24:225-246.

17. Brown NA, Carter JD: Urticarial vasculitis. *Curr Rheumatol Rep* 2007;9:312-319.

18. Lee JS, Loh TH, Seow SC, et al: Prolonged urticaria with purpura: the spectrum of clinical and histopathologic features in a prospective series of 22 patients exhibiting the clinical features of urticarial vasculitis. *J Am Acad Dermatol* 2007;56:994-1005.

19. Simons FE: Advances in H1-antihistamines. *N Engl J Med* 2004;351:2203-2217.

20. Zuberbier T, Bindslev-Jensen C, Canonica W, et al: EAACI/GA-2LEN/EDF guideline: management of urticaria. *Allergy* 2006;61:321-331.

21. Huston DP, Bressler RB: Urticaria and angioedema. *Med Clin North Am* 1992;76:805-840.

22. Paul E, Bodeker RH: Treatment of chronic urticaria with terfenadine and ranitidine. A randomized double-blind study in 45 patients. *Eur J Clin Pharmacol* 1986;31:277-280.

23. Bleehen SS, Thomas SE, Greaves MW, et al: Cimetidine and chlorpheniramine in the treatment of chronic idiopathic urticaria: a multi-centre randomized double-blind study. *Br J Dermatol* 1987;117:81-88

10

24. Erbagci Z: The leukotriene receptor antagonist montelukast in the treatment of chronic idiopathic urticaria: a single-blind, placebo-controlled crossover clinical study. *J Allergy Clin Immunol* 2002;110:484-488.

25. Bressler RB, Sowell K, Huston DP: Therapy of chronic idiopathic urticaria with nifedipine: demonstration of beneficial effect in a double-blind, placebo-controlled, crossover trial. *J Allergy Clin Immunol* 1989;83:756-763.

26. Sloane DE, Lee CW, Sheffer AL: Hereditary angioedema: Safety of long-term stanozolol therapy. *J Allergy Clin Immunol* 2007;120:654-658.

27. Cicardi M, Zingale LC, Zanichelli A, et al: The use of plasma-derived C1 inhibitor in the treatment of hereditary angioedema. *Expert Opin Pharmacother* 2007;8:3173-3181.

28. Prematta M, Gibbs JG, Pratt EL, et al: Fresh frozen plasma for the treatment of hereditary angioedema. *Ann Allergy Asthma Immunol* 2007;98:383-388

Chapter 11

Atopic and
Contact Dermatitis

A topic dermatitis and contact dermatitis are common allergic inflammatory disorders of the superficial layer of the skin and are associated with intense pruritus. Despite these similarities, the pathologic mechanisms, natural history, distribution of lesions, and treatments for each disorder are quite different. This chapter reviews the clinical features and therapy for each of these disorders.

Atopic Dermatitis

Atopic dermatitis is a chronic skin disorder characterized by pruritus, dry skin, and excoriation, which may be localized to a few patches or involve large portions of the body. Atopic dermatitis tends to occur in individuals who have a personal or family history of allergic rhinitis, asthma, or eczema,[1] and it is most common in children. As with the other atopic diseases, its incidence appears to be increasing, and recent studies have estimated that between 10% and 20% of children are affected in most Western countries.[2,3]

Early lesions of atopic dermatitis typically include dry patches with small red papules, mild scaling, and areas of excoriation. Chronically affected areas show accentuated skin lines and thickening of the skin (lichenification). Postinflammatory pigmentation abnormalities are also common. Pruritus is universally present, and scratching is a major factor in the pathogenesis of acute and chronic skin lesions. Moist and oozing lesions are also common and suggest the possibility of superficial infection.

Several features of the natural history of atopic dermatitis are distinctive. Atopic dermatitis usually begins early in life, typically in the second 6 months of the first year. The pattern of distribution of atopic dermatitis lesions changes with age. Affected areas in infants include the cheeks, trunk, and extensor surfaces of the extremities. During childhood and adolescence, the distribution shifts to the flexural areas of the extremities and neck. The hands and feet may also be involved and, in fact, this can be the only manifestation of atopic dermatitis in some patients. In addition, some patients experience a seasonal increase in severity, either in the dry winter months, or less commonly, in the summertime. As with other atopic diseases, the severity of atopic dermatitis tends to decrease after childhood, although increased skin sensitivity and occasional outbreaks of localized disease persist in most patients. However, active disease can be extremely uncomfortable and unsightly, and this underscores the importance of education and preventive therapy for this chronic disease.

Atopic dermatitis is associated with an increased susceptibility to skin infections, especially those involving *Staphylococcus*, *Streptococcus,* and herpes simplex. Topical or oral treatment with acyclovir (Zovirax®) may be necessary for persistent or severe herpes infections. It has also been suggested that immunoglobulin E (IgE) specific for the opportunistic yeast *Malassezia* species could also contribute to the severity of atopic dermatitis in adults.[4] Severe atopic dermatitis may also be complicated by psychological problems,[5] decreased growth velocity,[6] and cataracts.[7]

Progress has been made in understanding the pathogenesis of atopic dermatitis. The wide range in prevalence of atopic dermatitis among countries inhabited by similar ethnic groups suggests that environmental factors play a major role in determining the risk of the disorder.[3] Histologic features include intracellular edema (spongiosis) with formation of vesicles; hyperplasia of the epidermis; infiltration of inflammatory cells such as CD4+ T lymphocytes, dendritic cells, Langerhan's cells, and macrophages in acute lesions; and epidermal thickening and fibrosis in chronic lesions.[8] Circulating eosinophil counts are commonly elevated and correlate with disease severity.[8] Finally, certain bacterial proteins such as staphylococcal and streptococcal toxins may contribute to the pathogenesis of atopic dermatitis through superantigen activation of T cells in the skin,[8] and there is evidence that atopic dermatitis is associated with reduced levels of endogenous antibacterial peptides in the skin.[9] Finally, genetic studies indicate that polymorphisms in genes regulating immune responses and skin barrier function modify the risk of disease.[8,10]

Diagnosis

Atopic dermatitis is a clinical diagnosis based on the typical appearance and clinical course of the disorder.[11] Distinguishing features of atopic dermatitis include early age of onset; the distribution of the lesions, with characteristic shifting in distribution between infancy and later childhood; coexistence with other atopic diseases; the chronic nature of the disorder; and the prominent symptom of pruritus. Although circulating eosinophil counts and serum IgE levels are commonly elevated in atopic dermatitis, these findings are not specific and are usually not helpful in establishing the diagnosis.

Identifying factors that trigger flares of atopic dermatitis (Table 11-1) is essential in designing a rational treatment regimen. Sudden worsening of atopic dermatitis strongly suggests superficial bacterial infection of the skin. This is usually accompanied by a dramatic increase in pruritus, and the lesions may appear red, crusted, or weepy.

Irritants, including detergents, perfume, or other skin-care products, can also trigger acute symptoms. It is im-

Table 11-1: Triggers of Atopic Dermatitis

- Abrasion
  - Scratching
  - Rough clothing
- Infection
  - *Staphylococcus*
  - *Streptococcus*
- Allergens
  - Food (in children)
  - Epidermal allergens
    - house dust mite
- Climate
  - Cold, dry winter air
- Stress
- Sweating
- Contact dermatitis

portant to consider handwashing habits because frequent abrasion from washing and drying the skin can produce local outbreaks of eczema. Occupational exposure to food products, plant material, and the handling of other proteins or chemicals can cause atopic dermatitis, contact urticaria, or contact dermatitis. Allergic contact dermatitis, which is addressed in the second half of this chapter, can also trigger pruritus and eczema.

Studies have shown that food allergy is key in the pathogenesis of atopic dermatitis in some infants and young children and that it is especially common in children with severe disease that is relatively unresponsive to traditional therapy.[12] Allergic reactions to food often involve several organ systems, most commonly the skin, the gastrointestinal (GI) tract, and the respiratory system. Skin manifestations, such as flushing, urticaria, and angioedema, tend to occur soon after the offending food is eaten. In contrast, changes in atopic dermatitis typically appear hours or days after food ingestion, which makes it more difficult to identify the offending allergen. Evaluation involves a careful history and testing for food-specific IgE by either radioallergosorbent test (RAST) or skin testing. False-positive skin test or RAST results are common. Blinded food challenges can be helpful in determining the validity of these test results.[13] Food allergy associated with eczema seems to be uncommon in adults.

Several investigators have suggested that respiratory allergens, such as house dust mite or pollens, may contribute to the pathogenesis of atopic dermatitis,[14,15] and measures directed at decreasing the levels of house dust mite allergen in the environment have produced dramatic clinical improvement in some cases. Patch testing using epidermal allergens is performed in some centers.[16]

Treatment

Treatment of atopic dermatitis involves maintaining good skin hygiene, avoiding factors known to trigger symptoms, and treating flares of dermatitis when they occur.[8] As is the case with most chronic diseases, patient education is needed to achieve optimum results. General measures that may be helpful in the long-term control of atopic dermatitis include the use of skin moisturizers and avoiding heavy or irritating fabric, such as woolen clothes, because these may trigger scratching and, thus, skin rash. Frequent bathing followed by the immediate (within 2 to 3 minutes) application of creams or ointments moisturizes the skin and reduces the risk of secondary bacterial infections. Wet wraps can be used to treat troublesome areas, and they have been shown to improve the barrier function of the skin.[17]

Topical corticosteroids are used to maintain healthy skin and to treat exacerbations of dermatitis.[8] A low-potency corticosteroid (Table 11-2) such as 1% hydrocortisone cream (Hytone®) can be applied to affected areas of the skin twice daily for mild manifestations of atopic dermatitis. Medium-potency corticosteroids, such as 0.025% to 0.1% triamcinolone (Kenalog®) can be used to treat localized patches of more severely affected skin. Facial skin

Table 11-2: Topical Glucocorticoid Potency Ranking

Class I
    Betamethasone dipropionate 0.05% (cream and ointment)
    Clobestasol propionate 0.05% (cream and ointment)
    Diflorasone diacetate 0.05% (ointment)
    Halobetasol propionate 0.05% (cream and ointment)

Class II
    Amcinonide 0.1% (ointment)
    Betamethasone dipropionate 0.05% (cream and ointment)
    Desoximetasone 0.25% (cream)
    Desoximetasone 0.05% (gel)
    Diflorasone diacetate 0.05% (ointment)
    Fluocinonide 0.05% (cream, gel, ointment, and solution)
    Halcinonide 0.1% (cream)
    Mometasone furoate 0.1% (ointment)

Class III
    Amcinonide 0.1% (cream and lotion)
    Betamethasone dipropionate 0.05% (cream)
    Betamethasone valerate 0.1% (ointment)
    Desoximetasone 0.05% (cream)
    Diflorasone diacetate 0.05% (cream)
    Fluocinonide 0.05% (cream)
    Fluticasone propionate 0.005% (ointment)
    Halcinonide 0.1% (ointment and solution)
    Triamcinolone acetonide 0.1% (ointment)

Class IV   Hydrocortisone valerate 0.2% (ointment)
Flurandrenolide 0.05% (ointment)
Fluocinolone acetonide 0.025% (ointment)
Mometasone furoate 0.1% (cream)
Triamcinolone acetonide 0.1% (cream)

Class V   Betamethasone dipropionate 0.05%
(lotion)
Betamethasone valerate 0.1% (cream)
Fluticasone acetonide 0.025% (cream)
Fluticasone propionate 0.05% (cream)
Flurandrenolide 0.05% (cream)
Hydrocortisone valerate 0.2% (cream)
Prednicarbate 0.1% (cream)

Class VI   Alclometasone dipropionate 0.05%
(cream and ointment)
Betamethasone valerate 0.05% (lotion)
Desonide 0.05% (cream)
Fluocinolone acetonide 0.01%
(cream and solution)
Triamcinolone acetonide 0.1% (cream)

Class VII   Hydrocortisone hydrochloride 1%
(cream and ointment)
Hydrocortisone hydrochloride 2.5%
(cream, lotion, and ointment)
Hydrocortisone acetate 1%
(cream and ointment)
Hydrocortisone acetate 2.5%
(cream, lotion, and ointment)
Pramoxine hydrochloride 1.0%
(cream, lotion, and ointment)
Pramoxine hydrochloride 2.5%
(cream, lotion, and ointment)

is highly vascular, leading to great absorption of topical corticosteroids and increased susceptibility to side effects such as skin atrophy, striae, or telangiectasia. Therefore, corticosteroid use on the face should be restricted to low-potency preparations such as 1% hydrocortisone (Table 11-2). Intertriginous areas such as the groin and axilla are also more sensitive to corticosteroid side effects.

Corticosteroid skin preparations are classified by potency (Table 11-2), and clinicians should become familiar with one or two in each of the classes. High-potency (class I or II) corticosteroids are rarely needed in the treatment of atopic dermatitis. Patients who initially respond to one particular cream may develop tolerance to it and can benefit from the use of a different corticosteroid of the same potency. Contact dermatitis caused by hypersensitivity to a topical corticosteroid can also lead to treatment failure.[18]

For patients with severe atopic dermatitis that is refractory to standard therapy, the use of 0.03% to 0.1% tacrolimus (FK506) ointment (Protopic®) or pimecrolimus 1% cream (Elidel®) can produce marked improvement in skin signs and symptoms.[19] Fortunately, these medications do not inhibit collagen synthesis, so their use is not associated with atrophic skin changes. Side effects can include burning of the skin after application, which is more common with tacrolimus, and increased severity of cutaneous viral infections (eg, herpes simplex). Although both medications are labeled with a black box warning for a potential association with cancer, several expert review panels have subsequently affirmed that these medications have an excellent safety record.[20]

In addition to moisturization and corticosteroid creams, oral antihistamines (eg, hydroxyzine [Vistaril®], diphenhydramine) can be helpful in controlling acute bouts of pruritus. Long-term daily use of a second-generation antihistamine appears to have relatively little effect on the control of dermatitis.[21] Use of topical antihistamines (eg, lotions containing diphenhydramine) should be avoided because of the high incidence of contact dermatitis associated

Table 11-3: Management of Acute Flares of Atopic Dermatitis

I. Administer soaking baths* in cool or lukewarm water for 20 minutes twice daily, then:

  a. Immediately apply medium-potency topical corticosteroid (eg, 0.025%-0.1% triamcinolone cream) to affected skin, except the face, and

  b. Immediately apply 1% hydrocortisone cream to facial rash or less severely affected areas of the skin, and

  c. Immediately apply a moisturizing cream or ointment to other areas of dry skin.

II. Prescribe antistaphylococcal antibiotic therapy for severe flares, or for those accompanied by lesions that are weeping or crusted or have marked erythema.

  a. Consider performing skin culture when prescribing antistaphylococcal therapy because of the prevalence of resistant bacterial strains.

III. Prescribe an antihistamine for relief of pruritus.

IV. Schedule a follow-up visit to assess improvement and adjust the maintenance regimen as needed.

*For localized eruptions, as a substitute for bathing, the affected area may be wrapped in a wet cloth for 20 minutes.

with these preparations. Finally, written treatment plans are essential, especially for patients with more severe degrees of eczema. Finally, the National Institute of Arthritis and Musculoskeletal and Skin Diseases (http://www.niams.nih.gov/health_info/Atopic_Dermatitis/default.asp) and the National Eczema Association (http://www.nationaleczema.org)

maintain websites with many fine educational materials and handouts for patients with atopic dermatitis.

Acute Exacerbations of Atopic Dermatitis

Acute flares of atopic dermatitis should be treated with a combination of anti-infective therapy and intense local skin care (Table 11-3). Localized breakouts of atopic dermatitis should be cleaned and hydrated either by bathing or by wrapping a wet towel around the affected area for 15 or 20 minutes 2 to 3 times/day, followed immediately by the application of a moisturizing cream or ointment and a medium-potency corticosteroid. Infection should be strongly suspected in cases characterized by a sudden dramatic increase in severity, especially if the skin lesions are very red, weepy, or crusted. Surface cultures of the skin should be obtained because of the increasing frequency of antibiotic-resistant bacteria. Institution of topical (mupirocin [Bactroban®, Centany™]) or systemic (eg, erythromycin, cephalexin [Keflex®]) antibiotic therapy directed at *Staphylococcus* and *Streptococcus* often produces dramatic resolution of the skin rash within 2 to 3 days.

Systemic corticosteroids can be considered in some cases of acute severe outbreaks of eczema. However, their use should be avoided in the daily management of this disorder because of the significant side effects associated with long-term corticosteroid use.

Contact Dermatitis

Contact dermatitis is a common skin disease caused by exposure to irritants or allergens, producing skin inflammation and pruritus that is usually limited to the area of exposure.[22,23] The lesions are characterized by erythema, superficial edema that produces a firm texture, and vesiculation that typically begins with microvesicles that may coalesce to form larger blisters. Unroofing of the vesicles through scratching results in weeping and crusting of the lesions. Although the clinical appearance of the individual lesions

Table 11-4: Causes of Contact Dermatitis

A. Irritant dermatitis

- Soaps, detergents
- Abrasion (handwashing)
- Occlusion
- Acids
- Alkali
- Solvents

B. Allergic contact dermatitis

Source	Allergen
Topical medicines	Neomycin Bacitracin Benzocaine Corticosteroids Diphenhydramine
Medicine or cosmetic additives	Thimerosal Quaternium-15 Fragrances Balsam of Peru Formaldehyde Lanolin
Sunscreen	PABA
Jewelry Pocket change Belt buckles	Nickel Cobalt
Hair dye	Paraphenylenediamine
Cement, leather	Dichromate
Plants	Various
Shoes Rubber products	Thiuram Stabilizers

11

is nonspecific, the distribution of skin lesions is usually diagnostic because it corresponds with the application of the inciting agent.

Different mechanisms are responsible for allergic and irritant contact dermatitis. Allergic contact dermatitis is caused by a type IV hypersensitivity reaction involving sensitization of allergen-specific T cells in regional lymph nodes. The sensitized T cells home back to the skin and are reactivated by the contact allergen to secrete cytokines that activate macrophages and other effector cells at the site of inflammation.[24] The activated cells in the skin cause the dermatitis. In contrast, irritant dermatitis does not involve an immunologic mechanism and instead results from contact with a substance that damages, or irritates, the skin. Consequently, an irritant can cause dermatitis after the first exposure because no period of sensitization is required.

Because immunologic sensitization is a prerequisite to the development of allergic contact dermatitis, it follows that the rate of sensitization largely depends on the frequency and duration of exposure to potential allergens. For example, Europeans are not sensitive to poison ivy or poison oak because these are 'New World' plants. As another example, the rate of nickel sensitivity is up to 10 times higher in women, presumably because of increased exposure to nickel-containing alloys in jewelry.

Treatment of allergic contact dermatitis is based on avoidance of the inciting agent, so it is essential to carefully evaluate the history and pattern of distribution of skin lesions to identify the allergen. Clinicians should 'step into the patient's shoes' to obtain a complete history of daily activities, including the use of cosmetics, toiletries, hair preparations and dyes, and topical medications. Occupational exposures are important, as many industrial chemicals, proteins, and irritants have been implicated in contact dermatitis.[22,23] In fact, skin-related complaints account for up to 90% of all claims for workers' compensation. Exposure to potential allergens through hobbies and housework should also be explored. Finally, because many topical medications can cause contact dermatitis, it is crucial to get a complete history of the treatments that have been used on the rash.

Common skin sensitizers and their sources are listed in Table 10-4.[22,23,25] The association of a known skin sensitizer with the onset of a localized dermatitis establishes a provisional diagnosis, and presumptive therapy can then be started. However, contact dermatitis often follows the application of preparations with many ingredients, making it difficult to identify the offending allergen. In this situation, patch testing can be used to identify the allergen, opening the way to effective treatment and avoidance measures. Despite recent advances in the standardization of allergen preparations and techniques,[24] patch testing is still an art and should only be performed by physicians formally trained in this technique. There are many causes of false-positive and false-negative results,[25] and these limitations are even more evident when testing with materials that have not been standardized. Regrettably, this is often necessary because of the limited number of commercially available standardized extracts.

Treatment

The primary treatment for allergic contact dermatitis is avoidance of the allergen, but lesions may persist for weeks without additional anti-inflammatory therapy. Corticosteroids speed the resolution of skin lesions and associated symptoms. If topical therapy is used, a class I or class II corticosteroid can be prescribed (Table 11-2), but therapy should be limited to 2 weeks to avoid cutaneous side effects. In addition, potent corticosteroid preparations should never be used on the face because of the high incidence of side effects. For severe outbreaks of contact dermatitis on the body, or moderate-to-severe lesions on the face, oral corticosteroids are the most effective treatment,[26] if there are no medical contraindications. A 2- to 3-week course of prednisone, starting with 40 to 60 mg/day in adults or 1 mg/kg/day in children given in split doses followed by a slow taper, produces satisfactory relief in most patients. However, relapses are common if the prednisone is tapered over a shorter period.

Other supportive measures include the use of cool compresses with either Burow's solution or saline to relieve local discomfort, cleaning the affected area, and speed drying of the lesions. Antihistamines such as hydroxyzine can be used to treat pruritus, although topical antihistamine or anesthetic agents should be avoided because they are potent skin sensitizers. Secondary bacterial infections should be treated with oral antibiotics with good coverage of staphylococcal and streptococcal bacteria.

References

1.   Dold S, Wjst M, von Mutius E, et al: Genetic risk for asthma, allergic rhinitis, and atopic dermatitis. *Arch Dis Child* 1992; 67:1018-1022.

2.   Horii KA, Simon SD, Liu DY, et al: Atopic dermatitis in children in the United States, 1997-2004: visit trends, patient and provider characteristics, and prescribing patterns. *Pediatrics* 2007;120:e527-e534.

3.   Williams H, Robertson C, Stewart A, et al: Worldwide variations in the prevalence of symptoms of atopic eczema in the international study of asthma and allergies in childhood. *J Allergy Clin Immunol* 1999:103:125-138.

4.   Scheynius A, Johansson C, Buentke E, et al: Atopic eczema/ dermatitis syndrome and Malassezia. *Int Arch Allergy Immunol* 2002;127:161-169.

5.   Daud LR, Garralda ME, David TJ: Psychosocial adjustment in preschool children with atopic eczema. *Arch Dis Child* 1993; 69:670-676.

6.   Massarano AA, Hollis S, Devlin J, et al: Growth in atopic eczema. *Arch Dis Child* 1993;68:677-679.

7.   Niwa Y, Iizawa O: Abnormalities in serum lipids and leukocyte superoxide dismutase and associated cataract formation in patients with atopic dermatitis. *Arch Dermatol* 1994;130: 1387-1392.

8.   Akdis CA, Akdis M, Bieber T, et al: Diagnosis and treatment of atopic dermatitis in children and adults: European Academy

of Allergology and Clinical Immunology/American Academy of Allergy, Asthma and Immunology/PRACTALL Consensus Report. *J Allergy Clin Immunol* 2006;118:152-169.

9.   Ong PY, Ohtake T, Brandt C, et al: Endogenous antimicrobial peptides and skin infections in atopic dermatitis. *N Engl J Med* 2002;347:1151-1160.

10.   Chien YH, Hwu WL, Chiang BL: The genetics of atopic dermatitis. *Clin Rev Allergy Immunol* 2007;33:178-190.

11.   Hanifin JM, Rajka G: Diagnostic features of atopic eczema. *Acta Dermatol Venereol (Stockh)* 1980;92:44-47.

12.   Sampson HA: The evaluation and management of food allergy in atopic dermatitis. *Clin Dermatol* 2003;21:183-192.

13.   Bock SA, Sampson HA, Atkins FM, et al: Double-blind, placebo-controlled food challenge (DBPCFC) as an office procedure: a manual. *J Allergy Clin Immunol* 1988;82:986-987.

14.   Norris PG, Schofield O, Camp RD: A study of the role of house dust mite in atopic dermatitis. *Br J Dermatol* 1988;118: 435-440.

15.   Adinoff AD, Tellez P, Clark RA: Atopic dermatitis and aeroallergen contact sensitivity. *J Allergy Clin Immunol* 1988;81: 736-742.

16.   Darsow U, Vieluf D, Ring J: Atopy patch test with different vehicles and allergen concentrations: an approach to standardization. *J Allergy Clin Immunol* 1995;95:677-684.

17.   Lee JH, Lee SJ, Kim D, et al: The effect of wet-wrap dressing on epidermal barrier in patients with atopic dermatitis. *J Eur Acad Dermatol Venereol* 2007;21:1360-1368

18.   Rietschel RL: Patch testing for corticosteroid allergy in the United States. *Arch Dermatol* 1995;131:91-92.

19.   Alomar A, Berth-Jones J, Bos JD, et al: The role of topical calcineurin inhibitors in atopic dermatitis. *Br J Dermatol* 2004;151;3-27.

20.   Munzenberger PJ, Montejo JM: Safety of topical calcineurin inhibitors for the treatment of atopic dermatitis. *Pharmacotherapy* 2007;27:1020-1028.

21.   Diepgen TL, Early Treatment of the Atopic Child Study Group: Longterm treatment with cetirizine of infants with atopic dermatitis: a multi-country, double-blind, randomized, placebo-controlled trial (the ETAC trial) over 18 months. *Pediatr Allergy Immunol* 2002;13:278-286.

22.   Rietschel RL: Occupational contact dermatitis. *Lancet* 1997; 349:1093-1095.

23.   Slodownik D, Nixon R: Occupational factors in skin diseases. *Curr Probl Dermatol* 2007;35:173-189.

24.   Fyhrquist-Vanni N, Alenius H, Lauerma A: Contact Dermatitis. *Dermatologic Clinics* 2007;25:614-623.

25.   Marks JG, Belsito DV, DeLeo VA, et al: North American Contact Dermatitis Group: patch test results for the detection of delayed-type hypersensitivity to topical allergens. *J Am Acad Dermatol* 1998;38:911-918.

26.   Spector SL: Oral steroid therapy for asthma and contact dermatitis. *JAMA* 1992;268:1926.

Chapter 12

Food Allergy

F ood allergies are most common in early life, but can affect all ages. Surveys have estimated that approximately 30% of people believe that they or their children are allergic to one or more foods, but the true incidence of food allergy is much lower.[1-3] Studies using double-blind, placebo-controlled food challenges indicate that between 2% and 7.5% of children actually have food allergy, and the incidence in adults is significantly lower.[2,3] Presumably, the remainder of these self-reported reactions are caused by food intolerance or are mistakenly identified as food-caused symptoms. Overdiagnosis of food allergy is undesirable because it can lead to needless dietary restriction and, in some cases, to nutritional deficiencies.[4]

It is important to understand the difference between the two types of adverse reaction to foods—food allergy and food intolerance.[5] Food allergy is caused by an immunologic reaction to a specific food protein, including immunoglobulin E (IgE)-dependent and -independent mechanisms. In contrast, food intolerance may stem from one of a number of different nonimmunologic mechanisms (Table 12-1). Examples of food intolerance include lactose intolerance, resulting in an inability to digest the primary sugar in milk; food poisoning, which may be caused by toxins or microbes

Table 12-1: Food Intolerances

Metabolic deficiencies
- Lactase deficiency
- Phenylketonuria

Pharmacologic properties of food
- Caffeine → insomnia
- Serotonin → migraine headaches

Food poisoning
- Histamine (scombroid fish)
- Staphylococcal enterotoxin

Irritant reactions
- Capsaicin → heartburn
- Sulfites → bronchospasm

contaminating the food; or pharmacologic reactions to food ingredients, such as sleeplessness caused by the ingestion of caffeine. Scombroid fish poisoning is an example of a food poisoning that closely mimics an allergic reaction. In this case, the breakdown of histidine contained in the dark meat of deep-swimming ocean fish such as tuna or swordfish causes a buildup of histamine within the fish.[6] Ingestion of fish containing large amounts of histamine can produce symptoms that are almost indistinguishable from those caused by allergy, including gastrointestinal (GI) distress, facial flushing, urticaria, respiratory distress, and even hypotension.

Several important distinctions exist between food intolerance and food allergy. First, food allergic reactions are precipitated by food proteins, of which only a small amount is needed to set off an allergic reaction. In contrast, people with food intolerance are often able to ingest a small amount of the offending food and develop symptoms only if larger amounts are eaten. For instance, most people with primary lactose intolerance can drink up to several ounces of milk without experiencing any adverse reactions.[7] Furthermore, allergic reactions are reproducible because they occur after eating or drinking any food containing the offending food protein. For example, a person allergic to milk protein will experience symptoms after drinking milk or eating ice cream, cheese, or butter. In contrast, a person with lactose intolerance may be able to tolerate yogurt, which contains less lactose than milk, whereas drinking a similar amount of whole milk may lead to GI symptoms.

Clinical Manifestations

Historical information, such as the timing of symptoms in relation to food ingestion and the organ systems affected, provides important clues about whether an adverse reaction is from food allergy, food intolerance, or some other cause. Allergic reactions typically occur soon after the ingestion of the offending food, often within minutes and nearly always within 2 hours.[8,9] Delayed reactions, although uncommon, can occur if food absorption is delayed or if the allergic reaction is from a mechanism other than type I hypersensitivity.[5]

Food allergy can affect several different organ systems, including the GI tract, the skin, the cardiovascular system, the respiratory tract, and the central nervous system (CNS) (Table 12-2).[8-11] The GI tract and the skin are the most commonly affected organ systems. Many people with food allergy develop unpleasant sensations in the mouth, such as itching, burning, or tingling, within seconds after ingesting the food. Abdominal pain, nausea, vomiting, and diarrhea are common GI symptoms. Cutaneous manifestations of food allergy include urticaria, angioedema, and flushing, especially of the face, neck, and ears. Patients with atopic dermatitis may experience a generalized itching sensation after ingesting a food allergen. This may be followed hours later by an increase in the severity of eczema.[9] Respiratory symptoms are the next most

Table 12-2: Clinical Manifestations of Food Allergy

Allergic Syndrome	Organ System
IgE-mediated	Skin
	Gastrointestinal
	Respiratory
	Neurologic
	Cardiovascular
Non-IgE immune mechanism	Gastrointestinal
	Cardiovascular

IgE=immunoglobulin E

common manifestation of food allergy. These may range from mild symptoms, such as watering of the eyes and rhinorrhea, to severe bronchospasm or obstruction of the upper airway. Upper airway obstruction may be insidious in nature and may begin with mild symptoms, such as hoarseness of the voice or slight swelling of the tongue. These symptoms may progress

Rapid Onset	**Delayed Onset**
Urticaria	Eczema
Angioedema	
Flushing	
Pruritus	
Mouth pruritus	Failure to thrive
Vomiting	Iron deficiency
Abdominal pain	Protein loss
Diarrhea	
Rhinorrhea	↑ Asthma
Tearing	
Wheezing	
Laryngeal edema	
Migraine (rare)	
Seizures (rare)	
Shock	Shock
Hematochezia	Iron deficiency
Vomiting	Protein loss
Abdominal pain	Failure to thrive
Diarrhea	
Hypovolemia	Hypovolemia
Shock	

either rapidly or over several hours to produce severe respiratory distress. It is unusual, however, for respiratory symptoms to be the only manifestation of food allergy.[11]

Life-threatening allergic reactions to food may also involve the cardiovascular system, producing capillary leakage, diminished cardiac output, and hypotension. Three different patterns

247

can be observed with an allergic reaction to food.[12,13] The first pattern is typical of an immediate response, with symptoms appearing within minutes of food ingestion and resolving within 30 minutes to 1 hour. Biphasic responses may also be observed, in which symptoms are initially prominent, followed in succession by a quiescent period and then reappearance of symptoms. Finally, some reactions begin with mild manifestations that progressively worsen over several hours. Thus, it is important to monitor patients for at least 3 to 4 hours after an acute reaction, and not to underestimate the severity of a reaction simply because the initial manifestations are mild.

The potential association between food allergy and neurologic reactions precipitated by food allergy has generated considerable controversy. Migraine headaches can be triggered by the ingestion of foods such as chocolate and aged cheeses, although this association is probably due to a pharmacologic, rather than an allergic, response to the food. The use of diets restricted in sugar and food additives (eg, the Finegold diet), or oligoallergenic diets in the treatment of attention-deficit disorder (ADD) or other behavioral disorders have not been validated and should be avoided.[3,14,15] Multiple vague complaints, such as lethargy and headache, in the absence of signs or symptoms of hypersensitivity are unlikely to be caused by food allergy.[16]

Food-induced enterocolitis syndrome is an example of a food allergy that occurs independently of food-specific IgE, because skin and radioallergosorbent tests (RASTs) are often negative.[17] This disorder occurs most often in 3- to 6-month-old infants, and symptoms develop 4 to 6 hours after ingestion of formulas containing either soy or milk protein. Affected infants develop GI symptoms, including vomiting, hematochezia, diarrhea, and hypovolemia. Chronic allergen exposure may produce anemia, failure to thrive, and hypovolemia. Celiac disease is another non-IgE-mediated disorder in which an immunologic reaction to grain glutens produces mucosal damage to the small intestine that leads to chronic malabsorption.[18]

Diagnosing Food Allergy

Systematic evaluation of data obtained with the medical history and physical examination, along with determination of food-specific IgE and food challenge procedures, can be used to accurately diagnose food allergy (Table 12-3).[3,5] Historical information should be evaluated with a few key points in mind, including the timing of the adverse reaction in relation to when the food was ingested; the reproducibility of the adverse reaction after repeated exposure to the same food protein; and the involvement of the typical organ systems as described previously. Physical examination is important to exclude other possibilities in the differential diagnosis, such as primary GI disorders. Testing for food-specific IgE using either prick skin testing or RAST can provide valuable data to support or disprove the possibility of food allergy. However, it is important to realize the limitations of these tests. Both tests have a high (>90% for most allergens) negative predictive value and can reliably exclude the possibility of IgE-mediated food allergy,[19] although it is important to remember that infants with food-induced enterocolitis usually have negative skin tests and RASTs. The positive predictive value of skin tests is <50%, although large positive skin test results may have greater predictive accuracy. The quantity of serum food-specific IgE, as measured by carefully standardized tests such as the UniCAP system, is related to the probability of clinical reactivity to the food ingestion. Therefore, measuring food-specific IgE can help with the diagnosis of food allergy, and also with decisions related to food challenges and resolution of food allergy.[20-22] Consequently, it is important to verify food allergies suspected on the basis of positive skin tests or RASTs either with solid historical data or with food challenge procedures.

In some cases, eliminating suspect foods from the diet for 1 or 2 weeks may provide helpful information. A clear-cut improvement in symptoms suggests food allergy, but negative or equivocal responses may require further evaluation

Table 12-3: Diagnosing Food Allergy

History
- Temporal association of symptoms with ingestion of a specific food
- Reproducible reactions each time the food protein is eaten
- Reaction involves typical organ systems (ie, skin, gastrointestinal [GI], respiratory)

Physical examination
- Signs of atopic disease
- Exclude other disorders

Laboratory
- Prick skin tests
- Radioallergosorbent test (RAST)

Trial elimination diet
- Exclude suspect foods from diet for 1 to 2 weeks
- If results are not clear, consider food challenge

Food challenges
- Open challenge
- Double-blind, placebo-controlled food challenge
- Be prepared to treat possible adverse reactions

because of the limitations inherent in compliance with dietary restrictions. If the elimination diet is being used as a diagnostic tool, the patient should return to the clinic for follow-up in 2 to 4 weeks to ensure that the dietary restrictions do not become permanent without verification of food allergy.

Most cases of food allergy can be diagnosed on the basis of characteristic clinical manifestations that are temporarily associated with eating a particular food, detection of food-specific IgE, and improvement when the food is eliminated from the diet. Additional diagnostic studies may be needed in some cases, such as for unusual symptoms or for delayed reactions to food, or when allergy to multiple foods is suspected. Under these circumstances, food challenges are useful in verifying or disproving food allergies.[3,23] Challenge procedures can be performed using several formats—open, single-blind, or double-blind with a placebo control. Open challenges are particularly useful for quickly excluding food allergy in low-risk individuals, as in the case of a patient with negative skin tests. Because psychologic factors can strongly influence subjective reactions, blind challenges are helpful in many cases. Blinding the observer as well allows for unbiased observations that have greater clinical validity. In setting up a double-blind, placebo-controlled food challenge, it is often useful to enlist the help of a dietitian who can prepare the challenge substances in a suitable vehicle to disguise their taste. The general principle behind food challenge is to initially administer a low dose of the suspected allergen, then increase the dose at timed intervals until the subject has either eaten a typical portion of the food or shows manifestations of allergy. Standards and safeguards for performing food challenges have been proposed.[3,23] Because severe reactions can occur even under controlled conditions, food challenges should only be performed at a medical facility where resuscitative equipment is available, such as epinephrine, respiratory support, and intravenous fluids. It is neither advisable nor necessary to conduct oral challenge tests on patients with a straightforward history of severe anaphylaxis and evidence of food-specific IgE.

Treatment of Food Allergy

The only treatment that has proven to be effective in food allergy is to completely exclude the offending food protein from the patient's diet (Table 12-4).[3,5] Although this is sim-

Table 12-4: Food Allergy Management Checklist

Exclude the offending food protein(s) from the diet

- Read food ingredient labels
- Carry pocket-sized reference cards
- Meet with schoolteachers or other caregivers of allergic children
- Take extra care when eating away from home
- Label hospital charts

Prescribe treatment for accidental ingestions

- Diphenhydramine 1 mg/kg/dose (50 mg maximum) orally, every 4-6 hours for reactions limited to the skin
- Epinephrine (1:1,000) 0.01 mL/kg/dose (0.3 mL maximum) intramuscularly every 15-20 min for systemic or respiratory reactions
- If epinephrine is used, the patient should be transported to a medical facility as soon as possible
- Observe patient for at least 3-4 hours after accidental ingestion, and consider hospitalization for severe reactions

Consider purchasing a medical alert bracelet

Re-evaluate patients every 1-3 years to determine if the allergy has resolved

- Exceptions: peanut, tree nut, fish, and shellfish allergies tend to be lifelong

Table 12-5: Recommended Dietary Allowances

Age	Calcium (mg)	Vitamin D (μg)*
0-6 months	210	5
7-12 months	270	5
1-3 years	500	5
4-8 years	800	5
9-18 years	1,300	5

From National Institutes of Health, Office of Dietary Supplements. Available at: http://ods.od.nih.gov/factsheets/calcium. asp and http://ods.od.nih.gov/factsheets/vitamind.asp

*5 μg=200 international units (IU)

ple in principle, accidental ingestion of allergenic foods is common, even among highly motivated patients.[24] Patients or parents must be taught to carefully read the labels of prepared foods and to recognize all forms of the allergenic protein. For example, casein, whey, and sodium caseinate are all forms of cow's milk protein. In addition, special precautions must be taken when eating away from home. Restaurant and school personnel often misunderstand food allergy or do not really know what is in the food they are serving. In two surveys of fatal or near-fatal food-induced anaphylaxis, eating away from home was identified as a major risk factor for unsuspected ingestion of a known allergen.[12,13] Parents sending children with food allergy to school or day care for the first time should meet with teachers or other caretakers to clearly explain dietary restrictions and contingency plans for the treatment of accidental ingestion of an allergen.[25]

Excluding one or two foods from the diet is unlikely to lead to nutritional deficiencies, with the possible exception

Table 12-6: Infant Formulas With Reduced Antigenicity

	Nutramigen®	Pregestamil®
Manufacturer	Mead Johnson (Princeton, NJ)	Mead Johnson
Protein source	Casein hydrolysate	Casein hydrolysate
Recommended for milk-allergic patients	Yes*	Yes*
Recommended for prevention of food allergy/AD	Yes	Yes
Comments		Fat source: medium-chain triglycerides (Tgs)

*Allergic reactions to formulas based on extensively hydrolyzed milk protein are rare but have been reported.

of cow's milk allergy in an infant or young child. Milk is an important source of vitamin D and calcium, and supplements may be necessary to ensure that the recommended daily allowance of these nutrients is achieved (Table 12-5). Several infant formulas have been developed to have reduced antigenicity (Table 12-6).[26,27] Infants who are allergic to milk and soy usually do well when they are fed formulas that have either extensive hydrolyzed protein or

Good Start®	Alimentum®	Neocate®
Nestle/ Carnation (Glendale, CA)	Ross Products/ Abbott Laboratories (Abbott Park, IL)	Scientific Hospital Supplies (Gaithersburg, MD)
Partial whey hydrolysate	Casein hydrolysate	Amino acids
No	Yes*	Yes
?	Yes	Yes
Commonly causes allergic symptoms in children with cow milk allergy		Amino acids are often tolerated by infants who have adverse reactions to hydrolyzed milk protein

amino acids as the protein source. It should be noted that Good Start® formula contains partially hydrolyzed milk protein and is not suitable for milk-allergic patients. Finally, patients who exclude multiple food proteins from their diet should be re-evaluated because allergy to more than a few foods is uncommon.

Non-IgE-mediated milk and/or soy protein intolerance in infants also requires allergen avoidance.[5,17] These disorders commonly resolve spontaneously by 1 to 2 years of age. Eosinophilic esophagitis, gastritis, and enteritis sometimes respond to removing food allergens from the diet.[17] These disorders are best evaluated and managed with the help of a gastroenterologist, and mucosal biopsies are helpful in the diagnosis and monitoring of disease activity.

Accidental ingestion of known food allergens is a common problem, and all patients with food allergy should be prepared for this possibility.[24,25] For reactions that are limited to the skin, a fast-acting antihistamine such as diphenhydramine (Benadryl®) should be administered (Table 12-4). For more serious reactions involving recurrent vomiting or evidence of respiratory or cardiovascular compromise, epinephrine should be administered immediately. Delaying the use of epinephrine may lead to more severe or even fatal reactions.[12,13] Patients with food allergy should routinely be prescribed epinephrine autoinjectors (eg, EpiPen® [0.3 mg] and EpiPen® Jr. [0.15 mg]) and should carry it with them at all times. Medical alert bracelets are also recommended for patients who have experienced anaphylactic reactions in the past.

The Food Allergy & Anaphylaxis Network (10400 Eaton Place, Suite 107, Fairfax, VA 22030-2208, telephone 703-691-3179, http://www.foodallergy.org) is a support organization that was founded by parents of children with food allergy and is a valuable source of information, such as how to deal with schools, special recipes for food-allergic individuals, and pocket-sized guides to reading ingredient labels.

Natural History of Food Allergy

Most affected children eventually outgrow food allergy. Many infants who are allergic to common allergens such as egg, milk, soy, and wheat lose their allergies by the time they are school-aged.[3,9] Children with food allergies should therefore be periodically re-evaluated to see whether their allergies are still active. Allergies to peanuts, tree nuts, and seafood are less likely to resolve and may be lifelong afflictions.[3,24,28]

Summary

Most food allergies are recognized and treated by primary care providers. Careful evaluation of the history and physical findings, performance of RAST or prick skin testing, and use of elimination diets provide sufficient information to evaluate many food-related complaints. Supplemental use of food challenge procedures is helpful in clarifying cases with lingering uncertainties. After food allergy is diagnosed, treatment is based on excluding the food allergen from the diet. It is essential to prepare patients with food allergy for the accidental (and inevitable) ingestion of food allergens. Finally, it is important to realize that most children will eventually lose their food allergy; therefore, food allergy should be re-evaluated periodically. Careful evaluation of food-related complaints results in accurate diagnosis of food allergies and the avoidance of unwarranted dietary restrictions and associated nutritional deficiencies.

References

1.   Sicherer SH, Munoz-Furlong A, Sampson HA: Prevalence of peanut and tree nut allergy in the United States determined by means of a random digit dial telephone survey: a 5-year follow-up study. *J Allergy Clin Immunol* 2003;112:1203-1207.

2.   Bock SA: Prospective appraisal of complaints of adverse reactions to foods in children during the first 3 years of life. *Pediatrics* 1987;79:683-688.

3.   American College of Allergy, Asthma, and Immunology: Food allergy: a practice parameter. *Ann Allergy Asthma Immunol* 2006; 96(3 suppl 2):S1-S68.

4.   David TJ, Waddington E, Stanton RH: Nutritional hazards of elimination diets in children with atopic eczema. *Arch Dis Child* 1984;59:323-325.

5.   Sampson HA: 9. Food allergy. *J Allergy Clin Immunol* 2003; 111(2 suppl):S540-S547.

6.   Morrow JD, Margolies GR, Rowland J, et al: Evidence that histamine is the causative toxin of scombroid-fish poisoning. *N Engl J Med* 1991;324:716-720.

7.   Heyman MB, Committee on Nutrition: Lactose intolerance in infants, children, and adolescents. *Pediatr* 2006;118:1279-1286.

8.   Bock SA, Atkins FM: Patterns of food hypersensitivity during sixteen years of double-blind, placebo-controlled food challenges. *J Pediatr* 1990;117:561-567.

9.   Sampson HA, McCaskill CC: Food hypersensitivity and atopic dermatitis: evaluation of 113 patients. *J Pediatr* 1985;107:669-675.

10.   Goldman AS, Anderson DW, Sellers WA, et al: Milk allergy. I. Oral challenge with milk and isolated milk proteins in allergic children. *Pediatrics* 1963;32:425-443.

11.   James JM, Bernhisel-Broadbent J, Sampson HA: Respiratory reactions provoked by double-blind food challenges in children. *Am J Respir Crit Care Med* 1994;149:59-64.

12.   Sampson HA, Mendelson L, Rosen JP: Fatal and near-fatal anaphylactic reactions to food in children and adolescents. *N Engl J Med* 1992;327:380-384.

13.   Yunginger JW, Sweeney KG, Sturner WQ, et al: Fatal food-induced anaphylaxis. *JAMA* 1988;260:1450-1452.

14.   Warner JO: Behavior and adverse food reactions. In: Metcalfe DD, Sampson HA, Simon RA, eds: *Food Allergy: Adverse Reactions to Foods and Food Additives*, 2nd ed. Cambridge, MA, Blackwell Science, 1997, pp 511-518.

15.   Ferguson A: Food sensitivity or self-deception? *N Engl J Med* 1990;323:476-478.

16.   Pearson DJ, Rix KJ, Bentley SJ: Food allergy: how much in the mind? A clinical and psychiatric study of suspected food hypersensitivity. *Lancet* 1983;1:1259-1261.

17.   Maloney J, Nowak-Wegrzyn A: Educational clinical case series for pediatric allergy and immunology: allergic proctocolitis, food protein-induced enterocolitis syndrome and allergic eosinophilic gastroenteritis with protein-losing gastroenteropathy as manifestations of non-IgE-mediated cow's milk allergy. *Pediatr Allergy Immunol* 2007; 18:360-367.

18.   Green PH, Cellier C: Celiac disease. *N Engl J Med* 2007;357: 1731-1743.

19.   Yunginger JW, Ahlstedt S, Eggleston PA, et al: Quantitative IgE antibody assays in allergic diseases. *J Allergy Clin Immunol* 2000;105:1077-1084.

20. Sampson HA: Utility of food-specific IgE concentrations in predicting symptomatic food allergy. *J Allergy Clin Immunol* 2001;107:891-896.

21. Perry TT, Matsui EC, Kay Conover-Walker M, et al: The relationship of allergen-specific IgE levels and oral food challenge outcome. *J Allergy Clin Immunol* 2004;114:144-149.

22. Shek LP, Soderstrom L, Ahlstedt S, et al: Determination of food specific IgE levels over time can predict the development of tolerance in cow's milk and hen's egg allergy. *J Allergy Clin Immunol* 2004;114:387-391.

23. Bock SA, Sampson HA, Atkins FM, et al: Double-blind, placebo-controlled food challenge (DBPCFC) as an office procedure: a manual. *J Allergy Clin Immunol* 1988;82:986-997.

24. Bock SA, Atkins FM: The natural history of peanut allergy. *J Allergy Clin Immunol* 1989;83:900-904.

25. Munoz-Furlong A: Food allergy in schools: concerns for allergists, pediatricians, parents, and school staff. *Ann Allergy Asthma Immunol* 2004;93(5 suppl 3):S47-S50.

26. Hill DJ, Murch SH, Rafferty K, et al: The efficacy of amino acid-based formulas in relieving the symptoms of cow's milk allergy: a systematic review. *Clin Exp Allergy* 2007;37:808-822.

27. American Academy of Pediatrics, Committee on Nutrition. Hypoallergenic infant formulas. *Pediatrics* 2000;106:346-349.

28. Daul CB, Morgan JE Lehrer SB: The natural history of shrimp hypersensitivity. *J Allergy Clin Immunol* 1990;86:88-93.

Chapter 13

Iatrogenic Allergies: Drugs and Latex

Adverse reactions to medications are among the most common problems encountered by health-care providers. Such drug reactions occur in 2% to 3% of hospitalized patients[1] and in a sizable proportion of outpatients who are treated with a variety of medications. When evaluating an adverse reaction to a medication, it is important to distinguish drug hypersensitivity from more predictable reactions that are likely to occur given a sufficient dose or duration of treatment.[1,2] Examples of predictable reactions include drug overdose, side effects, complications, or interactions. In contrast, hypersensitivity reactions affect only a subset of patients, and they can be difficult to predict. Hypersensitivity reactions that have an immunologic basis are referred to as drug allergy. In most instances, a careful review of the medical history and the physical findings is sufficient to distinguish drug allergies from other reactions, but in some cases skin testing or in vitro testing for drug-specific immunoglobulin E (IgE) are needed to provide definitive information.

Clinical Manifestations and Mechanisms of Adverse Drug Reactions

Immunologic reactions to drugs or latex can occur via several different mechanisms. The timing of an allergic reaction after a drug administration and the organ systems that are affected are important clues to the relevant pathogenic mechanism and have significant diagnostic and therapeutic implications. Reactions that occur rapidly after the first or second dose of a medicine course are likely to be caused by immediate, or type I, hypersensitivity, which involves the activation of mast cells and subsequent release of noxious mediators such as histamine and leukotrienes (see Chapter 2). Once released, mast cell mediators rapidly induce allergic signs and symptoms. Therefore, mast cell mediated allergic reactions to intravenous or inhaled allergens usually begin within minutes of allergen exposure. Reactions that follow oral medications are sometimes delayed by 1 to 2 hours, probably because of the time required to absorb the allergen. Immediate hypersensitivity reactions can involve several organ systems, including the skin, gastrointestinal (GI) tract, respiratory system, cardiovascular system, and central nervous system (CNS) (Table 13-1).

Mast cells can be triggered via several different pathways, including the cross-linking of surface IgE, the generation of anaphylatoxins (C3a, C5a), or the direct effects of a drug on mediator release. Many low-molecular-weight (LMW) drugs (eg, penicillin) act as haptens and must first bind to a carrier protein to form a complex large enough to cross-link IgE and trigger the mast cell. In contrast, some medications trigger mast-cell mediator release directly, and this produces clinical findings that are indistinguishable from IgE-mediated allergy.[3] These reactions are called anaphylactoid reactions and are most commonly triggered by codeine and other opiates, by intravenous contrast dye, and by protamine.

Nonsteroidal anti-inflammatory drugs (NSAIDs), such as aspirin, produce adverse reactions in a subset of patients through pharmacologic effects on prostaglandin and leukotriene metabolism.[4] In affected individuals, aspirin or related drugs inhibit prostaglandin E_2, leading to overproduction of leukotrienes and mast-cell activation. In addition, intraven-

Table 13-1: Clinical Manifestations of Immediate Drug Hypersensitivity	
Organ System	**Signs and Symptoms**
Skin	Urticaria
	Angioedema
	Facial flushing
	Pruritus
Gastrointestinal	Oral pruritus
	Vomiting
	Abdominal pain
	Diarrhea
Respiratory	Rhinorrhea
	Tearing
	Wheezing
	Laryngeal edema
Neurologic	Obtundation
	Loss of consciousness
Cardiovascular	Tachycardia
	Hypotension

ous infusion of γ-globulin can cause immediate reactions that occur through an immune complex mediated mechanism. During rapid infusion of intravenous γ-globulin, small amounts of immune complexes present in the preparation can activate complement, causing fever, chills, skin rashes, and sometimes hypotension.

In contrast to immediate hypersensitivity reactions, some responses appear days or weeks after the initiation of therapy. Serum sickness, which is the most common form of delayed drug reaction, was first described in the early 1900s in patients who were treated with infusions of horse serum for various infectious diseases. Similar reactions have been observed in recent years after administration of antithymocyte globulin (also derived from horse serum), which is used in preparative regimens before transplantation. The mechanism of serum sickness is related to the production of drug-specific immunoglobulin M (IgM) and IgE antibodies. After 7 to 10 days of drug administration, the antibodies reach concentrations similar to that of the drug, leading to the formation of immune complexes that subsequently activate complement and other inflammatory cascades. Clinical manifestations usually begin insidiously,[5] and recognition of early signs and symptoms requires a high index of suspicion. Skin manifestations vary and include urticaria, erythema multiforme, and vasculitic rashes. Systemic manifestations of serum sickness reactions include fever, myalgia, abdominal pain, and generalized malaise. Joint swelling, liver inflammation, and eosinophilia also frequently occur. If these reactions are not recognized at an early stage, severe dermatitis and mucosal desquamation (Stevens-Johnson syndrome [SJS]) can develop. Sulfisoxazole, phenytoin (Dilantin®), cefaclor, and penicillin are the medications most commonly associated with serum sickness reactions.

Drug reactions produced by delayed hypersensitivity (type IV) reactions are usually limited to the skin or conjunctiva. An example is a skin rash that begins a few days after starting treatment with a topical eye drop or ointment. This type of reaction requires prior sensitization, during which drug-specific CD4$^+$ T cells were stimulated.[6] Within 48 hours of re-exposure, antigen-specific T cells home to the area of exposure and orchestrate local inflammation, which can be intense. The hallmark of the resulting contact dermatitis is that skin findings, which usually include redness, pruritus, and dermal edema or vesiculation, are usually sharply demarcated and correspond to the area to which the medication was applied.[6,7]

Medications can also trigger anemia, thrombocytopenia, or neutropenia by binding to cellular proteins and setting off an autoimmune reaction. For example, penicillin can initiate type II hypersensitivity reactions by binding to the surface of red blood cells, creating a 'neoantigen' that is recognized by circulating antibodies, leading to activation of complement and phagocytic cells.[8]

Skin Testing in the Clinical Evaluation of Drug Allergy

Immediate hypersensitivity skin tests or a radioallergosorbent test (RAST) should only be considered when the history and clinical findings are compatible with a type I reaction. Skin test reagents are available for penicillin and penicillin derivatives, although there have been supply problems in recent years. Skin testing protocols to detect allergy to other medications, including sulfa, insulin, and local anesthetics, have been published, but relatively little data exist regarding their sensitivity or specificity.

Skin testing for penicillin allergy is highly predictive of future reactions to penicillin and related medications.[9,10] However, skin tests that are negative for penicillin do not exclude the possibility of cephalosporin allergy.[11] The results of a penicillin skin test reflect the current state of sensitization and do not predict whether the patient will become resensitized in the future after additional courses of penicillin. Patients who have a history of hypersensitivity reactions to penicillin but have negative penicillin skin tests have only a 1% to 3% chance of developing a urticarial reaction during penicillin therapy. This risk is similar to that of the general population.[1,10] The risk of an anaphylactic reaction to penicillin following negative skin tests is approximately 1:1,000.[1,10] On the other hand, patients with a history of penicillin hypersensitivity who have positive skin tests have a 50% to 60% chance of developing a systemic reaction after penicillin administration.[1,10]

Patch testing can be helpful in identifying the offending medication in cases of drug-induced contact dermatitis, although the diagnosis is often made on clinical grounds. However, if preparations with many ingredients have been applied to the skin and if the identity of the allergen is unclear, it is important to positively identify the allergen to avoid future problems. Despite recent advances in the standardization of allergen preparations and techniques, there are many causes of false-positive and false-negative results.[12,13] This problem is even more evident when testing with materials that have not been standardized, which is often necessary because of the limited number of commercially available standardized extracts. Thus, patch testing should be performed only by physicians who have been formally trained in this technique.

Treatment of Allergic Reactions to Drugs

Managing allergic reactions to drugs involves five principles: (1) identifying the relevant mechanism; (2) identifying the drug causing the reaction; (3) deciding whether to discontinue the medication; (4) providing supportive care to involve medical therapy for anaphylactic symptoms as well as less severe reactions such as urticaria; and (5) consideration of desensitization therapy. The decision whether to stop treatment with a particular medication or to continue treatment in the face of a drug reaction depends on several factors. In most instances, it is best to discontinue a medication that is causing an allergic reaction, but sometimes it is in a patient's best interest to continue the offending medication while carefully monitoring the course of a mild allergic reaction, such as intermittent urticaria. In the case of a severe allergic reaction, the offending drug should be discontinued unless there is a compelling reason not to do so. However, if erythema multiforme or mucosal involvement is present, then the offending medication should be stopped immediately to minimize the chances of SJS, a potentially life-threatening disorder.

If a drug with similar pharmacologic effects will be substituted, the clinician should avoid using antigenically similar drugs (eg, erythromycin, clarithromycin [Biaxin® XL]) because of cross-reactivity. If a patient has a penicillin al-

Table 13-2: Oral Desensitization Regimen for β-Lactam Medications*

Step (15-min Intervals)	Drug Concentration (mg/mL)
1	0.5
2	0.5
3	0.5
4	0.5
5	0.5
6	0.5
7	0.5
8	5
9	5
10	5
11	50
12	50
13	50
14	50

After step 14, observe the patient for 30 minutes. If there is no adverse reaction, administer 1 g of the same agent intravenously.

lergy, it is best to avoid use of all medications that share the basic penicillin backbone, including semisynthetic penicillins, some cephalosporins, and imipenem (Primaxin®). Aztreonam (Azactam®), a monobactam, has negligible cross-reactivity with penicillin and can thus be used with a high degree of safety in penicillin-allergic patients.[14] The newer

Volume* (mL)	Dose Given (mg)	Cumulative Dose (mg)
0.1	0.05	0.05
0.2	0.1	0.15
0.4	0.2	0.35
0.8	0.4	0.75
1.6	0.8	1.6
3.2	1.6	3.2
6.4	3.2	6.4
1.2	6	12
2.4	12	24
4.8	24	48
1	50	98
2	100	198
4	200	398
8	400	798

*Modified from Sullivan,[19] used with permission.
**Dilute the drug suspension into 30 mL water for ingestion.

cephalosporins, which are distinct from penicillin, can also be used safely in most patients with penicillin allergy.[15]

Anaphylactic reactions to medications should be treated as outlined in Chapter 15. Reactions that are limited to the skin often respond to the use of antihistamines to relieve itching or urticaria. Drug-induced urticaria can last several weeks even after the offending medication has been discontinued. Manifestations of serum sickness reactions, such as myalgia and joint swelling, are treated with NSAIDs or, in severe cases, with oral corticosteroids.

Preventive measures to reduce the chances for future allergic reactions include desensitization, prophylactic use of medications before anticipated exposure to allergens, and communicating information about a patient's drug allergies to all members of the health-care team. Desensitization regimens are effective for treating allergy to several medications, including sulfa, penicillin, and aspirin.[1,16,17] Desensitization is best achieved via the oral route, which is as effective as parenteral desensitization but is associated with a lower incidence of anaphylaxis.[1] Desensitization should only be performed under close observation, such as in a hospital ward that allows for cardiac monitoring of the patient and that is fully equipped to treat anaphylaxis. Table 13-2 depicts a standard oral desensitization regimen for penicillin.[1]

In patients with a known hypersensitivity to intravenous radiocontrast material, premedication regimens may decrease, but not necessarily eliminate, the frequency or the severity of allergic reactions. These regimens include pretreatment with antihistamines and corticosteroids (see Chapter 15). The use of a nonionic radiocontrast material should also be considered in high-risk individuals.[18] Finally, flagging the patient's medical record and notifying inpatient or outpatient pharmacies of drug reactions are important precautionary measures. Medical alert bracelets or necklaces may be appropriate for patients with particularly severe allergies.

Latex Allergy

Although contact sensitivity to natural rubber or latex has been recognized for more than a century, IgE-mediated reactions to latex have only been widely recognized in the past decade. The reason for the recent surge in the incidence of allergy to natural rubber is unknown, but it is probably related

Table 13-3: Risk Factors for Latex Allergy

- Spina bifida
- Urologic abnormalities
- Health-care workers
- Latex industry workers
- Food allergy
- Repeated surgeries
- Unexplained intraoperative anaphylaxis

to the widespread use of latex gloves in the hospital as part of universal precautions to inhibit the spread of infectious diseases. Certain groups are at much higher risk for latex allergy than the general population and are listed in Table 13-3.[20] The common factor uniting these groups is increased exposure to natural rubber products, either in the health-care setting or in the workplace. In some groups, such as individuals with spina bifida or those with urologic abnormalities who have required several surgeries, the risk of latex sensitivity is high enough to warrant latex avoidance precautions even in the absence of signs or symptoms of latex allergy.[21]

Clinical manifestations of latex allergy depend on the mechanism of the immunologic reaction.[20] Signs and symptoms of latex-induced contact dermatitis, which is a type IV reaction mediated by sensitized T cells, are limited to the skin. These include redness, itching, and edema, accompanied by vesiculation and, occasionally, localized urticaria. The skin rash typically follows exposure to latex within 24 to 72 hours, although the temporal relationship may be obscured if exposure to latex is chronic. IgE-mediated latex reactions, on the other hand, are characterized by skin, respiratory, and systemic manifestations typical of type I allergy. It is important to realize that some patients may

Table 13-4: Latex Exposure in the Home and Office

- Balloons
- Adhesive tape
- Elastic bands in clothing
- Rubber erasers
- Sports balls
- Carpet backing
- Rubber bands
- Rubber trees

Note: 'Latex' paint is actually made of acrylic instead of natural rubber and does not pose a threat to latex-allergic patients.

become exquisitely sensitive to latex proteins and develop symptoms when exposed to minute amounts of latex, such as airborne dust particles from gloves that are opened in the same room as the patient.[22] Several foods also contain proteins that cross-react with latex allergens and can provoke allergic reactions in latex-allergic patients. These foods include bananas, avocados, cherries, plums, and chestnuts.[21,23]

The diagnosis of latex allergy is often clinically obvious because exposure to latex is common in the home, at work, and in health-care environments. Skin tests or RAST can be used to verify the presence of latex-specific IgE, which strongly supports the diagnosis of type I latex allergy.[23] This can also be helpful in evaluating whether urticaria secondary to latex exposure is from contact dermatitis or IgE-mediated allergy. A latex-specific RAST is available in the United States, but negative results should be interpreted with caution because up to 25% of all patients with proven latex allergy may have negative RAST results.[24] A latex antigen extract is being developed, and a multicenter clinical trial found that this skin test reagent had a high degree of safety and diagnostic accuracy.[25] Pending approval of a standardized test, skin testing may be performed using unstandardized latex extracts, which are prepared by soaking cut-up glove fragments in diluent. However, the concentration of latex proteins in such preparations varies considerably. In addition, systemic reactions to latex skin testing can occur, and thus skin testing with latex should not be performed in patients who are suspected of being exquisitely sensitive to latex.

The only proven therapy for latex allergy is avoidance. Because latex-derived products are ubiquitous in modern society (Table 13-4), this requires a dedicated effort. In addition, hospital and clinic staff should prepare protocols to ensure the safety of latex-allergic patients.[21,26] This should include having on hand supplies of latex-free materials such as gloves, urologic catheters, and tourniquets (Table 13-5). The Spina Bifida Association of America (4590 MacArthur Boulevard NW, Suite 250, Washington, DC 20007; 800-621-3141, http://www.sbaa.org) is an excellent source of information about latex-free medical supplies.

As with drug allergy, it is critically important to indicate in the hospital and clinic that the patient is latex allergic to avoid inadvertent exposure. This can be achieved by posting 'latex allergy' signs and stickers on the patient's hospital room, door, bed, and charts. Maintaining a latex-safe environment for an inpatient can be difficult, given the many people who enter the typical hospital room during any 24-hour period, and can only be accomplished by careful planning and staff education. Perhaps the most effective means of reducing exposure in the medical environment is to gradually replace latex-containing materials with nonlatex substitutes. In addition, it has recently been proposed that powdered latex gloves be replaced with either nonlatex gloves or powder-free low-protein latex gloves, which shed much less allergen into the environment.

It is especially challenging to provide a latex-safe environment in the operating room.[26] Many hospitals have set aside one hospital operating room in which no latex-containing equipment or supplies are used. In addition, patients who are scheduled for the operating room can be started on

Table 13-5: Latex Exposure in the Clinic and Hospital

Items Containing Latex	Latex-Free Replacements*
Adhesive tape, bandage strips	Paper tape, plastic tape, silk tape
Latex gloves	Gloves made of vinyl, nitrile, neoprene, or other synthetic materials
Urologic catheters	Silicone or plastic catheters
Stethoscope tubing	Plastic tubing
Tourniquets	Plastic tourniquets (or apply tourniquet over clothing)
Blood pressure cuffs	Plastic cuff (or apply cuff over clothing)
Ambu bag	Silicone or vinyl bags, masks, and reservoirs
Syringes	Glass syringes
Injection ports	Flush tubing and cover latex ports (use stopcock to infuse medications)
Medication vial stoppers	Single-use glass ampules

*Always check with the manufacturer or supplier to determine whether an individual product contains latex.

a prophylactic regimen of antihistamines and corticosteroids similar to that used in patients with radiocontrast hypersensitivity (see Chapter 15), although this regimen has not yet been evaluated in controlled trials.

References

1.   Adkinson NF Jr: Drug allergy. In: Adkinson NF, Jr., Yunginger JW, Busse WW, et al, eds. *Middleton's Allergy: Principles & Practice*, 6th ed. St. Louis, MO, Mosby, 2003, pp 1679-1694.

2.   Greenberger PA: 8. Drug allergy. *J Allergy Clin Immunol* 2006;117(2 Suppl Mini-Primer):S464-S470.

3.   Greenberger PA: Anaphylactic and anaphylactoid causes of angioedema. *Immunol Allergy Clin North Am* 2006;26:753-767.

4.   Szczeklik A, Sanak M. The broken balance in aspirin hypersensitivity. *Eur J Pharmacol* 2006;533:145-155.

5.   Lawley TJ, Bielory L, Gascon P, et al: A prospective clinical and immunologic analysis of patients with serum sickness. *N Engl J Med* 1984;311:1407-1413.

6.   Militello G, Jacob SE, Crawford GH: Allergic contact dermatitis in children. *Curr Opin Pediatr* 2006;18:385-390.

7.   Klaus MV, Wieselthier JS: Contact dermatitis. *Am Fam Physician* 1993;48:629-632.

8.   Dove AF, Thomas DJ, Aronstam A, et al: Haemolytic anaemia due to penicillin. *Br Med J* 1975;3:684.

9.   Sogn DD, Evans R 3d, Shepherd GM, et al: Results of the National Institute of Allergy and Infectious Diseases Collaborative Clinical Trial to test the predictive value of skin testing with major and minor penicillin derivatives in hospitalized adults. *Arch Intern Med* 1992;152:1025-1032.

10.   Pichichero ME, Pichichero DM: Diagnosis of penicillin, amoxicillin, and cephalosporin allergy: reliability of examination assessed by skin testing and oral challenge. *J Pediatr* 1998;132:137-143.

11.   Romano A, Mayorga C, Torres MJ, et al: Immediate allergic reactions to cephalosporins: cross reactivity and selective responses. *J Allergy Clin Immunol* 2000;106:1177-1183.

12.   Brasch J, Henseler T, Aberer W, et al: Reproducibility of patch tests. A multicenter study of synchronous left- versus right-sided patch tests by the German Contact Dermatitis Research Group. *J Am Acad Dermatol* 1994;31:584-591.

13.   Oshima H, Kawahara D, Hashimoto Y, et al: An approach to evaluating patch test results. *Contact Dermatitis* 1994;31:189-191.

14.   Moss RB: Sensitization to aztreonam and cross-reactivity with other beta-lactam antibiotics in high-risk patients with cystic fibrosis. *J Allergy Clin Immunol* 1991;87(1 pt 1):78-88.

13

15.   Anne S, Reisman RE: Risk of administering cephalosporin antibiotics to patients with histories of penicillin allergy. *Ann Allergy Asthma Immunol* 1995;74:167-170.

16.   Kletzel M, Beck S, Elser J, et al: Trimethoprim-sulfamethoxazole oral desensitization in hemophiliacs infected with human immunodeficiency virus with a history of hypersensitivity reactions. *Am J Dis Child* 1991;145:1428-1429.

17.   Bush RK, Asbury D: Aspirin-sensitive asthma. In: Busse WW, Holgate ST, eds: *Asthma and Rhinitis*. Boston, MA, Blackwell Scientific, 1995, pp 1429-1439.

18.   Bush WH, Swanson DP: Radiocontrast. In: Virant SL, ed: *Systemic Reactions*. Philadelphia, PA, WB Saunders Co., 1995, pp 597-612.

19.   Sullivan TJ: Drug Allergy. In: Adkinson NF, Yunginger JW, Busse WW, et al, eds: *Middleton's Allergy: Principles and Practice*, 6th ed. St. Louis, MO, Mosby, 2003, pp 1726-1746.

20.   Poley GE Jr, Slater JE: Latex allergy. *J Allergy Clin Immunol* 2000;105(6 pt 1):1054-1062.

21.   Kelly KJ: Management of the latex-allergic patient. *Immunol Allergy Clin North Am* 1995;15:139-157.

22.   Sussman GL, Tarlo S, Dolovich J: The spectrum of IgE-mediated responses to latex. *JAMA* 1991;265:2844-2847.

23.   Granady LC, Slater JE: The history and diagnosis of latex allergy. *Immunol Allergy Clin North Am* 1995;15:21-29.

24.   Hamilton RG, Biagini RE, Krieg EF: Diagnostic performance of Food and Drug Administration-cleared serologic assays for natural rubber latex-specific IgE antibody. The Multi-Center Latex Skin Testing Study Task Force. *J Allergy Clin Immunol* 1999;103 (5 pt 1):925-930.

25.   Hamilton RG, Adkinson NF Jr: Diagnosis of natural rubber latex allergy: multicenter latex skin testing efficacy study. Multicenter Latex Skin Testing Study Task Force. *J Allergy Clin Immunol* 1998;102:482-490.

26.   Reines HD, Seifert PC: Patient safety: latex allergy. *Surg Clin North Am* 2005;85:1329-1340.

Chapter 14

Diagnosis and Treatment of Insect Sting Allergy

Most allergic reactions associated with insect stings are caused by members of the Hymenoptera order, which includes bees, wasps, hornets, yellow jackets, and fire ants. The offending insects vary with geographic location—in the United States, yellow jackets account for most allergic reactions, while in Europe, >95% of insect sting reactions are caused by honeybees and wasps.[1] Allergic reactions to fire ants are becoming more common in the southern United States, coinciding with expansion of the insect's habitat northward from Central America and Mexico. Allergic reactions to biting insects, which include mosquitoes, horse flies, deer flies, and fleas, are relatively uncommon and will not be examined in this chapter.

When evaluating allergic reactions, medical personnel should have a basic understanding of the life cycle of stinging insects.[2,3] Because yellow jackets nest in the ground, they often sting victims who are mowing the lawn or walking barefoot outdoors. These insects are attracted by food and beverages such as meat, fish, fruit juices, colas, and beer. It is common to encounter swarms of yellow jackets around garbage or compost receptacles. Yellow jackets are aggressive and often sting even if unprovoked. Bumblebees also nest in the ground but are relatively docile. In general, bumblebees and honeybees sting only if their nests are disturbed or if they are trapped inside clothes. The exception is the Africanized bee, or so-called killer bee, which is more aggressive than domestic bees. These insects have spread from Mexico into Texas and other parts of the Southwest, where cases involving multiple stings are becoming more common. Wasps and hornets typically nest well above the ground, so it is unusual for stings to occur unless the nest is disturbed. One difference between these insects and the honeybee is that wasps and hornets can inflict multiple stings. Finally, the fire ant is found primarily in the southern United States.[4] Nests can be recognized by their low hills with multiple entrances. The hallmark of the fire ant sting is the appearance of a sterile pustule within 24 hours.

Adverse Reactions to Insect Stings

Adverse reactions to insect stings can be classified as toxic reactions, large local reactions, urticarial reactions, and anaphylaxis. Each of these reactions typically appears a few minutes to several hours after the insect sting. Reactions that occur many hours after an insect sting are reported less commonly.[5] The pathogenesis for these late-onset reactions has not clearly been established.

Toxic reactions

Toxic reactions only occur after multiple stings and are caused by pharmacologic effects of the cumulative dose of venom.[2,3] Clinical manifestations of toxic reactions can closely resemble anaphylactic reactions, so they may be difficult to distinguish clinically. If there is doubt about the nature of the reaction, skin testing or radioallergosorbent test (RAST) can be performed after the patient has recovered to help test for the possibility of allergy and to determine if desensitization therapy is warranted.

Large local reactions

Large local reactions that occur as the result of insect sting include localized swelling, itching, and pain that may begin minutes to hours after the sting. Peak symptoms usually occur within several days, and the swelling may persist for up to 1 week. Although large local reactions are uncomfortable, they are not dangerous. Furthermore, patients who have experienced local reactions are unlikely to develop more severe reactions after future insect stings.[6] For this reason, skin testing and desensitization therapy are not warranted after a large local reaction. The pathogenesis of these reactions is not known but may involve immunoglobulin E (IgE) antibodies in some cases. Treatment of large local reactions consists of providing symptomatic relief: cold compresses, nonsteroidal anti-inflammatory drugs (NSAIDs), and antihistamines can help relieve associated symptoms.

Generalized urticarial reactions

One of the more common adverse reactions to insect stings is urticaria, which can be either generalized or confined to the region surrounding the sting. The natural history of generalized urticarial reactions has been evaluated in a study of 242 children, including 86 children who did not receive immunotherapy.[7] In 196 repeat stings, only 9.2% of children developed systemic reactions, and none of these reactions was more severe than the original episode of generalized urticaria. Due to a lack of similar data in adults, it is generally recommended that adults with generalized urticaria undergo skin testing and be considered for venom immunotherapy.

Anaphylaxis

The estimated incidence of insect sting anaphylaxis in the general population is 0.3% to 3%.[1,2] Considering that these reactions can be fatal, it is surprising that about 50% of people with insect sting hypersensitivity never seek help for this problem. This is tragic considering that venom immunotherapy is highly effective for lowering the risk for subsequent anaphylactic reactions. Anaphylactic reactions occur most often in people under the age of 20; however, anaphylactic reactions are more likely to be fatal in the elderly. Another factor that increases the risk of fatality from an insect sting is the use of β-blocker medications such as propranolol (Inderal®, Inderal® LA).[8]

Atopic individuals are not at increased risk for stinging insect allergy.[9] Several studies have been conducted to determine the natural history of severe insect sting hypersensitivity. In the United States, individuals who experience a sting-related anaphylactic reaction have a 50% to 60% risk for anaphylaxis after subsequent insect stings[2,3] while studies performed in Europe suggest that the risk is approximately 30%.[10]

Anaphylaxis triggered by insect stings produces the same clinical manifestations found in anaphylaxis from other triggers (see Chapter 15). Signs and symptoms usually occur within minutes of the sting and include urticaria, angioedema, bronchospasm, laryngospasm, abdominal pain, tachycardia, hypotension, and loss of consciousness.

Testing for Insect Sting Hypersensitivity

Skin testing is the preferred method for confirming the diagnosis of insect sting hypersensitivity, but it should be reserved for those patients who are candidates for venom desensitization (Table 14-1).[2,3,11] These include adults or children with a history of anaphylactic reactions to insect stings and adults with generalized urticarial reactions. Toxic reactions, large local reactions, and generalized urticarial reactions in children do not warrant skin testing because the results would not alter the subsequent treatment. Standardized venom preparations are now available for all of the major members of the Hymenoptera order, including yellow jackets, honeybees, white-faced hornets, wasps, and fire ants. Immediate skin test reactions to insect venom at the concentration of ≤1 μg/mL indicate the presence of venom-specific IgE.[2,3]

Extensive cross-reactivity exists among the major allergens in the Hymenoptera order, especially among the vespids (yellow jackets, hornets, and wasps). Therefore, it is common to develop positive skin tests to multiple venoms after having an allergic reaction to a single vespid. When the insect cannot be positively identified and there are multiple positive skin tests, immunotherapy with mixed venom preparations is recommended.

Some patients have anaphylactic reactions to insect stings, and yet have minimal amounts of venom-specific IgE. In cases where the patient history is convincing for anaphylaxis, and yet venom skin tests are negative, tests for venom-specific IgE (RAST) should be ordered.[2,3] If the RASTs are also negative, patients should be retested in 6 months. Additional indications for using RASTs for diagnosis include daily use of β-blockers, dermatographism, or generalized skin disease that precludes skin testing.

Therapy

Treatment of insect stings depends on the nature and severity of the reaction. Most stings need no specific treatment, but significant local or systemic reactions may require acute medical management as well as preventive measures to decrease the chances of future reactions (Table 14-2).

Treatment of acute symptoms

Allergic reactions to insect stings should be treated in the same fashion as allergic reactions caused by other triggers.[2,3] Generalized reactions that are limited to skin should be treated with oral antihistamines such as diphenhydramine (Benadryl®, 1 mg/kg/dose q6h for children, 25 to 50 mg PO q 6 h for adults). If the reaction includes extracutaneous allergic manifestations, then subcutaneous epinephrine (1:1,000; 0.01 mL/kg for children, 0.3 to 0.5 mL for adults) should be administered. Epinephrine (EpiPen®, EpiPen® Jr.) has a short half-life, and the dose may need to be repeated every 15 to 30 minutes. Patients who do not promptly and completely respond to 1 or 2 doses of epinephrine require insertion of a large-gauge intravenous catheter and prompt resuscitation with intravenous fluids (other measures are reviewed in Chapter 15). Patients who present with particularly severe reactions or those with protracted symptoms should be hospitalized for observation and/or continued treatment.

Table 14-1: Insect Sting Reaction

Type of Reaction	Mechanism	Skin Testing Indicated?
Toxic	Pharmacologic effects of venom	No
Large local	Local inflammation	No
Urticaria	IgE-mediated or complement activation	Adults - yes Children - no
Anaphylaxis	IgE-mediated	Yes

*If skin tests are positive

IgE=immunoglobulin E, NSAIDs=nonsteroidal anti-inflammatory drugs

Preventive measures

Several commonsense precautions are useful to people who would like to avoid insect stings in the future, regardless of whether the reactions are IgE-mediated (Table 14-2). Most unprovoked stings are from yellow jackets, but the risk of being stung by these insects can be diminished by avoiding eating or drinking uncovered drinks outdoors during the yellow jacket season. These insects congregate around compost or garbage, so it is best to keep these items separated as far as possible from living quarters. Fishermen are at especially high risk for yellow jacket stings because these insects are attracted by fish. Other precautions include wearing long-sleeved shirts, pants, and shoes outdoors to avoid stepping on insects. Common insect repellents have little or no effect on stinging insects.[12]

People at risk for repeated occurrences of anaphylaxis, such as those who are just starting venom immunotherapy or

Acute Therapy	Immunotherapy Indicated?
Supportive	No
Cool packs, NSAIDs, antihistamines	No
Antihistamine, close observation	Adults - yes* Children - no
Epinephrine subcutaneous, other resuscitation as needed	Yes*

those who refuse venom therapy, should carry epinephrine in a self-administered form. It is also important to prescribe epinephrine to patients who have had systemic reactions to insect stings and who are awaiting an allergic evaluation.

Venom Immunotherapy

Venom immunotherapy is essentially curative for the treatment of anaphylactic reactions to insect stings.[13,14] Patients who are candidates for venom immunotherapy include those with anaphylactic reactions as well as adults who have had generalized urticarial reactions. Immunotherapy involves injecting gradually increasing amounts of purified insect venom or, in the case of the fire ant, whole body extracts, to alter the immune response. Although the precise mechanism for venom immunotherapy is unknown, clinical protection is associated with increases in venom-specific immunoglobulin G (IgG) and decreases in venom-specific IgE.[15]

Table 14-2: Overview of Therapy for Insect Sting Allergies

Medical therapy for acute symptoms

Avoidance measures

- Avoid outdoor eating or drinking
- Wear shoes outdoors
- Wear long pants and long-sleeved shirts
- Keep garbage or compost far away from living areas

Immunotherapy

Medical alert bracelets

Epinephrine for self-administration

- EpiPen®, EpiPen® Jr.

Venom immunotherapy can be administered according to standard protocols that take 2 to 3 months to reach a maintenance dose or as a rush immunotherapy schedule that is especially helpful for fishermen and beekeepers, for whom a re-sting is extremely likely.[2,3,16] Regardless of the schedule, once maintenance doses have been achieved, immunotherapy is usually continued monthly for an extended period. The optimum duration for immunotherapy is controversial, but most allergists agree that a 3- to 5-year treatment regimen is sufficient to produce permanent desensitization in many cases.[2,3,17] Longer courses of immunotherapy may be appropriate for people who have had more severe anaphylactic reactions.[18] Repeating venom skin tests can also be helpful in deciding when to stop immunotherapy.[3]

Summary

Insect sting hypersensitivity is a common clinical problem. Primary care providers can treat most sting symptoms by administering symptomatic relief and by advising patients how to avoid stings in the future. For severe reactions, including anaphylaxis and generalized urticarial reactions in adults, referral to an allergist is recommended, especially because venom immunotherapy can prevent future episodes of anaphylaxis.

References

1.   Muller UR: Epidemiology of insect sting allergy. *Monogr Allergy* 1993;31:131-146.

2.   Golden DBK: Insect allergy. In: Adkinson NF, Yunginger JW, Busse WW, et, al, eds: *Middleton's Allergy: Principles and Practice*, 6th ed. St. Louis, MO, Mosby 2003, pp 1475-1486.

3.   Moffitt JE, Golden DB, Reisman RE, et al: Stinging insect hypersensitivity: a practice parameter update. *J Allergy Clin Immunol* 2004;114:869-886.

4.   Freeman TM: Imported fire ants: the ants from hell! *Allergy Proc* 1994;15:11-15.

5.   Reisman RE, Livingston A: Late-onset allergic reactions, including serum sickness, after insect stings. *J Allergy Clin Immunol* 1989;84:331-337.

6.   Mauriello PM, Barde SH, Georgitis JW, et al: Natural history of large local reactions from stinging insects. *J Allergy Clin Immunol* 1984;74(4 pt 1):494-498.

7.   Valentine MD, Schuberth KC, Kagey-Sobotka A, et al: The value of immunotherapy with venom in children with allergy to insect stings. *N Engl J Med* 1990;323:1601-1603.

8.   Jacobs RL, Rake GW Jr, Fournier DC, et al: Potentiated anaphylaxis in patients with drug-induced beta-adrenergic blockade. *J Allergy Clin Immunol* 1981;68:125-127.

9.   Chafee FH: The prevalence of bee sting allergy in an allergic population. *Acta Allergol* 1970;25:292-293.

10.   van der Linden PW, Struyvenberg A, Kraaijanhagen RJ, et al: Anaphylactic shock after insect-sting challenge in 138 persons with a previous insect-sting reaction. *Ann Intern Med* 1993;118: 161-168.

14

11. Hunt KJ, Valentine MD, Sobotka AK, et al: Diagnosis of allergy to stinging insects by testing with Hymenoptera venoms. *Ann Intern Med* 1976;85:56-59.

12. Greene A, Breisch NL: Avoidance of bee and wasp stings: an entomological perspective. *Curr Opin Allergy Clin Immunol* 2005;5:337-341.

13. Hunt KJ, Valentine MD, Sobotka AK, et al: A controlled trial of immunotherapy in insect hypersensitivity. *N Engl J Med* 1978; 299:157-161.

14. Graft DF, Schuberth KC, Kagey-Sobotka A, et al: Assessment of prolonged venom immunotherapy in children. *J Allergy Clin Immunol* 1987;80:162-169.

15. Golden DB, Lawrence ID, Hamilton RH, et al: Clinical correlation of the venom-specific IgG antibody level during maintenance venom immunotherapy. *J Allergy Clin Immunol* 1992;90 (3 pt 1):386-393.

16. Birnbaum J, Charpin D, Vervloet D: Rapid Hymenoptera venom immunotherapy: comparative safety of three protocols. *Clin Exp Allergy* 1993;23:226-230.

17. American Academy of Allergy, Asthma and Immunology: The discontinuation of Hymenoptera venom immunotherapy. Report from the Committee on Insects. *J Allergy Clin Immunol* 1998;101:573-575.

18. Reisman RE: Duration of venom immunotherapy: relationship to the severity of symptoms of initial insect sting anaphylaxis. *J Allergy Clin Immunol* 1993;92:831-836.

Chapter 15

Anaphylaxis

A naphylaxis, which is derived from the Latin words ana (against) and phylaxis (protection), is a term that was coined by Portier and Richet at the turn of the 20th century to describe an immune reaction that was harmful, rather than protective, to the host. Today, anaphylaxis is used to describe a sudden, immunologically mediated reaction to a foreign substance that produces a severe and potentially life-threatening reaction. Clinical manifestations of anaphylaxis vary widely, but typically involve the skin, respiratory tract, cardiovascular system, gastrointestinal (GI) system, and central nervous system (CNS) (Table 15-1).[1,2] Respiratory signs and symptoms range from mild rhinorrhea or watering of the eyes to laryngospasm, laryngeal edema, or severe bronchospasm. Skin manifestations include urticaria, generalized facial flushing, or pruritus. Cardiovascular manifestations of anaphylaxis include tachycardia, decreased cardiac contractility, capillary leakage, and hypotension. Abdominal pain is also common, especially with ingested allergens, and may be accompanied by either vomiting or diarrhea. Uterine contractions can also be triggered by anaphylaxis, producing severe abdominal pain. Disorientation, panic, and loss of consciousness indicate CNS involvement. In fatal cases of

Table 15-1: Clinical Manifestations of Anaphylaxis

Organ System	Signs and Symptoms
Skin	Flushing Urticaria Angioedema Pruritus
Gastrointestinal	Abdominal pain Vomiting Diarrhea Uterine contractions
Respiratory	Wheezing Hoarseness of the voice Stridor Coughing
Neurologic	Disorientation Seizures
Cardiovascular	Tachycardia Hypotension

anaphylaxis, petechial hemorrhages and laryngeal edema have been recorded. However, there are no specific findings in up to 50% of cases, probably reflecting the role of shock and the rapidity of death.

Although most anaphylactic reactions occur soon after exposure to an inciting agent, there are three patterns of systemic anaphylaxis.[3] Unimodal anaphylaxis usually begins rapidly, and the clinical manifestations are usually short-lived. Bimodal anaphylaxis can also begin within minutes of exposure, but 1 to 8 hours after a transient clinical improvement, the reactions return. Finally, protracted anaphylaxis can begin suddenly or gradually, but the clinical manifestations are prolonged, sometimes requiring hours or even days of intense resuscitation. Considering these three different clinical presentations, it is important that a patient who has suffered an anaphylactic episode be observed for an adequate length of time.[3,4] For milder reactions, this is typically 3 to 4 hours, but patients who have had severe reactions should be hospitalized overnight for observation.

Several mechanisms may produce general systemic reactions. These can be classified in terms of the underlying pathophysiology (Table 15-2). Proteins or smaller molecules (haptens) that are bound to native proteins can bind to allergen-specific immunoglobulin E (IgE) that is present on the surface of mast cells, triggering a type I hypersensitivity reaction.[5] Most authors classify reactions that are mediated by allergen-specific IgE as *anaphylactic*, while clinically indistinguishable reactions that occur via other mechanisms are termed *anaphylactoid* reactions.[6] Examples of anaphylactoid reactions include immune complex activation of complement during administration of human serum proteins such as intravenous γ-globulin or direct triggering of mast cell mediator release by substances such as radiocontrast materials, opiates, and dextran.[5,6] Nonsteroidal anti-inflammatory drugs (NSAIDs), such as aspirin, may produce anaphylactoid reactions in some patients through a mechanism involving mast cell activation and production of leukotrienes.[7]

Diagnosis

Anaphylaxis is a clinical diagnosis. In most cases, there is a clear history of a sudden and sometimes catastrophic reaction after the administration of an inciting agent (Table 15-1). An agent is sometimes never identified, and, as a result, some patients experience recurrent anaphylaxis of idiopathic origin.[8] Because anaphylaxis can evolve rapidly, patients must be reassessed frequently, especially in terms of the respiratory and cardiovascular systems. Laboratory evaluation is usually neither helpful nor necessary during the acute reaction, but increased blood levels of tryptase, a marker of

Table 15-2: Classification of Anaphylactic and Anaphylactoid Reactions

IgE-mediated (type I hypersensitivity)

- Food—peanuts, tree nuts, seafood, eggs
- Drugs—penicillin, cephalosporins, insulin, serum, allergenic extracts
- Stinging insect (Hymenoptera) venom—bees, yellow jackets, wasps, fire ants
- Other—latex, seminal proteins

Direct stimulation of mast-cell degranulation

- Drugs—opiates, vancomycin
- Radiocontrast material
- Physical stimuli—exercise, cold
- Idiopathic

Increased leukotriene synthesis

- Aspirin and other nonsteroidal anti-inflammatory drugs (NSAIDs)

Complement activation

- Transfusion reaction
- Immunoglobulin

Other

- Sulfite-induced bronchospasm
- Scombroid fish poisoning

IgE=immunoglobulin E

mast cell activation, can retrospectively confirm the diagnosis of anaphylaxis; even though it is not a very sensitive test and is often normal, especially in cases of food-induced anaphylaxis.[9] Because many cases of anaphylaxis are initially unwitnessed, health-care providers should check the patient for a medical alert bracelet or necklace bearing information about allergies and carefully review the medical record for any mention of allergies or systemic reactions.

Treatment

Treatment of anaphylactic reactions is based upon the same principles, regardless of the precipitating cause (Table 15-1).[1] Treatment should be tailored to the severity of the reaction and to the organ systems involved (Table 15-3). Mild anaphylactic reactions with manifestations limited to the skin should be treated with antihistamines such as diphenhydramine (Benadryl®) or hydroxyzine (Vistaril®). These antihistamines have a quick onset of action and provide effective relief of urticaria, pruritus, and flushing. Nevertheless, patients who present with cutaneous reactions should be monitored closely for signs of respiratory or cardiovascular compromise.

The initial treatment of choice for anaphylactic reactions involving organs other than the skin is the rapid intramuscular administration of epinephrine (EpiPen®, EpiPen® Jr.).[1,10] This is especially important because surveys of fatal or near-fatal anaphylactic reactions have identified the delayed use of epinephrine as a poor prognostic factor.[10-12] The intramuscular route for administering epinephrine is preferred over subcutaneous injection because of more rapid absorption.[13]

In addition to administration of epinephrine, patients should be placed in Trendelenburg's position, if tolerated, to maximize blood flow to the vital organs, and all patients with respiratory compromise should promptly receive supplemental oxygen. Nebulized albuterol should also be administered (in addition to intramuscular epinephrine) to patients with bronchospasm. Oral or parenteral corticosteroids administered early in therapy may help to prevent prolonged or recurrent symptoms. These measures, plus close observation, adequately treat most cases of anaphylaxis.

Table 15-3: Treatment of Anaphylaxis

Remove the stimulus for anaphylaxis, if possible

- Stop infusion of offending drug or blood products
- For stings or injections, consider tourniquet proximal to site to retard absorption*

Perform rapid assessment

Airways

Breathing

Circulation

Vital signs

Activate emergency medical systems for transfer, if necessary

Treatment of mild cutaneous reactions

- Antihistamine
  - Diphenhydramine 1 mg/kg PO (maximum=50 mg/dose) q 4-6 h
- Observation

Treatment of severe cutaneous reactions or reactions with extracutaneous manifestations

Initial treatment:

- Administer oxygen
- Epinephrine 1:1,000 0.01 mL/kg (maximum=0.3 mL) intramuscularly
- Trendelenburg's position (if tolerated)
- Antihistamine
  - Diphenhydramine 1 mg/kg PO (maximum=50 mg), IV, or IM

---

*Tourniquets should be tight enough to impede venous return without obliterating distal pulses.

Initial treatment: *(continued)*

- Nebulized β-adrenergic agonist as needed for bronchospasm
- Corticosteroid
  - Prednisone 0.5 mg/kg PO, or
  - Methylprednisolone 1-2 mg/kg IV q 6 h

For severe symptoms or inadequate response:

- Repeat epinephrine 1:1,000 0.01 mL/kg (maximum= 0.3 mL) IM every 5 minutes, *and*

For respiratory symptoms:

- Continue oxygen
- Continue nebulized β-agonists for bronchospasm
- Intubation for upper airway obstruction or impending respiratory failure

For cardiovascular symptoms:

- Rapid administration of normal saline
- Sympathomimetic drug via continuous infusion (eg, dopamine)
- Application of medical antishock trousers
- Glucagon 1-5 mg (20-30 μg/kg [maximum=1 mg] in children) IV over 5 min followed by 5-15 μg/min infusion

Reassess condition frequently

- Consider hospitalization

Consider referral to an allergist for prevention of future episodes

IM=intramuscular, IV=intravenous

Additional measures are required for patients who present with severe anaphylaxis or do not respond to initial treatment. Epinephrine administration should be repeated every 5 minutes as needed to treat persistent hypotension or respiratory compromise. For persistent bronchospasm, nebulized β-agonists should be continued, and intravenous aminophylline and corticosteroids may be added. Intubation may be required for patients with significant laryngeal edema who do not respond to subcutaneous epinephrine or who have impending respiratory failure.

All patients with significant cardiovascular compromise should have a large-gauge intravenous catheter inserted quickly. Hypotension should be aggressively treated with intramuscular epinephrine, rapid infusion of intravenous normal saline, and Trendelenburg positioning (if tolerated). In patients who are refractory to epinephrine and fluid resuscitation, vasopressors such as dopamine, ephedrine, or norepinephrine, given via a constant intravenous drip can be useful in restoring blood pressure.[1,5] Medical antishock trousers have also been used successfully to treat refractory hypotension associated with anaphylaxis.[14] Any patient with severe respiratory or cardiovascular compromise should be hospitalized, and monitoring in an intensive care unit (ICU) should be considered.

Special measures may be needed to treat anaphylaxis in patients taking β-adrenergic blockers such as propranolol (Inderal®, Inderal® LA) because these patients can develop refractory hypotension and bradycardia.[15] Epinephrine is still the first-line therapy for these patients,[15,16] although its use in the presence of β-adrenergic blockade may lead to undesirable effects such as peripheral and coronary vasoconstriction from unopposed α-adrenergic stimulation. Glucagon may be helpful in treating cardiovascular symptoms in patients receiving β-blockers because it exerts inotropic and chronotropic effects via a nonadrenergic mechanism.[15] In addition, atropine (Atropen®) (0.3 to 0.5 mg subcutaneous or intramuscular every 10 minutes to a maximum of

2 mg) can be used to treat bradycardia in the presence of β-adrenergic blockade, although atropine does not improve inotropy.[15]

It is important to identify the agent responsible for triggering the anaphylactic episode so that adequate preventive measures can be followed. If the cause of a systemic reaction is unclear, or if preventive therapy is possible, referral to an allergist is strongly recommended.

Prevention

As is the case with most serious medical disorders, the most effective treatment for anaphylaxis is prevention (Table 15-4). Although most cases of anaphylaxis are unforeseen, a disturbing number of serious allergic reactions are caused by repeated exposure to a known allergen.[4,17,18] While it seems that avoiding a known food or drug allergen would be straightforward, in practice, it may be difficult. For example, in a survey of fatal or near-fatal reactions to foods, each of the patients had reacted to the same food previously and was making a conscious effort to avoid the food.[4] Many of the accidental exposures occurred away from home, where there is less control of the ingredients in meals. Patients should be taught to carefully read labels of food ingredients and be especially vigilant when eating away from home.

Multiple safeguards are required to adequately protect drug- or latex-allergic patients from re-exposure to allergens. Hospital charts should be flagged, and it is prudent to also notify the hospital and outpatient pharmacy of medication allergies to increase the level of safety. Hospital, outpatient clinic, and ancillary service (phlebotomy, radiology) protocols should be developed ahead of time to ensure the safety of these patients.[19]

Patients who are at risk for repeat anaphylaxis should prepare an emergency action plan for potential future allergic reactions. This is of primary importance for children with food allergy who are enrolled in school or day care.[20] The plan should include emergency contact telephone

Table 15-4: Preventive Measures

Avoid re-exposure to the inciting agent

- Medications
  - Flag the medical record
  - Notify the patient's pharmacy
- Foods
  - Totally exclude the offending food protein from the diet
  - Teach the patient to read product labels
- Stinging insects
  - Avoid eating outdoors during warm-weather months
  - Avoid wearing perfumes outdoors
  - Avoid wearing floral colors during warm-weather months
- Latex
  - Avoid latex exposure in the medical setting
  - Provide lists of home products that contain latex
- Physical stimuli
  - Cold
  - Exercise

numbers, prescriptions with instructions to administer oral antihistamines for cutaneous reactions, and epinephrine to treat systemic reactions involving other organ systems. Unfortunately, surveys have indicated that epinephrine is often not administered to children who are experiencing anaphylaxis, even when it is available in the home or at school.[21] Moreover, although most paramedics can administer epinephrine, basic-level emergency medical technicians, who are often the first to respond to an emergency, are not

Prepare the patient for accidental exposures to inciting agents

- Oral antihistamine administration for reactions that are limited to the skin
- Epinephrine for self-administration (EpiPen®, EpiPen® Jr.) for more severe reactions

Preventive therapy

- Immunotherapy for stinging insect hyper-sensitivity
- Aspirin desensitization
- Oral desensitization for penicillin (or other medication) allergy
- Prophylactic medication regimens

Medical alert bracelets

permitted to administer epinephrine in many states.[22] Until these regulations are revised, it is critical that high-risk children and adults carry epinephrine autoinjectors and know how and when to use them. Patients should be instructed to seek medical care immediately if epinephrine use is necessary, given the short half-life of this medication.

Several modes of therapy have been shown to be effective in preventing anaphylactic reactions. Immunotherapy for stinging insect hypersensitivity is 97% effective at

---

Table 15-5: Prophylactic Medications for Patients Allergic to Radiocontrast Material or Latex

The following doses are recommendations and should be adjusted according to a patient's health status, concurrent medications, and disease state. Choose either oral or intravenous regimen (not both):

1. **Oral regimen**

   Medication

   Diphenhydramine (Benadryl®)*

   Prednisone or prednisolone
   (Pediapred®, Prelone®)

---

2. **Intravenous regimen**

   Medication

   Diphenhydramine*

   Methylprednisolone
   (Depo-Medrol®, Solu-Medrol®)

*An H_2-receptor antagonist such as cimetidine can also be administered 1 h before the procedure if combined H_1 and H_2 blockade is desired.

---

preventing systemic reactions upon re-sting.[23] Effective desensitization regimens have also been established for many medications, including penicillin, sulfonamides, and aspirin.[5] Patients with exercise-induced anaphylaxis should

Pediatric Dose

1 mg/kg PO 1 h
preoperatively
(maximum=50 mg/dose)

1.0 mg/kg PO 13, 7, and
1 h preoperatively
(maximum=50 mg/dose)

Adult Dose

50 mg PO 1 h
preoperatively

50 mg PO 13, 7, and
1 h preoperatively

Pediatric Dose

1 mg/kg IV 1 h
preoperatively
(maximum=50 mg/dose)

1 mg/kg IV 13, 7, and
1 h preoperatively
(maximum=50 mg/dose)

Adult Dose

50 mg IV 1 h
preoperatively

50 mg IV 13, 7, and
1 h preoperatively

15

exercise only with a partner and should be aware of early
warning signs so that severe episodes can be avoided. Prophylactic use of antihistamines may decrease the severity
or frequency of idiopathic or exercise-induced anaphylaxis

in some patients, but responses vary considerably. Before undergoing radiologic procedures, patients with anaphylactoid reactions to radiocontrast material may be pretreated with an antihistamine along with a corticosteroid (Table 15-5) to decrease the frequency and severity of reactions.[24] Use of contrast material with low osmolality may be better tolerated by patients with a history of adverse reactions to standard media, although premedication is still advisable.[24] Similar regimens have been recommended for latex-allergic patients undergoing surgical procedures, although the use of prophylactic medications is not a substitute for avoiding contact with latex through the use of nonlatex gloves and other medical supplies.[19]

Finally, medical alert bracelets or necklaces containing information about allergies may be advisable for patients with a history of systemic reactions. These aids can help health-care providers arrive at a diagnosis quickly, so that appropriate treatments can be started without delay.

Summary

Systemic anaphylaxis is relatively rare, but the appropriate initial management of the medical emergency greatly increases the chances for a full recovery. Primary care providers and emergency department physicians are most likely to encounter patients with acute anaphylaxis and need to be familiar with its signs and symptoms as well as with resuscitation measures. It is important to identify the precipitating agent for anaphylaxis so that preventive measures can be taken to reduce the risk of future reactions.

References

1. Joint Task Force on Practice Parameters; American Academy of Allergy, Asthma and Immunology; American College of Allergy, Asthma and Immunology; Joint Council of Allergy, Asthma and Immunology: The diagnosis and management of anaphylaxis: an updated practice parameter. *J Allergy Clin Immunol* 2005;115 (3 suppl 2):S483-S523.

2.   Pumphrey RS, Roberts IS: Postmortem findings after fatal anaphylactic reactions. *J Clin Pathol* 2000;53:273-276.

3.   Stark BJ, Sullivan TJ: Biphasic and protracted anaphylaxis. *J Allergy Clin Immunol* 1986;78(1 pt 1):76-83.

4.   Sampson HA, Mendelson L, Rosen JP: Fatal and near-fatal anaphylactic reactions to food in children and adolescents. *N Engl J Med* 1992;327:380-384.

5.   Adkinson NF Jr: Drug Allergy. In: Adkinson NF Jr., Yunginger JW, Busse WW, et al, eds: *Middleton's Allergy: Principles and Practice*, 6th ed. St. Louis, MO, Mosby, 2003, pp 1679-1694.

6.   Greenberger PA: Anaphylactic and anaphylactoid causes of angioedema. *Immunol Allergy Clin North Am* 2006;26:753-767.

7.   Szczeklik A, Sanak M: The broken balance in aspirin hypersensitivity. *Eur J Pharmacol* 2006;533:145-155.

8.   Patterson R, Stoloff RS, Greenberger PA, et al: Algorithms for the diagnosis and management of idiopathic anaphylaxis. *Ann Allergy* 1993;71:40-44.

9.   Simons FE, Frew AJ, Ansotegui IJ, et al: Risk assessment in anaphylaxis: current and future approaches. *J Allergy Clin Immunol* 2007;120(1 suppl):S2-S24.

10.   Sicherer SH, Simons FE, and Section on Allergy and Immunology, American Academy of Pediatrics: Self-injectable epinephrine for first-aid management of anaphylaxis. *Pediatrics* 2007;119:638-646.

11.   Yunginger JW, Sweeney KG, Sturner WQ, et al: Fatal food-induced anaphylaxis. *JAMA* 1988;260:1450-1452.

12.   Frazier CA, Wynn SR, Munoz-Furlong A, et al: Anaphylaxis at school: etiologic factors, prevalence, and treatment. *Pediatrics* 1993;91:516.

13.   Simons FE, Gu X, Simons KJ: Epinephrine absorption in adults: intramuscular vs subcutaneous injection. *J Allergy Clin Immunol* 2001;108:871-873.

14.   Oertel T, Loehr MM: Bee-sting anaphylaxis: the use of medical antishock trousers. *Ann Emerg Med* 1984;13:459-461.

15.   Lieberman PL: Anaphylaxis and anaphylactoid reactions. In: Adkinson NF Jr., Yunginger JW, Busse WW, et al, eds: *Middleton's Allergy: Principles and Practice*, 6th ed. St. Louis, MO, Mosby, 2003, pp 1497-1522.

16.   Toogood JH: Risk of anaphylaxis in patients receiving beta-blocker drugs. *J Allergy Clin Immunol* 1988;81:1-5.

17.   Bock SA, Atkins FM: The natural history of peanut allergy. *J Allergy Clin Immunol* 1989;83:900-904.

18.   Gern JE, Yang E, Evrard HM, et al: Allergic reactions to milk-contaminated "nondairy" products. *N Engl J Med* 1991;324: 976-979.

19.   Reines HD, Seifert PC: Patient safety: latex allergy. *Surg Clin North Am* 2005;85:1329-1340.

20.   Anaphylaxis in schools and other childcare settings. AAAI Board of Directors, American Academy of Allergy, Asthma and Immunology. *J Allergy Clin Immunol* 1998;102:173-176.

21.   Gold MS, Sainsbury R: First aid anaphylaxis management in children who are prescribed an epinephrine autoinjector device (EpiPen).AAAI Board of Directors, American Academy of Allergy, Asthma and Immunology. *J Allergy Clin Immunol* 2000;106 (1 pt 1):171-176.

22.   Goldhaber SZ: Administration of epinephrine by emergency medical technicians. *N Engl J Med* 2000;342:822.

23.   Hunt KJ, Valentine MD, Sobotka AK, et al: A controlled trial of immunotherapy in insect hypersensitivity. *N Engl J Med* 1978; 299:157-161.

24.   Bush WH, Swanson DP: Radiocontrast. In: Virant SL, ed: *Systemic Reactions.* Philadelphia, PA, WB Saunders Co., 1995, pp 597-612.

Chapter 16

Complications of Allergic Diseases

Chronic cellular inflammation, mucous hypersecretion, and mucosal edema usually accompany respiratory allergies, and can promote complications including sinusitis and otitis media. Regional immunity in the upper and lower respiratory tracts depends on adequate drainage of respiratory air spaces. Obstruction of the eustachian tube or sinus ostia produces pooling of secretions that can increase the risk of secondary bacterial infections.

While inflammation clearly exerts mechanical effects on upper respiratory air spaces, evidence also suggests that pre-existing inflammation, such as that which accompanies respiratory allergies, leads to increased adherence of pathogens to respiratory epithelial cells. For example, treatment of endothelial or epithelial cells with inflammatory cytokines such as tumor necrosis factor-α (TNF-α) or interleukin-1 (IL-1) promotes binding of *Streptococcus pneumoniae* to the cell membrane and internalization of bacteria into the cell.[1] These cytokines are increased in allergic airways, suggesting a second mechanism linking allergy to bacterial respiratory infections.

Nasal polyposis, although not strongly associated with respiratory allergy per se, is strongly associated with aspirin hypersensitivity and with chronic sinusitis in allergic and nonallergic individuals. This chapter examines the diagnostic and therapeutic approaches to otitis media, sinusitis, and nasal polyposis.

Otitis Media

Nearly all children develop otitis media in the first six years of life, but a subset of these children have recurrent infections that may interfere with hearing, school attendance, and overall health. Several epidemiologic factors have been linked to an increased risk of otitis media, including bottle-feeding, low socioeconomic status, exposure to cigarette smoke, day-care center attendance, genetic predisposition, and viral infection. The role of allergy in the pathogenesis of otitis media has not been clearly defined. Allergy has been implicated as an epidemiologic risk factor for otitis media in some studies but not others.[2-4] There is evidence, however, which indicates that allergen exposure produces eustachian tube dysfunction and that allergic inflammation can extend into the middle ear.[5,6] These findings suggests that respiratory allergy could increase the risk of recurrent otitis media in some children.

Otitis media is classified into two categories: acute otitis media (AOM) and otitis media with effusion (OME), and guidelines for the assessment and treatment of each has been published.[4,7] Diagnostic criteria for AOM include acute onset, the presence of middle ear effusion on examination, and signs or symptoms of middle ear inflammation (eg, erythema, otalgia).[7] OME is defined as fluid in the middle ear without signs or symptoms of acute ear infection.[4] Signs of middle ear fluid include air fluid levels or bubbles visible in the middle ear, or impaired movement of the eardrum. Alternately, middle ear fluid can be diagnosed with tympanometry. The critical distinguishing feature between these two disorders is the presence of acute ear pain with AOM. OME is quite common and usually transient, and often does not require treatment. For AOM, treatment strategies depend on the type of otitis, age, the degree of symptoms, and a history of previous antibiotic treatment.

Table 16-1: Microbiology of Acute Otitis Media

- *Streptococcus pneumoniae*
- *Haemophilus influenzae*
- *Moraxella catarrhalis*
- Rhinovirus
- Respiratory syncytial virus (RSV)

Treatment of AOM

The microbiology of AOM is remarkable for both bacterial and viral pathogens (Table 16-1).[7,8] Therapeutic strategies are designed in consideration of the presence of multiple drug-resistant bacteria, including strains of penicillin-resistant *S pneumoniae*. It has recently been appreciated that a significant number of AOM resolve spontaneously, and this may be due to viral etiology or resolution through immune mechanisms. With this in mind, nontreatment and observation is an option that should be considered for selected cases, including children >2 years with illnesses that are not severe, and children >6 months of age if the illness is not severe and the diagnosis is in question. Pain control and follow-up should be addressed regardless of whether an antibiotic are prescribed.

If treatment includes antimicrobial therapy, the choice of antibiotic should be based on several factors, including age, severity of illness, suspected microbiology, cost, and individual histories of drug allergies or intolerance. Risk factors for antibiotic resistance include attendance at day-care facilities, age <2 years, and recent antibiotic treatment (Tables 16-2 and 16-3). Amoxicillin (Amoxil®) remains an effective and cost-conscious treatment for most children with otitis media, and high-dose treatment (80 to 90 mg/kg/day) is necessary to ensure the eradication of moderately resistant *S*

16

Table 16-2: Recommended Antibiotics for Patients with Acute Otitis Media

Temperature ≥39°C and/or severe otalgia	Initial Choice	
	Recommended	Alternative for penicillin allergy
No	Amoxicillin 80-90 mg/kg/d	Non-type I: cefdinir, cefuroxime sodium (Zinacef®), cefpodoxime; type I: azithromycin, clarithromycin
Yes	Amoxicillin/ clavulanate, 90 mg/kg/d of amoxicillin with 6.4 mg/kg/d of clavulanate	Ceftriaxone 1 or 3 days

From American Academy of Pediatrics Subcommittee on Management of Acute Otitis Media[7]

pneumoniae. For children with more severe illnesses, as indicated by high fever (≥39°C) or severe otalgia, amoxicillin/ clavulanate (Augmentin®, Augmentin® XR) (90 mg/kg/day amoxicillin component with 6.4 mg/kg/day of clavulanate in 2 divided doses) can be prescribed. This regimen can also be used if additional coverage for β-lactamase-positive *Haemophilus influenzae* and *Moraxella catarrhalis* is desired. Alternate medications are recommended for patients with allergies to the first-line choices (Tables 16-2 and 16-3).

Treatment failure at 48-72 hours after initial management with antibacterial agents

Recommended	Alternative for penicillin allergy
Amoxicillin/clavulanate, 90 mg/kg/d of amoxicillin with 6.4 mg/kg/d of clavulanate	Non-type I: ceftriaxone, 3 days; type I: clindamycin
Ceftriaxone 3 days	Tympanocentesis, clindamycin

Treatment guidelines have also been established for patients who do not improve in 48 to 72 hours (Table 16-2). In general, antibiotics should be prescribed for patients who were initially observed, and the illness has worsened. In addition, antibiotic treatment should be intensified for those already taking an antibiotic. For patients not responding to amoxicillin/clavulanate, options include intramuscular (IM) injection of ceftrizone for 3 days, an empiric course of clindamycin, or tympanocentesis for bacterial culture and sensitivity to guide future treatment.

Table 16-3: Antimicrobial Therapy for Otitis Media and Sinusitis in Children*

Medication	How Supplied	Dose
Penicillins		
amoxicillin (Amoxil®)	125 or 250 mg/5 mL 125 or 250 mg chewable tabs	40-80 mg/kg/d in 3 divided doses 80-90 mg/kg/d in 2 divided doses
amoxicillin/ clavulanate** (Augmentin®)	125/31.25, 200/28.5, 250/62.5, or 400/57 mg/5 mL oral suspensions 125/31.25, 200/28.25, 250/62.5, or 400/57 mg chewable tabs	40 mg/kg/d in 3 divided doses *or* 45 mg/kg/d in 2 divided doses
amoxicillin/ clavulanate ES (Augmentin ES-600®)	600/42.9 mg/5 mL oral suspension	90 mg/kg/d in 2 divided doses

*Children weighing >40 kg should be dosed according to adult guidelines (Table 16-5).

**Note that Augmentin® chewable tablets contain less clavulanate than Augmentin® tablets, which should only be used by children who weigh >40 kg.

Medication	How Supplied	Dose
Cephalosporins		
loracarbef	100, 200 mg/5 mL 200 mg caps	30 mg/kg/d in 2 divided doses
cefixime (Suprax®)	100, 200 mg/5 mL 400 mg tabs	8 mg/kg/d once daily
cefuroxime axetil (Ceftin®)	125, 250 mg/5 mL 125, 250, 500 mg tabs	30 mg/kg/d in 2 divided doses
cefdinir (Omnicef®)	125, 250 mg/5 mL 300 mg caps	14 mg/kg/d in 1 or 2 divided doses***
cefpodoxime (Vantin®)	50 and 100 mg/5 mL 100 and 200 mg tabs	10 mg/kg/d in 2 divided doses†
cefprozil (Cefzil®)	125 and 250 mg/5 mL 250 and 500 mg tabs	15 mg/kg q12h
ceftibuten (Cedax®)	90 mg/5 mL 400 mg capsules	9 mg/kg/d once daily
ceftriaxone (Rocephin®)	Vials containing 250 mg, 500 mg, or 1 g	50 mg/kg (not to exceed 1 g IM/d)

***The recommended duration of treatment for otitis media is 5-10 days for the b.i.d. regimen and 10 days if the medication is to be administered once daily.

†For otitis media, the recommended duration of treatment is 5 days.

Table 16-3: Antimicrobial Therapy for Otitis Media and Sinusitis in Children*

Medication	How Supplied	Dose
Macrolides		
azithromycin (Zithromax®)	100 or 200 mg/ 5 mL 250 mg tablets and capsules	10 mg/kg (maximum= 500 mg) on day 1, followed by 5 mg/kg (maximum= 250 mg) on days 2-5, in single daily doses
clarithromycin (Biaxin®)	125 or 250 mg/ 5 mL, 250, 500 mg tabs	15 mg/kg/day in 2 divided doses
Sulfa combinations		
trimethoprim/ sulfamethoxazole (Bactrim™, Septra®)	40 mg TMP + 200 mg SMX/ 5 mL	8/40 mg/kg/ day in 2 divided doses
erythromycin/ sulfisoxazole	200 mg erythro- mycin + 600 mg sulfisoxazole/ 5 mL	50/150 mg/ kg/day in 4 divided doses

Treatment of recurrent acute otitis media

Several strategies can help to reduce the frequency of AOM. Breastfeeding has a beneficial effect, while attendance in day care, supine bottle feeding ('bottle propping'), exposure to tobacco smoke, and respiratory allergies are all associated with an increased rate of ear infections. Influenza and conjugated pneumococcal vaccines each have modest effects to reduce AOM.[9,10] For patients with recurrent otitis media, prophylactic antibiotic regimens were used extensively in the past, but these regimens were often only marginally effective and likely contributed to the emergence of drug-resistant organisms.

Treatment of OME

Most cases of OME spontaneously without need for antibiotic therapy. In contrast, prolonged OME can impair hearing, and thereby adversely affect speech, language and learning. It is recommended that OME can be managed more aggressively in children who are at risk for developmental delay, and speech and hearing evaluations are recommended in this setting. For low-risk children, a 3-month waiting period is advised due to the likelihood of spontaneous resolution. For effusions lasting longer than 3 months, or if hearing loss is suspected, testing of hearing is recommended. For children with significant loss of hearing, referral to an otorhinolaryngologist for consideration of tympanostomy tubes is advised.[4,11] For children with persistent OME and normal hearing, additional watchful waiting is appropriate. Finally, in the absence of indications related to allergic rhinitis, antihistamines, decongestants, and topical corticosteroids are not effective treatments for OME and their use is not recommended.

Sinusitis

Sinusitis is one of the most common infections, affecting approximately 16% of the US population annually.[12] Respiratory allergies and viral respiratory infections are the two of the most important risk factors for the development of acute sinusitis.[13,14] Mucosal edema and overproduction of respiratory secretions are probably important factors that link respiratory allergy and bacterial sinusitis. Chronic sinusitis can also be caused by fixed obstruction of the sinus drainage tracts, caused by scar tissue, nasal polyps, or anomalies of the nasal bones. The occurrence of both recurrent sinusitis and lower respiratory tract infections strongly suggests the possibility of humoral immune deficiency or cystic fibrosis.[15]

In addition to increasing the risk of bacterial sinusitis, allergy can contribute to local inflammation in patients with fungal sinusitis.[16] Patients with allergic fungal sinusitis do not respond to antibiotic therapy and have positive cultures for fungi from the sinus cavity and evidence of fungus-specific immunoglobulin E (IgE) upon skin testing or radioallergosorbent test (RAST).

The clinical findings associated with sinusitis differ with age.[12,15] Typical findings in children include chronic nasal congestion, rhinorrhea, halitosis, fever, and chronic cough. Notably absent in most cases of childhood sinusitis are complaints of facial pressure or tenderness to palpation of the sinuses, both of which are relatively common findings in adults. Much of the difficulty in accurately diagnosing sinusitis stems from the fact that pathopneumonic findings of sinusitis, such as a purulent postnasal drip, are found in relatively few patients, and that most of the signs and symptoms of sinusitis are also produced by viral upper respiratory tract infections or respiratory allergy. The duration and timing of symptoms can be helpful clues: viral upper respiratory infections resolve within 7 to 10 days of onset, while sinus infections are more likely when symptoms endure for longer periods.[12,17] Symptoms that have a seasonal pattern are more likely to be allergic, although secondary sinus infections are common complications of respiratory allergy.

Radiologic evaluation of the sinuses is not routinely recommended, although imaging can be helpful when there is diagnostic uncertainty.[12] Sinus radiographs detect only 50% to 70% of bacterial sinus infections that are verified by culture of the maxillary sinuses. CT or magnetic resonance imaging (MRI) scans have a greater sensitivity, but the false-positive rate is also increased, and the cost of CT or MRI scans is difficult to justify for routine use in primary care medicine. Limited CT scanning of the sinuses, which provides a few key sectional views, is available in some centers and has the advantages of increased sensitivity and relatively low cost. In patients with chronic sinusitis for whom surgery is being considered, CT or MRI scanning is the procedure of choice for defining the anatomy of the ostiomeatal complex.

The microbiology of acute sinusitis in children is similar to that of otitis media (Table 16-4).[18,19] *S pneumoniae*, *Haemophilus influenzae*, and *Moraxella catarrhalis* are the bacteria most frequently recovered from maxillary sinus aspirates from children and adults with acute sinusitis. In prolonged or unusually severe sinusitis, the possibility of anaerobic bacteria, *Staphylococcus aureus*, or fungi should be considered.

Treatment of sinusitis should be tailored to the individual, depending on the patient's age, presence of chronic sinus disease, and whether there are predisposing factors such as allergy (Figure 16-1).[12,15,17] Amoxicillin is recommended for initial therapy of children and adults with uncomplicated disease, although high doses (80 to 90 mg/kg in children, 3 to 4 grams/day in adults) may be necessary to overcome bacterial resistance. Alternatively, amoxicillin/clavulanate combination therapy can be used if a β-lactamase-positive organism is suspected. If a patient is allergic to amoxicillin, alternate antibiotics are available, including third generation cephalosporins, macrolides, and trimethoprim/sulfamethoxazole (TMP/SMX). Suggested antibiotics for sinusitis in children and adults are listed in Tables 16-2 and 16-5, respectively.

Although most patients with sinusitis show clinical improvement after 3 or 4 days of therapy with an appropriate antibiotic, it is recommended that antibiotic therapy be continued for 10 to 14 days to decrease the chance of relapse. If

Table 16-4: Microbiology of Sinusitis

	Children		Adults	
Organism	Acute	Chronic	Acute	Chronic
S pneumoniae	+++	+++	+++	+
H influenzae	+++	+++	+++	+
M catarrhalis	+++	+++	++	+
Anaerobes		+	+	+++
S aureus		+	+	++
Fungi		+		+
Viruses	+		+	

+ = reported, ++ = occasional, +++ = common

symptoms do not improve, imaging or rhinoscopy should be considered to confirm the diagnosis (Figure 16-1). Resistent cases in children can be treated with amoxicillin/clavulanate, or if this was the initial antibiotic, cefdinir, cefuroxime sodium (Zinacef®), or cefpodoxime can be prescribed. Intramuscular ceftriaxone should be considered for more severe illnesses and those accompanied by significant vomiting. For adults, quinolones are also a possibility. If anaerobes are suspected, clindamycin or metronidazole might be considered in combination with a broad-spectrum antibiotic.[12] Further lack of improvement should trigger consultation with an otorhinolaryngologist for consideration of sinus aspiration and culture. A sinus CT scan at this stage is usually advisable to determine whether anatomic abnormalities of the sinus drainage tracts exist.

Several adjuvant therapies, including use of antihistamines, decongestants, topical vasoconstrictors, and mucolytic agents, are widely used for treating sinusitis, despite a paucity

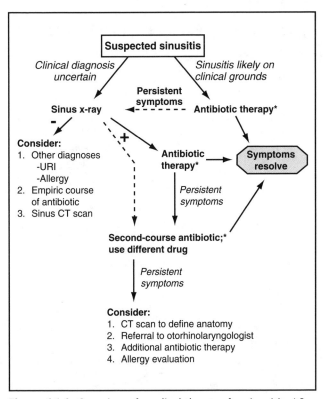

Figure 16-1: Overview of medical therapy for sinusitis. *See Tables 16-2 and 16-4 for suggested antibiotics for use in children and adults with sinusitis. Topical nasal corticosteroid sprays (see Chapter 6, Table 6-3) may also be beneficial in some patients with sinusitis. URI=upper respiratory infection

of data regarding efficacy. Topical vasoconstrictors cause rebound congestion if used for more than 4 or 5 days, and their chronic use should be avoided. There is evidence that saline nasal rinses can help to speed recovery,[20] and several studies have shown that topical nasal corticosteroids have efficacy when used together with antibiotics.[21]

Table 16-5: Treatment of Sinusitis in Adults*

Medication	How Supplied
Acute sinusitis	
amoxicillin (Amoxil®)	250 or 500 mg caps
amoxicillin/clavulanate (Augmentin®, Augmentin® XR)	250-125, 500-125, or 875-125 mg tabs** 1,000-62.5 mg tabs †
azithromycin (Zithromax®)▲	250 mg caps, 250, 500, 600 mg tabs
cefixime (Suprax®)▲	200 or 400 mg tabs
cefuroxime axetil (Ceftin®)	125, 250, or 500 mg tabs
clarithromycin (Biaxin® XL)	250 or 500 mg tabs 500 mg extended-release tabs
loracarbef	200 or 400 mg caps
trimethoprim/ sulfamethoxazole (Bactrim™, Septra®)▲	80/400 or 160/800 mg tabs
levofloxacin (Levaquin®)	250, 500, 750 mg tabs
moxifloxacin (Avelox®)	400 mg tabs
cefdinir (Omnicef®)	300 mg tabs
cefprozil (Cefzil®)	250 and 500 mg tabs

* The duration of therapy should be 2-3 weeks (except 5 days for azithromycin) to decrease the likelihood of relapse; however, if there is no clinical response after 1 week, consider switching medications.

** The clavulanate dose is 125 mg for either the 250 or 500 mg tablets; therefore, the 500 mg dose should *not* be given as two 250 mg tablets.

Dose

500 mg PO q 8 h

250-500 mg PO t.i.d
500-875 mg PO b.i.d.
2 tabs (1,000-125 mg) PO b.i.d.

500 mg PO on day 1, then
250 mg PO on days 2-5

400 mg PO q day

250-500 mg PO b.i.d.

500 mg PO q 12 h, or
1 g extended-release tabs PO q 24 h

400 mg PO q 12 h

160/800 mg PO q 12 h

500 mg q day x 10-14 d or 750 mg q day x 5 d

400 mg q day

600 mg/d in 1 or 2 divided doses

250-500 mg q 12 h

▲ Medications that are widely used but not approved by the US Food and Drug Administration for the treatment of sinusitis.
†Use of Augmentin XR® should be reserved for infections that are proven or strongly suspected to be caused by resistant bacteria.

(continued on next page)

Table 16-5: Treatment of Sinusitis in Adults
(continued)

Medication	How Supplied
Chronic sinusitis***	
amoxicillin/clavulanate	250-125, 500-125, or 875-125 mg tabs
ciprofloxacin (Cipro®)	250, 500, or 750 mg tabs
clarithromycin	250 or 500 mg tabs
clindamycin (Cleocin®)▲	75, 150, or 300 mg caps
doxycycline (Doryx®, Vibramycin®)▲	50 or 100 mg caps or tabs
metronidazole (Flagyl®)▲	250, 375, or 500 mg tabs or caps
penicillin V	250 or 500 mg tabs

***Combination therapy to cover aerobes and anaerobes is often used. Treatment failures are common, even if appropriate antibiotics are chosen, when sinus drainage is blocked.

The epidemiologic association between sinusitis and respiratory allergy suggests that patients with recurrent sinusitis should be evaluated for respiratory allergies. Achieving adequate control of allergen-induced mucosal edema and hypersecretion of mucus by allergen avoidance, medications, and, in selected cases, immunotherapy, helps reduce chronic respiratory symptoms and the frequency of sinusitis.[12,22]

Nasal Polyps

Nasal polyps, which are outgrowths of nasal mucosa, are usually located on the lateral wall of the nose. The characteristic appearance of a nasal polyp is best described as round or pear-shaped, pale, and gelatinous, and resembling a peeled

Dose

500 mg PO q 8 h or 875 mg PO b.i.d.
(based on amoxicillin component)

500-750 mg PO q 12 h

500 mg PO q 12 h

150-300 mg PO t.i.d. or q.i.d.

100 mg PO q 12 h on day 1, then 50 mg PO q 12 h

375-500 mg PO t.i.d. or q.i.d.

500 mg PO q.i.d.

grape in texture. Most nasal polyps originate in the ethmoid sinus but may occur in other sinuses as well. Nasal polyps are most common among men over the age of 40 and especially in those individuals with aspirin-sensitive asthma.[23] The primary morbidity associated with nasal polyps is sinusitis, but it is not clear whether the recurrent sinusitis is the stimulus for polyp growth or vice versa. Polyps are unusual in patients with uncomplicated allergy, except in allergic individuals with recurrent sinusitis. The occurrence of nasal polyps in childhood strongly suggests the diagnosis of cystic fibrosis.

The histology of nasal polyps is remarkable only for normal tissue constituents with chronic cellular inflammation. A polyp consists of an epithelial layer surrounding edematous fibrous tissue infiltrated with eosinophils, mast cells, and lymphocytes.[24,25] Increased levels of immunoglobulin in nasal polyp fluid are further evidence of local activation of the immune system.

Signs and symptoms associated with nasal polyposis include nasal congestion, rhinorrhea, sneezing, postnasal drip, facial pain, and loss of sense of smell (anosmia). The clinical presentation thus resembles that of allergic rhinitis. Despite the lack of association with allergy, patients with nasal polyps have an increased incidence of bronchial hyperresponsiveness and asthma, especially patients with both asthma and aspirin sensitivity.

Treatments for nasal polyps include use of oral or topical corticosteroids and/or surgical removal.[26-28] Approximately 80% of patients with nasal polyps experience significant improvement after using topical corticosteroid sprays (see Chapter 6, Table 6-3). Patients who have an incomplete response to corticosteroids, indicated by persistent symptoms or recurrent sinus infections, should be referred to an otorhinolaryngologist for polypectomy. Polypectomy usually produces dramatic symptom relief, but the polyps almost invariably return over time. Postoperative use of topical corticosteroid sprays may decrease the regrowth of polypoid tissue.

References

1.   Cundell DR, Gerard NP, Gerard C, et al: Streptococcus pneumoniae anchor to activated human cells by the receptor for platelet-activating factor. *Nature* 1995;377:435-438.

2.   Chantzi FM, Kafetzis DA, Bairamis T, et al. IgE sensitization, respiratory allergy symptoms, and heritability independently increase the risk of otitis media with effusion. *Allergy* 2006;61: 332-336.

3.   Lasisi AO, Olayemi O, Irabor AE: Early onset otitis media: risk factors and effects on the outcome of chronic suppurative otitis media. *Eur Arch Otorhinolaryngol* 2007 [Epub ahead of print].

4.   American Academy of Family Physicians; American Academy of Otolaryngology-Head and Neck Surgery; American Academy of

Pediatrics Subcommittee on Otitis Media With Effusion: Otitis media with effusion. *Pediatrics* 2004;113:1412-1429.

5. Nguyen LH, Manoukian JJ, Tewfik TL, et al: Evidence of allergic inflammation in the middle ear and nasopharynx in atopic children with otitis media with effusion. *J Otolaryngol* 2004; 33:345-351.

6. Yeo SG, Park DC, Eun YG, et al: The role of allergic rhinitis in the development of otitis media with effusion: effect on eustachian tube function. *Am J Otolaryngol* 2007; 28:148-152.

7. American Academy of Pediatrics Subcommittee on Management of Acute Otitis Media: Diagnosis and management of acute otitis media. *Pediatrics* 2004;113:1451-1465.

8. Chantzi FM, Papadopoulos NG, Bairamis T, et al: Human rhinoviruses in otitis media with effusion. *Pediatr Allergy Immunol* 2006;17:514-518.

9. Fletcher MA, Fritzell B: Brief review of the clinical effectiveness of PREVENAR against otitis media. *Vaccine* 2007;25: 2507-2512.

10. Ozgur SK, Beyazova U, Kemaloglu YK, et al: Effectiveness of inactivated influenza vaccine for prevention of otitis media in children. *Pediatr Infect Dis J* 2006;25:401-404.

11. Mattila PS: Adenoidectomy and tympanostomy tubes in the management of otitis media. *Curr Allergy Asthma Rep* 2006;6: 321-326.

12. Slavin RG, Spector SL, Bernstein IL, et al: The diagnosis and management of sinusitis: A practice parameter update. *J Allergy Clin Immunol* 2005;116:S13-S47.

13. Corren J, Kachru R: Relationship between nonallergic upper airway disease and asthma. *Clin Allergy Immunol* 2007;19:101-114.

14. van Cauwenberge P, Van Hoecke H, Bachert C: Pathogenesis of chronic rhinosinusitis. *Curr Allergy Asthma Rep* 2006;6:487-494.

15. Zacharisen M, Casper R: Pediatric sinusitis. *Immunol Allergy Clin North Am* 2005;25:313-332.

16. Schubert MS: Allergic fungal sinusitis. *Clin Rev Allergy Immunol* 2006;30:205-216.

17. Wald ER: Beginning antibiotics for acute rhinosinusitis and choosing the right treatment. *Clin Rev Allergy Immunol* 2006: 143-152.

18. Wald ER, Milmoe GJ, Bowen A, et al: Acute maxillary sinusitis in children. *N Engl J Med* 1981;304:749-754.

19. Gwaltney JM Jr, Scheld WM, Sande MA, et al: The microbial etiology and antimicrobial therapy of adults with acute community-acquired sinusitis: a fifteen-year experience at the University of Virginia and review of other selected studies. *J Allergy Clin Immunol* 1992;90(3 pt 2):457-461.

20. Harvey R, Hannan SA, Badia L, et al: Nasal saline irrigations for the symptoms of chronic rhinosinusitis. *Cochrane Database Syst Rev* 2007;(3):CD006394.

21. Zalmanovici A, Yaphe J: Steroids for acute sinusitis. *Cochrane Database Syst Rev* 2007;(2):CD005149.

22. Mabry RL: Allergic and infective rhinosinusitis: differential diagnosis and interrelationship. *Otolaryngol Head Neck Surg* 1994;111(3 pt 2):335-339.

23. Slavin RG: Nasal polyps and sinusitis. *JAMA* 1997;278:1849-1854.

24. Stoop AE, van der Heijden HA, Biewenga J, et al: Eosinophils in nasal polyps and nasal mucosa: an immunohistochemical study. *J Allergy Clin Immunol* 1993;91:616-622.

25. Stoop AE, van der Heijden HA, Biewenga J, et al: Lymphocytes and nonlymphoid cells in human nasal polyps. *J Allergy Clin Immunol* 1991;87:470-475.

26. Patiar S, Reece P: Oral steroids for nasal polyps. *Cochrane Database Syst Rev* 2007;(1):CD005232.

27. Fokkens W: Role of steroids in the treatment of rhinosinusitis with and without polyposis. *Clin Allergy Immunol* 2007;20: 241-250.

28. Luong A, Marple BF: Sinus surgery: indications and techniques. *Clin Rev Allergy Immunol* 2006;30:217-222.

Chapter 17

Treatment Options for Allergy and Asthma

The best way to treat an allergic disease is to identify the offending allergen and remove it from the environment to prevent future reactions from occurring. Sometimes this goal is achieved, but more often, patients continue to be exposed to low levels of allergen or have intermittent and accidental exposures to allergens, such as often happens with food allergy. Consequently, although there is considerable value in identifying specific allergens and in striving to prevent contact with those allergens, other means of therapy are needed to treat acute symptoms, to reduce underlying chronic allergic inflammation, and to reduce the risk of future allergic reactions. This is especially true in treating diseases such as atopic dermatitis and nonallergic asthma, in which the inflammatory mechanisms are similar to allergy but specific allergens are usually not implicated in the disease process. This chapter examines the roles of allergen avoidance, medications, immunotherapy, and other precautionary measures in the treatment of asthma and atopic disorders (Table 17-1).

Allergen Avoidance

In addition to causing seasonal and perennial rhinoconjunctivitis, overwhelming evidence indicates that respira-

Table 17-1: Overview of Therapy for Allergic Diseases

Allergen avoidance

Symptomatic medications

- Antihistamines
- Decongestants
- β-adrenergic agonists
- Anticholinergics

Preventive medications

- Mast cell stabilizing agents
- Corticosteroids
- Leukotriene modifiers

Allergen desensitization

Precautionary measures

- Epinephrine for self-administration
- Indicate allergies on hospital and pharmacy records
- Medical alert bracelets

tory allergies are a significant factor in the pathogenesis of asthma, especially in children. Limiting exposure to relevant indoor allergens can lead to reductions in asthma symptoms, bronchial hyperresponsiveness, and use of asthma medications.[1] Therefore, patients with significant asthma should be evaluated for respiratory allergies, and the asthma treatment plan should always include detailed instructions to the patient, child, and family to help minimize exposure to relevant allergens (Table 17-2). Avoidance measures are especially effective in decreasing exposure to indoor allergens such as pet dander, house dust mite, and mold. Avoiding contact with cat or dog allergens is straightforward in

Table 17-2: Control of Indoor Allergens

House dust mite

- Encase mattress in an airtight cover
- Encase pillows, or wash weekly in hot water
- Wash blankets and bed linens in hot (>130°F) water every 10-14 days
- Avoid upholstered furniture
- If feasible, remove carpets in the bedroom
- If possible, keep humidity <50%

Pets

- Remove from the house (especially if contributing to asthma)

Mold

- Use a dehumidifier in the basement
- Remove carpets laid over concrete
- If possible, keep humidity <50%
- Fix leaks in roof, bathrooms, etc.

principle: find another home for the pet. Some patients with allergic rhinitis may be willing to tolerate significant upper airway symptoms to keep a beloved pet, but when the animal contributes to asthma, removing the pet from the home is clearly the best choice in light of the morbidity and even mortality associated with asthma. Unfortunately, reports that washing pets or treating them with acepromazine can reduce their allergen shedding and thus limit allergy symptoms have not been substantiated.[2]

House dust mites are arachnids that are too small to be seen with the naked eye. These highly allergenic creatures cohabitate, eat skin scales and are thus found in high concentrations in bedding, upholstered furniture, and carpets. Successful methods of controlling dust mite allergen concentrations include encasing mattresses and pillows in plastic, washing bed covers and linens in hot (>130°F) water, and removing carpets and upholstered furniture.[3] Acaricides such as malathion also reduce mite numbers, but few people are willing to use insecticides indoors. Tannic acid solutions denature mite proteins and render them less allergenic; however, tannic acid can stain furniture and carpets, and clinical benefits after treatments with it have not been demonstrated.[4] Maintaining indoor humidity at <50% is an effective way to control dust mites and molds.[3] Important sources of indoor mold include damp carpets, especially carpet laid on concrete slab, and construction materials that are water damaged from leaks or flooding. Faulty ventilation systems can also increase exposure to allergenic molds.

Controlling exposure to outdoor allergens such as pollens and molds is difficult, but a few measures can be helpful. Closing the windows and using either air conditioning or a high-efficiency air filter help limit indoor mold spore and pollen counts. Limiting outdoor exercise during peak allergen seasons, especially in the morning hours, can also be beneficial.

Allergen avoidance is currently the only effective treatment for food allergy.[5] Patients and parents must be taught to carefully read the labels of prepared foods, and they must be able to recognize all forms of the allergenic protein. Although avoidance is simple in principle, accidental ingestion of foods identified as allergenic is common, especially when eating away from home.[6,7] Parents sending children with food allergy to school or day care for the first time should explain to teachers the dietary restrictions and contingency plans for the treatment of accidental ingestion of an allergen.[8] The Food Allergy & Anaphylaxis Network (11781 Lee Jackson Hwy., Suite 160, Fairfax, VA 22033-3309, 800-929-4040, http://www.foodallergy.org) is a parent-run organization that is a valuable source of information about living with food allergy.

Antihistamines

Antihistamines block the interaction between histamine and histamine-specific receptors. H_1-receptor antagonists are the most useful drugs for treating allergic symptoms, although the addition of H_2 antihistamines may provide some additional relief for patients with chronic urticaria. Because histamine is one of many mediators involved in allergic inflammation, antihistamines usually provide only partial relief from allergic symptoms. In general, antihistamines are fairly effective for treatment of urticaria, sneezing, itching, and rhinorrhea, but they have relatively little effect on congestion,[9] which is one of the most troublesome symptoms of allergic rhinitis. Some antihistamines produce bronchodilation, but its effect is too small to be clinically significant in patients with asthma. Antihistamines do not cause mucous plugging in the lower airway and can be used safely in patients with asthma.

First-generation antihistamines are effective histamine-receptor blockers, but produce clinically apparent sedation in about one third of users. Studies using neural psychological testing or monitoring of brain waves have demonstrated that subtle central nervous system (CNS) effects can be demonstrated in a much greater fraction of subjects taking standard antihistamines.[10,11] Furthermore, tests in a sophisticated driving simulator suggest that effects of standard doses of diphenhydramine (Benadryl®) on driving performance are similar to those caused by a blood alcohol level of 0.1 mg/mL.[12] Second-generation antihistamines, which are lipophobic and do not cross the blood-brain barrier (with the exception of cetirizine [Zyrtec®]), retain potent antihistaminic effects, have relatively long half-lives, and produce sedation in very few individuals (see Chapter 6, Table 6-3).[9] Although antihistamines are generally safe, cardiac arrhythmias can occur with overdoses of certain antihistamines or with standard doses if administered to patients with liver disease, to patients taking medications such as erythromycin and ketoconazole (Nizoral®)

that slow hepatic clearance, or to patients with prolonged corrected QT (QTc) interval.[9] Fexofenadine (Allegra®), loratadine (Alavert®, Claritin®), cetirizine, and levocetirizine (Xyzal®) do not produce cardiac side effects because they do not prolong the QTc interval.[9]

Topical antihistamines, such as levocabastine, can be used on an as-needed basis for the symptomatic relief of allergic rhinitis and conjunctivitis. Some topical H_1-blockers (eg, azelastine [Astelin®], ketotifen) may also have anti-inflammatory effects, including inhibition of eosinophil recruitment and mast-cell and eosinophil activation.[9]

Decongestants and Vasoconstrictors

α-Adrenergic agonists have potent vasoconstrictive effects when administered either orally or topically and are widely used as adjunctive medications for allergic rhinoconjunctivitis. Antihistamines are often combined in drug mixtures with decongestants, which may counteract the sedative effect of antihistamines to some degree and potentiate the decongestive effects of the antihistamine. Unfortunately, oral decongestants sometimes produce side effects that limit their clinical utility, including tremor, insomnia, nervousness, and restriction of urinary flow in males.[13] Topical α-adrenergic agonists such as oxymetazoline (Afrin® nasal spray) or phenylephrine (Neo-Synephrine®) are potent vasoconstrictors, but these medications produce rebound congestion if used for more than a few days and so are unsuitable for treating patients with chronic allergic rhinitis.

Bronchodilators

Drug delivery systems

Aerosol delivery of medications would seem to be ideally suited for asthma therapy because it maximizes drug delivery to the small airway while minimizing the systemic effects of medications. Although there are definite theoretic advantages to drug delivery via inhalation, clinical responses to aerosolized medications vary widely. The principal reason for these inconsistent responses is that the mechanics of breathing (eg, inspiratory flow, duration of breath-holding) greatly affect the amount of medicine that reaches the lungs.

Inhaled medications are usually administered either by nebulizer or pressurized metered-dose inhaler (MDI), although some medications are also available in dry powder inhalers. The optimum particle size for lower airway deposition is 1 mm to 5 mm. Larger droplets are likely to stay in the upper airway.[14] MDIs generate relatively smaller 'respirable' particles compared with nebulizers, which may explain why nebulizer doses of β-agonists must be 3 to 10 times larger to achieve the same degree of bronchodilation. MDIs have the additional advantages of being more portable and quicker to use, and they cost 50% to 75% less per treatment than nebulizers. Although nebulizers have traditionally been used in medical facilities for treating acute asthma, MDIs provide bronchodilation that is faster and of equal or greater magnitude, although larger than standard doses may be required.[15]

MDIs that contain chlorofluorocarbons (CFCs) contribute to the depletion of stratospheric ozone. As a result of the consequent health hazards, CFCs have been internationally banned. Although a temporary medical exemption has been granted, MDIs with CFC propellants are being replaced with alternative aerosol products. New MDIs are driven by an alternate propellant using hydrofluoroalkane (HFA-134a), which does not deplete ozone.

Unfortunately, many patients do not use inhalers correctly (see Chapter 7, Table 7-5) and thus do not derive full benefit from the medications contained within them. Spacer devices can improve the efficacy of medications delivered via MDI in patients who are unable to master correct inhaler technique.[16,17] These devices work by trapping most of the large aerosol droplets while holding the smaller particles in a reservoir until they are inhaled. Some spacer devices, such as the Aerochamber® and Inspirease®, can be equipped with variable-size masks suitable for use by young children. For older children, spacers equipped with mouthpieces are preferred because the nose may filter out particles that would otherwise be deposited in the lung. In addition to improving drug delivery to the lower airways, the use of a spacer with inhaled corticosteroids also reduces the incidence of side effects such as oral candidiasis and hoarseness.

Epinephrine and β-adrenergic agonists

Epinephrine is a catecholamine that has long been used to relieve acute symptoms of allergy. Because epinephrine is inactivated in the gastrointestinal (GI) tract, it must be either inhaled or injected. The potent α-adrenergic (increased heart rate, stroke volume, and vascular tone) and β-adrenergic (bronchodilator) effects of epinephrine make it the drug of choice for treating anaphylactic reactions. Delayed use of epinephrine in anaphylactic reactions has been associated with a poorer outcome.[6,7] Epinephrine for self-administration should be prescribed for patients at risk for repeated anaphylaxis (eg, food allergy, idiopathic anaphylaxis) and may also be useful for patients with a history of severe paroxysmal asthma. Injectable epinephrine is available in several forms; however, the EpiPen® (0.3 mg) and EpiPen® Jr. (0.15 mg) are especially easy to use, which is a distinct advantage in an emergency. Medical alert bracelets are also advisable for patients who have experienced anaphylactic reactions in the past.

Inhaled selective β_2-agonists, which produce longer-lasting bronchodilation with less discomfort, have largely replaced injected epinephrine in the management of acute asthma (see Chapter 9). The availability of β_2-agonists in multiple forms (short-, intermediate-, and long-acting) and delivery systems (MDIs, nebulizer solutions, oral liquids and tablets, respirable powders) gives them wide clinical versatility. Short-acting β_2-agonists are the most effective medications for relieving bronchospasm and are the drugs of choice for treating acute asthma symptoms and exacerbations and for preventing exercise-induced bronchospasm (EIB). All patients with asthma, regardless of severity, should have access to a short-acting β_2-agonist at all times.[17] Paradoxically, the rapid onset of action and potent bronchodilator activity may lead to deterioration of asthma disease control if the patient uses β-agonists to the exclusion of anti-inflammatory medications, which do not produce any immediate positive feedback. Therefore, the increasing frequency of β_2-agonist use should be considered an indicator of inadequate disease control and a signal for the need for a medical evaluation. Delivery devices with dose counters (ie, Ventolin® HFA) can help patients track their use of a β_2-agonist. Side effects of selective β_2-agonists include tremor, tachycardia, and increased anxiety, but these occur infrequently when β_2-agonists are administered via inhalation.

Levalbuterol (Xopenex®) is the active R-isomer of albuterol. Clinical studies have shown that levalbuterol is as effective at lower doses as racemic albuterol.[18,19] For example, 0.63 mg levalbuterol causes bronchodilation that is similar to 2.5 mg racemic albuterol, and may have fewer side effects.[18] Therefore, levalbuterol should be considered an option for the treatment or prevention of bronchospasm, especially in patients who experience adverse effects after the use of racemic albuterol.

Long-acting β_2-agonists and combination medications

Long-acting β_2-agonists, ie, salmeterol (Serevent®) and formoterol (Foradil®, Perforomist™) are best used as adjuncts to anti-inflammatory medications to control persistent asthma.[17,20,21] For example, in patients who continue to have chronic asthma symptoms despite the use of a low-dose inhaled corticosteroid, adding a long-acting β_2-agonist to the regimen produces improved asthma control, including improved symptom relief, lung function, and protection from asthma exacerbations.[17,20,21] Currently, there are two combination medications (fluticasone/salmeterol [Advair Diskus®] and budesonide/formoterol [Symbicort®]), combining long-acting β_2-agonists with several different doses of inhaled corticosteroid. However, there is clinical evidence that treatment with a long-acting β_2-agonist alone (without the concomitant use of an inhaled corticosteroid) masks the symptoms of worsening asthma, and may increase the risk of severe exacerbations and even death.[22,23] These findings prompted the US Food and Drug Administration (FDA) to put a black box warning label on all products containing long-acting β_2-agonists, and in fact long-acting β_2-agonists alone should not be used to treat persistent asthma. In choosing a treatment regimen for moderate or severe asthma, this information needs to be weighed against the considerable body of evidence indicating that combination medications are both safe and effective.[17,23] Finally, salmeterol should not be used for the relief of acute asthma symptoms because of the relatively slow onset of action compared with short-acting β_2-agonists, ie, albuterol HFA (ProAir® HFA, Proventil® HFA, Ventolin® HFA).

Theophylline

Theophylline is a methylxanthine drug that produces bronchodilation by inhibiting phosphodiesterase, causing increases in smooth-muscle cyclic adenosine monophosphate. Several studies suggest that theophylline has anti-inflammatory effects, including inhibition of inflammatory cell mediator release. Theophylline is available in liquid, beaded capsule, and tablet forms, including several sustained-release formulations that may be given at 8- to 24-hour intervals. Aminophylline, the amino salt of theophylline, is administered intravenously.

Theophylline is a safe and effective bronchodilator at serum concentrations of 5 µg/mL to 15 µg/mL. Other beneficial effects of theophylline include attenuation of the early- and late-phase response to allergen, corticosteroid sparing, and improved exercise tolerance.[24] When compared with β_2-agonists, theophylline has a slower onset of action and a lower peak effect, making it less suitable for acute therapy.

Serum levels of theophylline are influenced by a number of variables, including age, diet, disease states, drug interactions, and hepatic clearance, all of which contribute to the

Table 17-3: Theophylline: Common Drug Interactions*

Medications that decrease serum theophylline levels

- Carbamazepine (Carbatrol®, Tegretol®)
- Phenobarbital
- Phenytoin (Dilantin®, Phenytek®)
- Rifampin (Rifadin®, Rimactane®)

Medications that increase serum theophylline levels

- Allopurinol (Aloprim®, Lopurin®, Zyloprim®)
- Cimetidine (Tagamet®)
- Ciprofloxacin (Cipro®)
- Disulfiram (Antabuse®)
- Macrolide antibiotics
- Mexiletine
- Oral contraceptives
- Propranolol (Inderal®, Inderal® LA)
- Verapamil (Calan®, Covera-HS®, Isoptin® SR, Verelan®)
- Zileuton (Zyflo®, Zyflo CR™)

Medications with accentuated side effects when administered with theophylline

- Cetirizine (Zyrtec®)
- Ephedrine
- Tetracycline

*This list is not all inclusive; consult the medical literature before prescribing other medications along with theophylline.

complexity of using this medication.[24] For example, tobacco and marijuana smoking increase theophylline metabolism, while febrile illnesses and high carbohydrate diets significantly decrease theophylline metabolism. Potential drug interactions require that the dose of theophylline be adjusted accordingly (Table 17-3). Because of the variability of theophylline metabolism, as well as its narrow therapeutic index, serum concentrations of theophylline should be monitored periodically.

Unfortunately, theophylline may produce a number of dose-related side effects, such as nausea, irritability, and insomnia. The frequency and severity of these side effects can be minimized by initiating therapy with a low dose of theophylline and gradually increasing the dose to achieve therapeutic serum concentrations.[24] Of concern to parents and teachers is the suggestion that chronic use of theophylline might adversely affect school performance, although studies have not substantiated this association. [25]

Anticholinergics

Anticholinergic medications such as atropine inhibit the muscarinic effects of acetylcholine, producing bronchodilation. Ipratropium bromide (Atrovent®) is a closely related quaternary ammonium compound that also causes bronchodilation, but because it is poorly absorbed into the systemic circulation, it has fewer side effects than atropine. Because the bronchodilation produced by anticholinergic medications has a slower onset of action and a smaller peak effect compared to β-agonists, their use in asthma is limited. Their role is best defined for use in chronic obstructive pulmonary disease. Ipratropium is available as an MDI, solution for nebulization, and a nasal spray. Ipratropium nasal spray acts directly on secretory glands to decrease the production of nasal secretions and has a mild decongestant effect. Ipratropium effectively inhibits rhinorrhea caused by vasomotor rhinitis or the common cold,[26] but its role in the management of allergic rhinitis remains to be determined.

Anti-Inflammatory Medications
Antiallergic medications

Cromolyn (Intal®) and nedocromil (Tilade®) are two structurally distinct asthma medications that have similar properties. Both medications inhibit inflammatory cell activation, mediator release, early and late allergen-induced bronchoconstriction, and airway hyperresponsiveness. Although cromolyn and nedocromil attenuate exercise- and allergen-induced bronchospasm, they do not have direct bronchodilating effects. Their mechanisms of action are not well understood but probably involve inhibition of chloride channels or neurokinins. Cromolyn is available in several forms: MDI (Intal®), solution for nebulization, nasal spray, and ophthalmic solution (Crolom®, Opticrom®). Nedocromil is available as an MDI and an ophthalmic. A third mast cell stabilizing agent, lodoxamide, is also available as an ophthalmic solution (Alomide®) for the treatment of allergic conjunctivitis.

Clinical studies have confirmed that regular use of cromolyn or nedocromil for asthma improves pulmonary function and reduces respiratory symptoms and the use of rescue medications.[27,28] The use of these drugs may be limited because they must be dosed four times daily, although the dosing frequency can usually be reduced to three times daily or twice daily in patients with a good initial response. Cromolyn nasal spray, which is available over the counter, is somewhat less effective for allergic rhinitis. Cromolyn and lodoxamide eyedrops are effective prophylactic treatments for ocular allergies when used regularly.[29,30] Cromolyn and nedocromil have excellent safety records.

Corticosteroids

Glucocorticosteroids are the most potent anti-inflammatory agents available for the treatment of allergic inflammation and asthma.[17] Their efficacy is related to many factors, including a diminution in inflammatory cell function and activation, stabilization of vascular leakage, a decrease in mucus production, and an increase in β-adrenergic response.

Unfortunately, chronic administration of oral glucocorticosteroids may result in multiple dose-dependent adverse effects, including hypothalamic pituitary adrenal axis suppression, osteoporosis, posterior subcapsular cataracts, hyperglycemia, hypertension, dermal thinning and striae, and the potential for growth retardation.[17] In addition, although short courses of oral corticosteroids rarely cause serious side effects, corticosteroid therapy may exacerbate pre-existing health problems such as hypertension or diabetes. Finally, case reports of fatal varicella infection associated with systemic corticosteroid use in children with asthma suggest a potential danger.[31] As a result, patients who contract varicella during or within 30 days of a course of oral corticosteroid may require additional treatments such as a course of oral acyclovir (Zovirax®). It is also prudent to administer varicella vaccine to children or adults without a history of chickenpox who are likely to require oral corticosteroids for asthma.

Fortunately, because inhaled corticosteroids are effective in children and adults, the need for oral corticosteroid regimens has diminished substantially. Inhaled corticosteroids are the most potent and effective anti-inflammatory therapy available for asthma and have few side effects when used at standard doses. The two most common side effects are hoarseness and oral candidiasis, occurring in less than 10% of patients. The incidence of these side effects is further reduced by using spacer devices and instructing patients to rinse their mouth and gargle after using an inhaled corticosteroid. It is clear, however, that high-dose inhaled corticosteroids (see Chapter 7, Table 7-6) can cause systemic side effects, especially when high-potency corticosteroids are used.

The potential effects of inhaled corticosteroids on growth are of interest to health-care providers caring for children with asthma. Standard doses of inhaled corticosteroids can temporarily slow short-term growth in some children,[32] although studies of long-term (>12 months) inhaled corticosteroid therapy have generally not found adverse effects on growth.[33,34] These data suggest that inhaled corticosteroids can be used safely in children with the following precautions. First, all children requiring prolonged oral or inhaled corticosteroid at any dose should be measured carefully at routine intervals to monitor effects on stature. In addition, once respiratory symptoms are controlled, the dose of corticosteroid should be tapered to the lowest effective dose.

Topical corticosteroid preparations are also the treatment of choice for moderate to severe allergic rhinitis.[13,35] They relieve a broad range of symptoms, including congestion, which is generally not affected by antihistamine therapy. Prolonged use of topical corticosteroids in the nose or lower airways is safe, as verified by biopsy studies after prolonged (up to 10 years) daily administration of beclomethasone dipropionate (Beconase AQ®). Side effects associated with topical nasal corticosteroids are uncommon but include nosebleeds and local nasal inflammation. Septal perforations have been reported rarely and are caused by overdosing or improper inhaler technique (see Chapter 6). However, topical corticosteroids in the eye should be used with extreme caution because of the effects on intraocular pressure, the risk of cataracts, and potentiation of ocular infections such as herpes keratitis. Patients who suffer severe rhinoconjunctivitis during the pollen allergy season may benefit significantly by taking a short course of an oral corticosteroid (eg, prednisone 20 mg PO twice daily x 5 days in adolescents or adults). This approach provides prompt and dramatic clinical relief and opens the airway so that topical nasal sprays can reach the target tissues.

Leukotriene Modifiers

The leukotrienes are potent inflammatory mediators that contribute to the pathogenesis of asthma and to nasal blockage in allergic rhinitis.[36-38] These compounds are synthesized from arachidonic acid in cell membranes through a series of enzymatically-controlled reactions (Figure 17-1). Leukotriene synthesis and effects of these mediators can

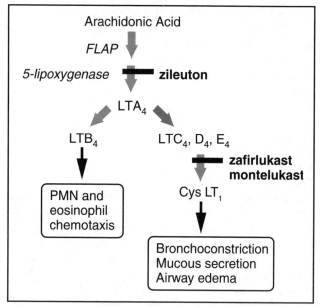

Figure 17-1: Leukotriene synthesis pathways and activities of leukotriene modifiers. FLAP=5-lipoxygenase activating protein

therefore be regulated at several points in this process. Compounds (eg, zileuton) that inhibit either 5-lipoxygenase or 5-lipoxygenase activating protein (FLAP) prevent synthesis of leukotrienes, while receptor antagonists (zafirlukast [Accolate®], montelukast) block binding of LTC_4, LTD_4, and LTE_4 to cystinyl leukotriene receptors ($CysLT_1$) on the surface of cells.

Although leukotriene synthesis inhibitors and receptor blockers exert their effects through distinct mechanisms, their clinical effects are similar. Both types of leukotriene modifiers produce bronchodilation beginning with the first dose, and chronic use can reduce daytime and nighttime symptoms, produce modest improvements in pulmonary function, and inhibit acute asthma symptoms triggered by exercise, allergen inhalation, and aspirin. In addition, leukotriene modifiers may have anti-inflammatory properties because they reduce circulating eosinophil counts and inhibit allergen-induced eosinophil recruitment to the airway.

Despite their similar effects, a few differences among these leukotriene modifiers can affect their clinical utility. Although these medications share the ease of oral administration and have few side effects, zileuton occasionally produces liver toxicity, and hepatic enzymes (ALT) should be monitored.[17] Zafirlukast and montelukast are less likely to cause hepatic inflammation and do not require monitoring of liver enzymes. Zafirlukast and zileuton are metabolized in the liver—zafirlukast can interfere with warfarin metabolism, and zileuton interferes with warfarin, theophylline, and terfenadine metabolism. In addition, zileuton must be given four times daily, although patients who have a good initial response may do well on a three times daily schedule. Montelukast (once daily) and zafirlukast (twice daily) are easier to use because of less frequent dosing, although zafirlukast should be taken on an empty stomach because food interferes with its bioavailability.

As a cautionary note, cases of Churg-Strauss syndrome (pulmonary eosinophilic vasculitis) have been reported in patients with severe asthma soon after starting therapy with zafirlukast or zileuton. It appears, however, that this might not be related to the leukotriene modifier, but rather to the reduction in systemic corticosteroids in a patient with Churg-Strauss syndrome that was previously unrecognized.

The updated National Heart, Lung, and Blood Institute *Guidelines for the Diagnosis and Management of Asthma*[17] classify these compounds as an alternative controller for the treatment of mild persistent asthma, and for adjunctive therapy for more severe asthma. Furthermore, double-blind, placebo-controlled studies have demonstrated that treatment with montelukast, a leukotriene-receptor blocker, can reduce the severity of a variety of symptoms associated with seasonal allergic rhinitis.[39,40]

Immunotherapy

Immunotherapy involves injecting gradually increasing amounts of an allergen into a sensitized patient in an effort to induce a state of tolerance to that allergen. Although the precise mechanism underlying the induction of tolerance is unknown, several hypotheses have been advanced. Clinical changes such as reduction in immediate and late-phase reactivity to allergens correspond with a number of immunologic alterations, including a rise in allergen-specific immunoglobulin G_4 (IgG_4) antibodies, decreased allergen-specific immunoglobulin E (IgE), and a shift in T-cell responses away from T helper 2 and toward a T helper 1-like cytokine response pattern.[41] Which one of these immunologic changes causes the clinical improvement is uncertain. Regardless of the mechanism, immunotherapy has proven efficacy for the treatment of several allergic disorders, including stinging insect hypersensitivity, allergic rhinoconjunctivitis, and, in some instances, asthma.[42-45]

Immunotherapy for stinging insect hypersensitivity is curative and reduces the incidence of subsequent systemic allergic reactions after a re-sting to that of the general population. Patients receiving immunotherapy for rhinoconjunctivitis usually experience partial relief of symptoms, enabling better symptom control with less medication. Because the combination of allergen avoidance and medications effectively controls allergy symptoms in most patients, most allergists reserve immunotherapy for patients who do not respond favorably to this combination. There is evidence that asthma can also be treated with immunotherapy.[44] Unstable asthma is a contraindication to immunotherapy because of increased risk of anaphylaxis and fatal reactions.

Immunotherapy for food allergy has been carefully evaluated in a large clinical trial.[45] Unfortunately, because of concerns about safety and efficacy, immunotherapy for food allergy cannot be recommended at this time.

New Directions in Medical Therapy

Several innovative treatments for allergic diseases are under investigation, including several new biologic response modifiers. Neutralizing monoclonal antibodies for IL-5 has been used successfully for the treatment of hypereosino-philic disorders and eosinophilic esophagitis.[46] However, to date this molecule has failed to demonstrate substantial benefits in clinical trials of asthma.[47] Likewise, clinical trials testing effects of a soluble form of the IL-4 receptor, as well as the T helper 1 cytokines IL-12 and interferon gamma, have yielded negative results.[48] Novel approaches to immunotherapy are also being tested.

One approach to provide effective immunotherapy with less risk to the patient has been to use omalizumab (anti-) to pretreat patients receiving rush immunotherapy to decrease the risk of treatment-related anaphylaxis.[49] In addition, high dose sublingual and oral immunotherapy is being tested for the treatment of respiratory allergies, and this form of therapy is now used in some European countries.[50] Clinical trials using these approaches for the treatment of food allergy are also underway.[51]

Finally, an innovative approach to the treatment of severe asthma is the use of thermoplasty, in which a bronchoscope is introduced into the lung and airways are treated with radio frequency energy in an effort to reduce the mass of smooth muscle to open obstructed airways.[52] Short-term improvements in lung function, medication use, and lung function have been demonstrated in a clinical trial, and long-term studies are ongoing. Time and additional testing in clinical studies will tell whether these approaches will eventually be useful in clinical practice.

References

1. Platts-Mills T, Leung DY, Schatz M: The role of allergens in asthma. *Am Fam Physician* 2007;76:675-680.

2. Klucka CV, Ownby DR, Green J, et al: Cat shedding of Fel d I is not reduced by washings, Allerpet-C spray, or acepromazine. *J Allergy Clin Immunol* 1995;95:1164-1171.

3. Platts-Mills TA, Vaughan JW, Carter MC, et al: The role of intervention in established allergy: avoidance of indoor allergens in the treatment of chronic allergic disease. *J Allergy Clin Immunol* 2000;106:787-804.

4. Woodfolk JA, Hayden ML, Couture N, et al: Chemical treatment of carpets to reduce allergen: comparison of the effects of tannic acid and other treatments on proteins derived from dust mites and cats. *J Allergy Clin Immunol* 1995;96:325-333.

5. Sampson HA: 9. Food allergy. *J Allergy Clin Immunol* 2003; 111(2 suppl):S540-S547.

6. Sampson HA, Mendelson L, Rosen JP: Fatal and near-fatal anaphylactic reactions to food in children and adolescents. *N Engl J Med* 1992;327:380-384.

7. Yuninger JW, Sweeney KG, Sturner WQ, et al: Fatal food-induced anaphylaxis. *JAMA* 1988;260:1450-1452.

8. Munoz-Furlong A: Food allergy in schools: concerns for allergists, pediatricians, parents, and school staff. *Ann Allergy Asthma Immunol* 2004;93(5 suppl 3):S47-S50.

9. Simons FE: Advances in H1-antihistamines. *N Engl J Med* 2004; 351:2203-2217.

10. Bender B, Milgrom H: Neuropsychiatric effects of medications for allergic diseases. *J Allergy Clin Immunol* 1995;95: 523-528.

11. Simons FE, Reggin JD, Roberts JR, et al: Benefit/risk ratio of the antihistamines (H1-receptor antagonists) terfenadine and chlorpheniramine in children. *J Pediatr* 1994;124:979-983.

12. Weiler JM, Bloomfield JR, Woodworth GG, et al: Effects of fexofenadine, diphenhydramine, and alcohol on driving performance. A randomized, placebo-controlled trial in the Iowa driving simulator. *Ann Intern Med* 2000;132:354-363.

13. Howarth PH: Allergic and nonallergic rhinitis. In: Adkinson NF Jr, Yuninger JW, Busse WW, et al, eds: *Middleton's Allergy:*

Principles and Practice, 6th ed. St. Louis, MO, Mosby, 2003, pp 1391-1410.

14. Morrow PE: Conference on the scientific basis of respiratory therapy. Aerosol therapy. Aerosol characterization and deposition. *Am Rev Respir Dis* 1974;110(6 pt 2):88-99.

15. Kerem E, Levison H, Schuh S, et al: Efficacy of albuterol administered by nebulizer versus spacer device in children with acute asthma. *J Pediatr* 1993;123:313-317.

16. Toogood JH: Helping your patients make better use of MDIs and spacers. *J Respir Dis* 1994;15:151-165.

17. National Asthma Education and Prevention Program, National Heart, Lung, and Blood Institute, National Institutes of Health: Expert Panel Report 3: Guidelines for the Diagnosis and Management of Asthma (Full Report 2007). Bethesda, MD, NIH publication number 08-5846, US Department of Health and Human Services, 2007. Available at: http://www.nhlbi.nih.gov/guidelines/asthma/asthgdln.htm. Accessed January 21, 2008.

18. Nelson HS, Bensch G, Pleskow WW, et al: Improved bronchodilation with levalbuterol compared with racemic albuterol in patients with asthma. *J Allergy Clin Immunol* 1998;102(6 pt 1):943-952.

19. Milgrom H, Skoner DP, Bensch G, et al: Low-dose levalbuterol in children with asthma: safety and efficacy in comparison with placebo and racemic albuterol. *J Allergy Clin Immunol* 2001;108:938-945.

20. Bateman ED, Boushey HA, Bousquet J, et al, and GOAL Investigators Group: Can guideline-defined asthma control be achieved? The Gaining Optimal Asthma ControL study. *Am J Respir Crit Care Med* 2004;170:836-844.

21. Kuna P, Creemers JP, Vondra V, et al: Once-daily dosing with budesonide/formoterol compared with twice-daily budesonide/formoterol and once-daily budesonide in adults with mild to moderate asthma. *Respir Med* 2006;100:2151-2159.

22. Nelson HS, Weiss ST, Bleecker ER, et al: The Salmeterol Multicenter Asthma Research Trial: a comparison of usual pharmacotherapy for asthma or usual pharmacotherapy plus salmeterol. *Chest* 2006;129:15-26.

23. Nelson HS: Is there a problem with inhaled long-acting beta-adrenergic agonists? *J Allergy Clin Immunol* 2006;117:3-16.

24. Weinberger M, Hendeles L: Theophylline in asthma. *N Engl J Med* 1996;334:1380-1388.

25. Bender B, Milgrom H: Theophylline-induced behavior change in children. An objective evaluation of parents' perceptions. *JAMA* 1992;267:2621-2624.

26. Grossman J, Banov C, Boggs P, et al: Use of ipratropium bromide nasal spray in chronic treatment of nonallergic perennial rhinitis, alone and in combination with other perennial rhinitis medications. *J Allergy Clin Immunol* 1995;95(5 pt 2):1123-1127.

27. Shapiro GG, Sharpe M, DeRouen TA, et al: Cromolyn versus triamcinolone acetonide for youngsters with moderate asthma. *J Allergy Clin Immunol* 1991;88:742-748.

28. Armenio L, Baldini G, Bardare M, et al: Double-blind, placebo controlled study of nedocromil sodium in asthma. *Arch Dis Child* 1993;68:193-197.

29. Blumenthal M, Casale T, Dockhorn R, et al: Efficacy and safety of nedocromil sodium ophthalmic solution in the treatment of seasonal allergic conjunctivitis. *Am J Ophthalmol* 1992;113: 56-63.

30. Juniper EF, Guyatt GH, Ferrie PJ, et al: Sodium cromoglycate eye drops: regular versus "as needed" use in the treatment of seasonal allergic conjunctivitis. *J Allergy Clin Immunol* 1994;94:36-43.

31. Silk HJ, Guay-Woodford L, Perez-Atayde AR, et al: Fatal varicella in steroid-dependent asthma. *J Allergy Clin Immunol* 1988;81:47-51.

32. Long-term effects of budesonide or nedocromil in children with asthma. The Childhood Asthma Management Program Research Group. *N Engl J Med* 2000;343:1054-1063.

33. Agertoft L, Pedersen S: Effect of long-term treatment with inhaled budesonide on adult height in children with asthma. *N Engl J Med* 2000;343:1064-1069.

34. Silverstein MD, Yunginger JW, Reed CE, et al: Attained adult height after childhood asthma: effect of glucocorticoid therapy. *J Allergy Clin Immunol* 1997;99:466-474.

35. Al Sayyad JJ, Fedorowicz Z, Alhashimi D, et al: Topical nasal steroids for intermittent and persistent allergic rhinitis in children. *Cochrane Database Syst Rev* 2007;(1):CD003163.

36. Israel E, Cohn J, Dube L, et al: Effect of treatment with zileuton, a 5-lipoxygenase inhibitor, in patients with asthma. A randomized

controlled trial. Zileuton Clinical Trial Group. *JAMA* 1996;275: 931-936.

37. Storms W: Update on montelukast and its role in the treatment of asthma, allergic rhinitis and exercise-induced bronchoconstriction. *Expert Opin Pharmacother* 2007;8:2173-2187.

38. Chervinsky P, Philip G, Malice MP, et al: Montelukast for treating fall allergic rhinitis: effect of pollen exposure in 3 studies. *Ann Allergy Asthma Immunol* 2004;92:367-373.

39. van Adelsberg J, Philip G, Pedinoff AJ, et al, and Montelukast Fall Rhinitis Study Group: Montelukast improves symptoms of seasonal allergic rhintis over a 4-week treatment period. *Allergy* 2003;58:1268-1276.

40. Nayak AS, Philip G, Lu S, et al, and Montelukast Fall Rhinitis Investigator Group: Efficacy and tolerability of montelukast alone or in combination with loratadine in seasonal allergic rhinitis: a multicenter, randomized, double-blind, placebo-controlled trial performed in the fall. *Ann Allergy Asthma Immunol* 2002; 88:592-600.

41. Durham SR, Till SJ: Immunologic changes associated with allergen immunotherapy. *J Allergy Clin Immunol* 1998;102:157-164.

42. Frew AJ: 25. Immunotherapy of allergic disease. *J Allergy Clin Immunol* 2003;111(2 suppl):S712-S719.

43. Durham SR, Walker SM, Varga EM, et al: Long-term clinical efficacy of grass-pollen immunotherapy. *N Engl J Med* 1999;341: 468-475.

44. Ross RN, Nelson HS, Finegold I: Effectiveness of specific immunotherapy in the treatment of asthma: a meta-analysis of prospective, randomized, double-blind, placebo-controlled studies. *Clin Ther* 2000;22:329-341.

45. Oppenheimer JJ, Nelson HS, Bock SA, et al: Treatment of peanut allergy with rush immunotherapy. *J Allergy Clin Immunol* 1992;90:256-262.

46. Simon D, Braathen LR, Simon HU: Anti-interleukin-5 antibody therapy in eosinophilic diseases. *Pathobiology* 2005;72:287-292.

47. Flood-Page P, Swenson C, Faiferman I, et al, and International Mepolizumab Study Group: A study to evaluate safety and efficacy of mepolizumab in patients with moderate persistent asthma. *Am J Respir Crit Care Med* 2007;176:1062-1071.

48. O'Byrne PM: Cytokines or their antagonists for the treatment of asthma. *Chest* 2006;130:244-250.

49. Klunker S, Saggar LR, Seyfert-Margolis V, et al, and Immune Tolerance Network Group: Combination treatment with omalizumab and rush immunotherapy for ragweed-induced allergic rhinitis: Inhibition of IgE-facilitated allergen binding. *J Allergy Clin Immunol* 2007;120:688-695.

50. Cox LS, Linnemann DL, Nolte H, et al: Sublingual immunotherapy: a comprehensive review. *J Allergy Clin Immunol* 2006; 117:1021-1035.

51. Nash SD, Steele PH, Kamilaris JS, et al: Oral peanut immunotherapy for peanut allergic patients. *J Allergy Clin Immunol* 2007;119:S158.

52. Pavord ID, Cox G, Thomson NC, et al, and RISA Trial Study Group: Safety and efficacy of bronchial thermoplasty in symptomatic, severe asthma. *Am J Respir Crit Care Med* 2007;176: 1185-1191.

Index

A

W

warfarin 131, 177, 337
wasps 41, 275, 276, 278, 288
weeds 41, 58, 59
Wegener's syndrome 22
weight gain 123, 125, 165, 169
wheals 54, 55, 61, 214, 215
wheat 60
wheezing 8, 20, 25, 27, 31, 35, 102, 104-107, 121, 132, 149-152, 154, 167, 173, 191, 247, 262, 286
Wiskott-Aldrich syndrome 30

X

Xolair® 128, 133, 141
Xopenex® 117, 155, 192, 329
Xopenex® HFA 118
Xyzal® 74, 326

Y

yellow jackets 41, 275, 278, 280, 288

Z

Zaditor® 71, 72, 80
zafirlukast (Accolate®) 117, 130, 131, 166, 176, 177, 336, 337
Zantac® 222
zileuton (Zyflo®, Zyflo CR™) 117, 130, 131, 135, 331, 336, 337
Zinacef® 304, 312
Zithromax® 308, 314
Zovirax® 228, 334
Zyflo® 117, 130, 331
Zyflo CR™ 117, 130, 331
Zyloprim® 331
Zyrtec-D 12-Hour® 89, 90
Zyrtec® 74, 89, 90, 221, 325, 331

NOTES

NOTES

NOTES

NOTES

NOTES

NOTES

NOTES

NOTES

NOTES

NOTES

NOTES

NOTES

NOTES

NOTES

NOTES